Y0-ALN-075

PROJECTS FOR THE WEEKEND

PROJECTS FOR THE WEEKEND

a Rockwell Publication

Tool Group
400 North Lexington Avenue
Pittsburgh, Pennsylvania 15208

Foreword

The projects in this book are basically simple, and most of them were designed to be completed in a single weekend's time. A look at the table of contents will reveal a wide range of styles and types of projects.

Most of the plans for the furniture pieces first appeared in *Flying Chips* (a former Rockwell publication). We would like to thank the Formica Corporation (subsidiary of Cyanamid) and the American Plywood Association for certain laminated plastic and plywood projects that appear in this book.

Before attempting to build any of the projects in the book, be certain to review and understand each step of construction and to verify all of the dimensions. While every effort has been made to ensure accuracy in these designs and drawings, the possibility of error always exists and the publisher cannot accept responsibility for materials improperly used or designs not first verified.

Published by Rockwell International

Text prepared and book designed by
Robert Scharff & Associates

Library of Congress Catalog Card Number: 78-66289

Manufactured in the United States of America

Contents

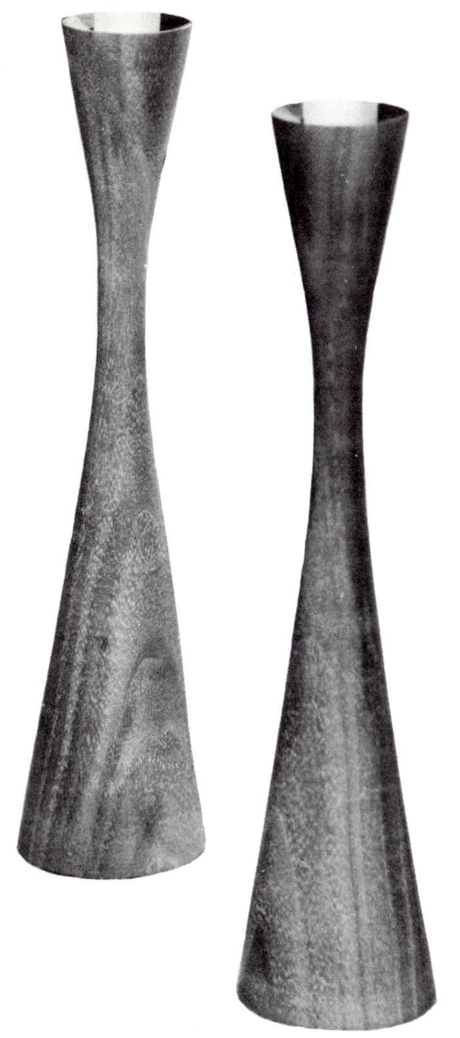

MODERN CANDLE HOLDER

The smooth sleek lines of these candle holders will make a very interesting lathe project as well as a decorative addition to your dining table.

A hard wood like walnut or mahogany would be best suited for this project. Glue up some stock to make a block 2-5/8″ square by 10-1/4″ long. While the stock is still in the square, bore a 7/8″ hole and a 1-5/16″ hole at the base as indicated in the drawing (Photo 1). Bore the 1-5/16″ hole 1/4″ deeper than what is called for on the drawing to allow for cutting the holder to the proper length while it is in the lathe. Insert a 7/8″ plug into the top hole which is fastened on the drive end in the lathe (Photo 2). The dead center is held in the larger hole of the stock. Turn the holder down to the finished size using the dimensions shown in the drawing. The dovetail effect of the bottom hole that secures the lead weight can be cut out with a bent point chisel. The lead weight can have straight sides and can be screw fastened to the candle holder (Fig. 1-A).

After the holder is turned down to shape, sand it thoroughly with first medium and then fine abrasive paper until all of the turning and scratch marks are removed. Wipe all of the dust off the turning with a tack rag. For a natural finish, apply two coats of satin polyurethane finish.

A French polish will give the holders that professional touch which will add greatly to their value. For complete data on French polishing, refer to the Rockwell Publication, *Practical Finishing Methods.*

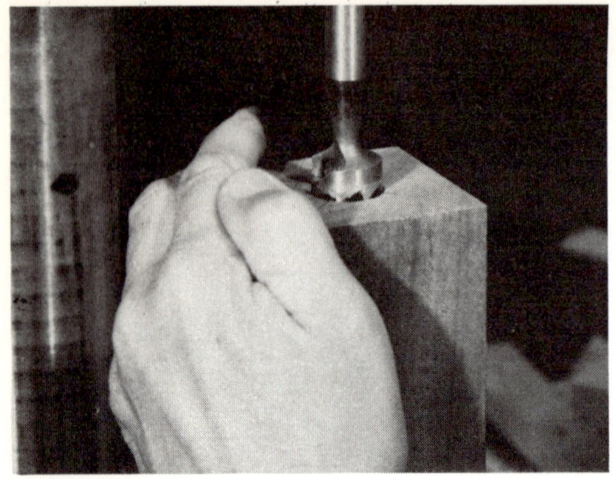
Photo 1: Before the holders are turned on the lathe, the candle hole and the lead weight hole are bored on the drill press with a multi-spur bit. Note: Use hand screws for holding the stock while it is being drilled.

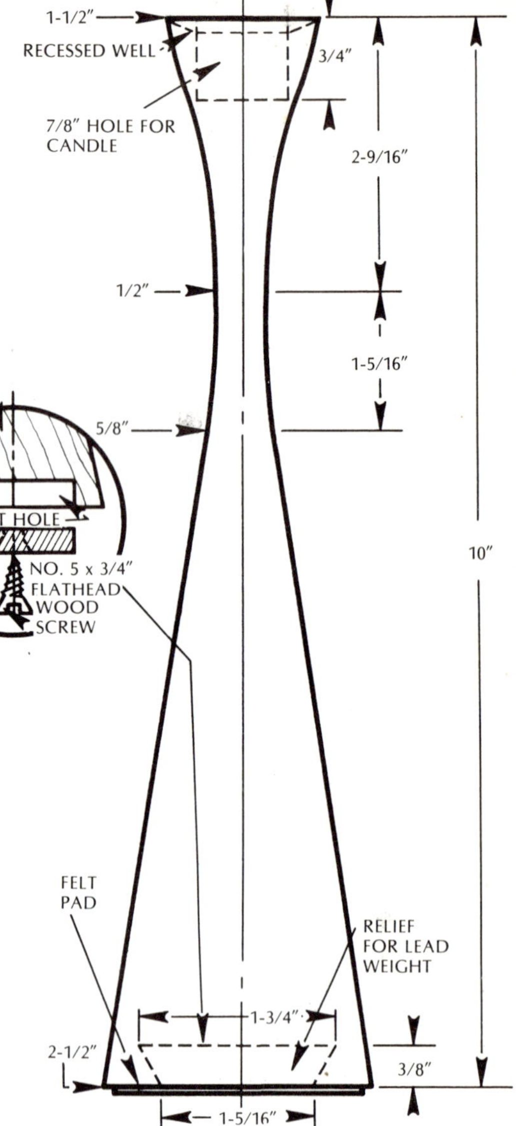

Photo 2: The outside shape of the holder is turned on the lathe with finishing cuts being made with a skew chisel. Note: The wood plug is inserted on the live end of the turning.

Photo 3: The recessed well on the end of the candle holder is made on the lathe using a parting tool.

TOY STORAGE BENCH

MATERIALS

Quantity	Description
2	3/4″ x 4′ x 8′ Plywood panels (A-A, A-B, or B-B Exterior grade marked)
16	1-1/2″ dia. x 3″ Long dowel for slot and tab assembly
12	Casters for drawers
8	Furniture glides for "tab" separators
-	8d Finishing nails for glue-nailing drawers
-	Glue (urea resin type recommended) for glue-nailing drawers
-	Filler for countersunk nail holes and, if necessary, for filling small gaps in cut plywood edges
-	Fine abrasive paper for smoothing plywood cut edges and filler material
-	Top-quality nontoxic paint for finishing. A prime coat is recommended

Turn a cluttered child's room into a well-ordered space with this practical toy storage bench. Made of a strong, rigid plywood, the sturdy knockdown unit has three pull-out compartments that are deep enough to hide all the playthings. A cinch to build, this space-saving project doubles as a perch for playmates. It can be painted, covered with fabric, or dotted with decals, but any way you look at it, this workshop wonder is a natural answer to the where-to-put-it question in children's bedrooms.

Following the panel layout (Fig. 1), draw all the parts on the plywood panels using a straightedge and a carpenter's square for accuracy. Use a compass to draw corner radii. Be sure to allow for saw kerfs when plotting dimensions; if in doubt, check the width of your saw cut.

For hand-sawing, use a 10 to 15 point crosscut. Support the panel firmly with its good face up. Use a fine-toothed coping saw for curves. For inside cuts, start the hole with a drill, then use a coping or keyhole saw. For power sawing, a plywood blade gives the best results, but a combination blade may be used. Place the good face down for hand power sawing. The good panel face should be up for table or radial power sawing. The first cuts will reduce the panel to pieces small enough for easy handling. The use of scrap lumber underneath the panel, clamped or tacked securely in place, prevents splintering on the back side. Plan to cut matching parts with the same saw setting. If available, you may use a jig saw, band saw, or scroll saw for curved cuts. In any case, be sure the blade enters the good face of the panel.

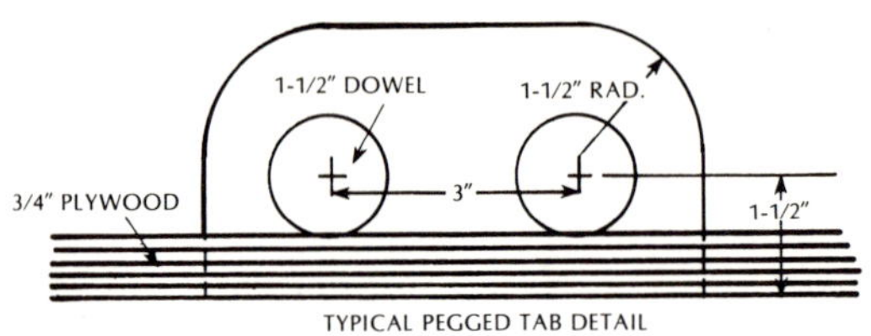

TYPICAL PEGGED TAB DETAIL

Panel Layout

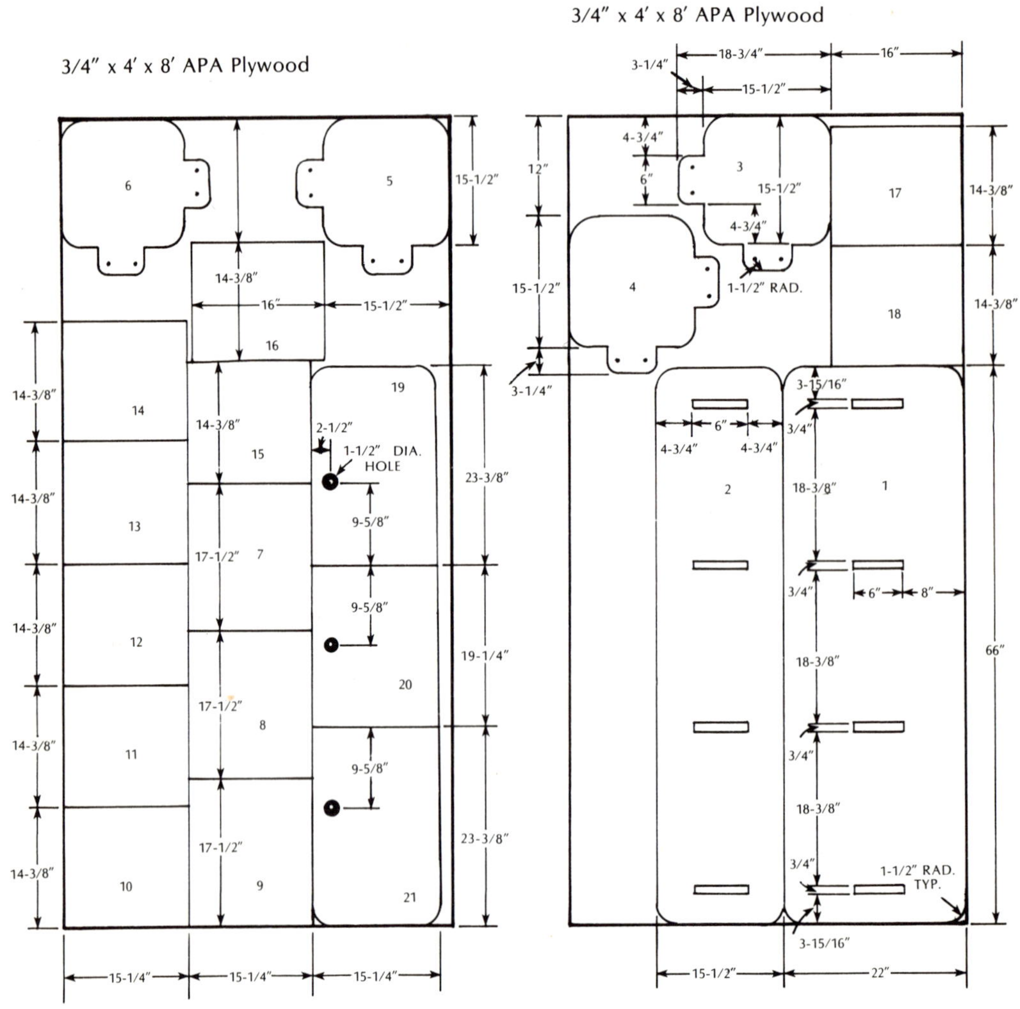

3/4" x 4' x 8' APA Plywood

3/4" x 4' x 8' APA Plywood

FIG. 1

Exploded View

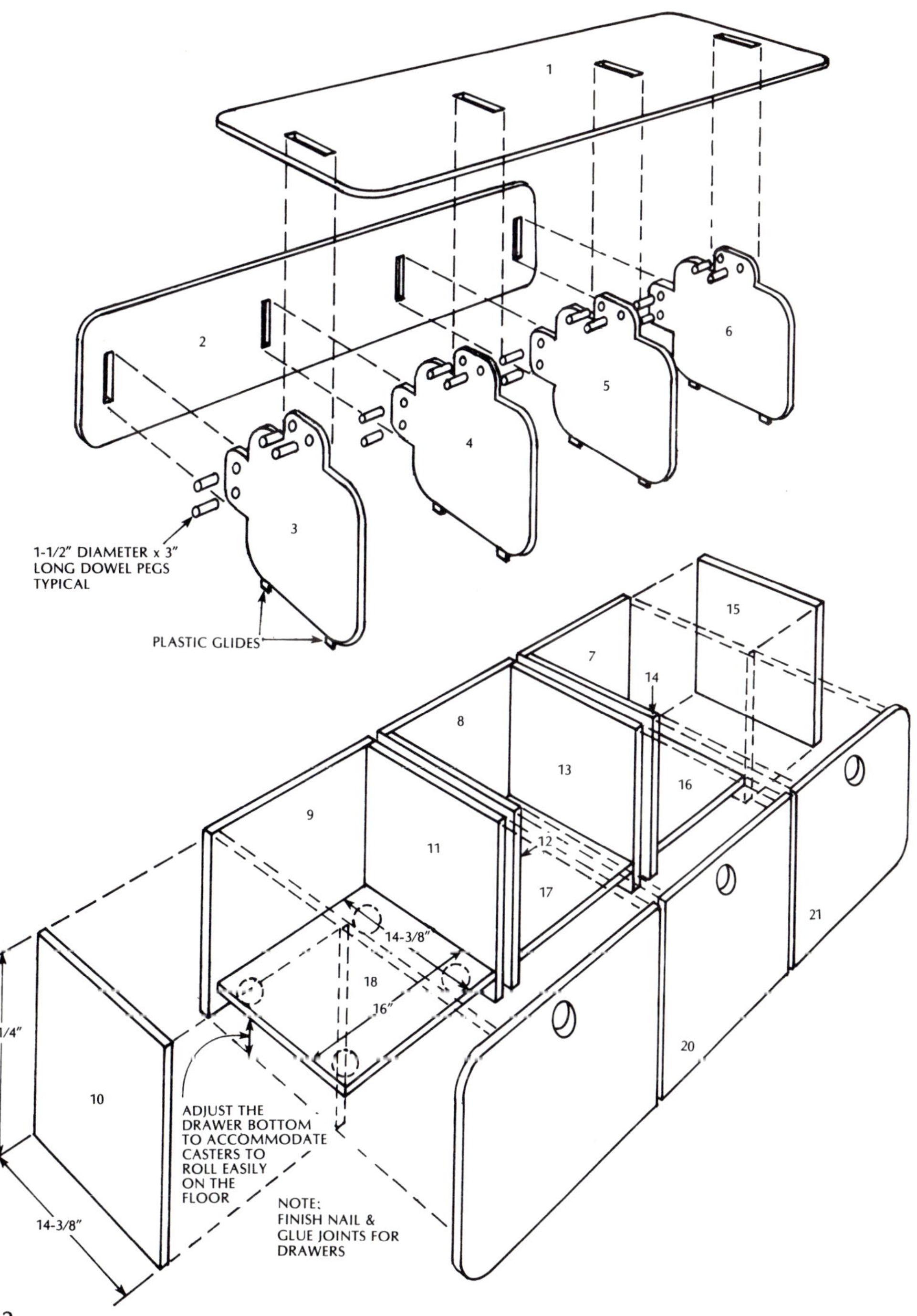

FIG. 2

COAT RACK

Keep frequently used hats, jackets, and coats handy — and at the same time, neatly stored — on this nifty, wall-mounted rack.

After all the parts are cut to size, assemble the coat rack as follows:

1. Glue each pair of (A) and (B) sections together.
2. When cutting the horizontal 3/4″ channel along each (B) section, take care to make the channel only 3/4″ longer than the width of the shelf. Use either a router and a straight cutter, or the dado head set-up in your table saw or radial saw to plough the channels.
3. Before assembling the rack, glue-nail the butt-ended 3/4″ half-round to sections (C) and (D), as shown in Fig. 1.
4. The ends of the 1-1/2″ half-rounds must be cut to a 45° angle. Glue-nail the half-rounds to the side sections, as shown.
5. Slide the shelf in place; glue-nail. Assemble the remaining sections; glue-nail.

Use A-B Interior, A-C Exterior or Medium Density Overlaid (MDO) American Plywood Association grade-trademarked plywood for the coat rack. If you use MDO plywood, you need no surface preparation and it is finished with conventional paints for an exceptionally smooth and durable surface. Sanded panels require very little preparation, primarily "touch sanding" (in the direction of the grain only) to smooth any filler or spackle applied to the minor openings in the panel face or to remove blemishes. Do not paint over dust, spots of oil, or glue. Any knots or pitch streaks should be touched up with sealer or shellac before painting.

MATERIALS

Quantity	Description
1/4	3/4″ x 2′ x 4′ Plywood panel
6′	1-1/2″ Half-rounds
10′	3/4″ Half-rounds
-	Coat hooks
-	Wood putty
-	Fine abrasive paper
-	White glue
-	8d Finishing nails
-	Interior semi-gloss enamel paint

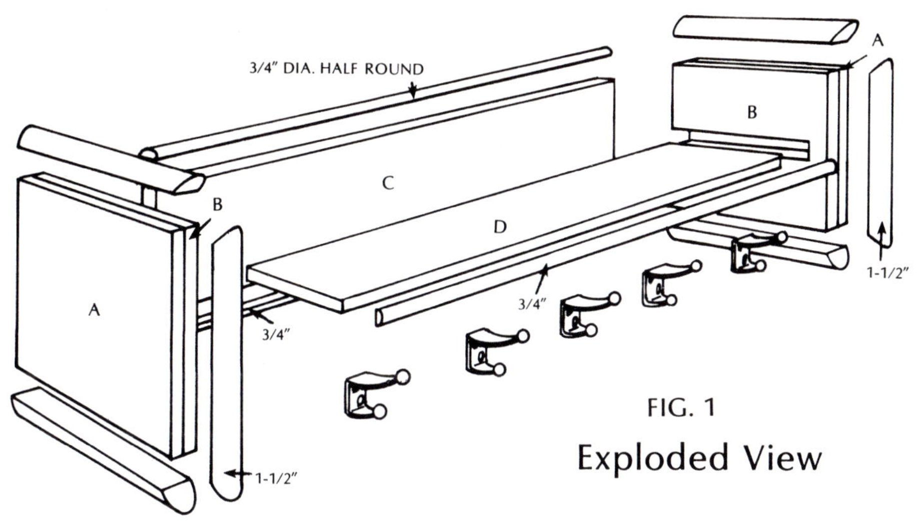

FIG. 1

Exploded View

3/4" x 2' x 4' PLYWOOD

A
8" x 10"
C
8" x 36-1/2"
A
D
7-3/4" x 37-7/8"
B
B
3-5/8"
3/4"
8" x 10"
8-1/2"

Panel Layout

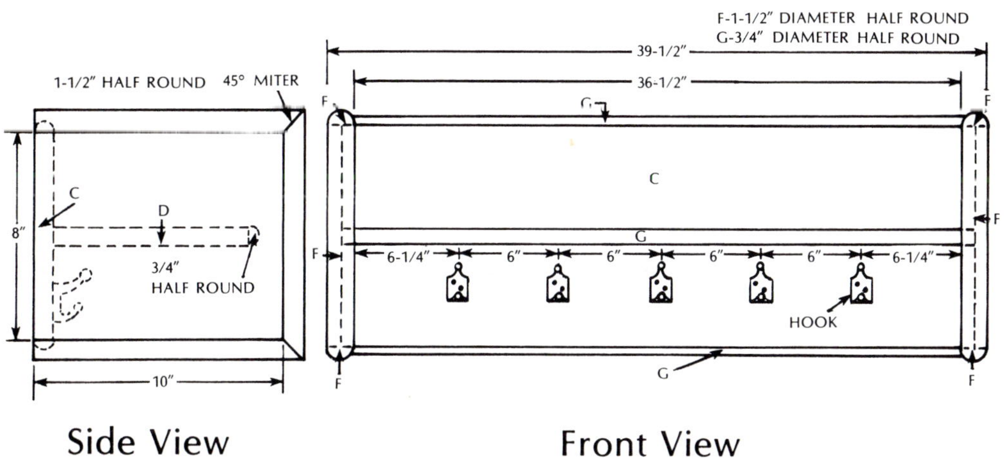

Side View

Front View

MESSAGE CENTER

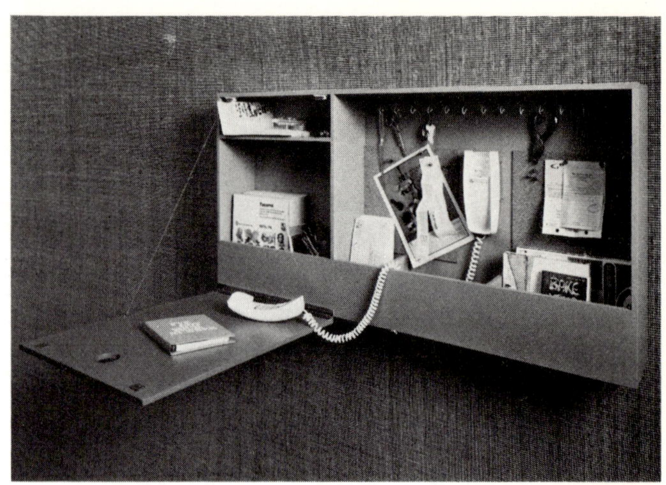

Conduct all your personal and business calls at this handy message center. There is plenty of room for telephone and address books, correspondence supplies, and note-taking.

The first cuts will help reduce the panel in size and thus make handling easier, especially when using a table or radial saw. The use of scrap lumber underneath the panel, clamped or tacked securely in place, prevents splintering on the back side. Plan to cut matching parts with the same blade setting. If available, you may use a jig saw, band saw, or scroll saw for the curved cuts. In any case, be sure the blade enters the good face of the panel.

When assembling the message center, be sure to keep these points in mind:

1. Glue-nail the smaller shelf and organizer partitions in place before assembling the larger pieces.
2. The chain should be attached to the shelf at the point where it holds the shelf level.
3. The number and the placement of the cup hooks and cork board can be varied to suit individual needs.

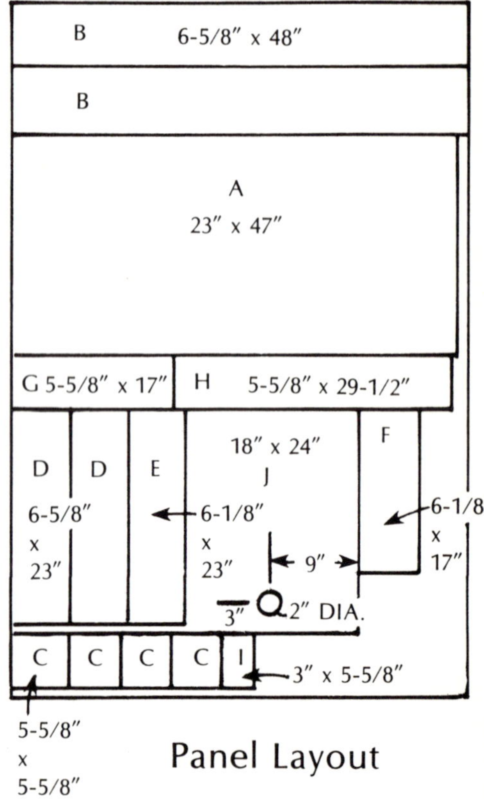

Panel Layout

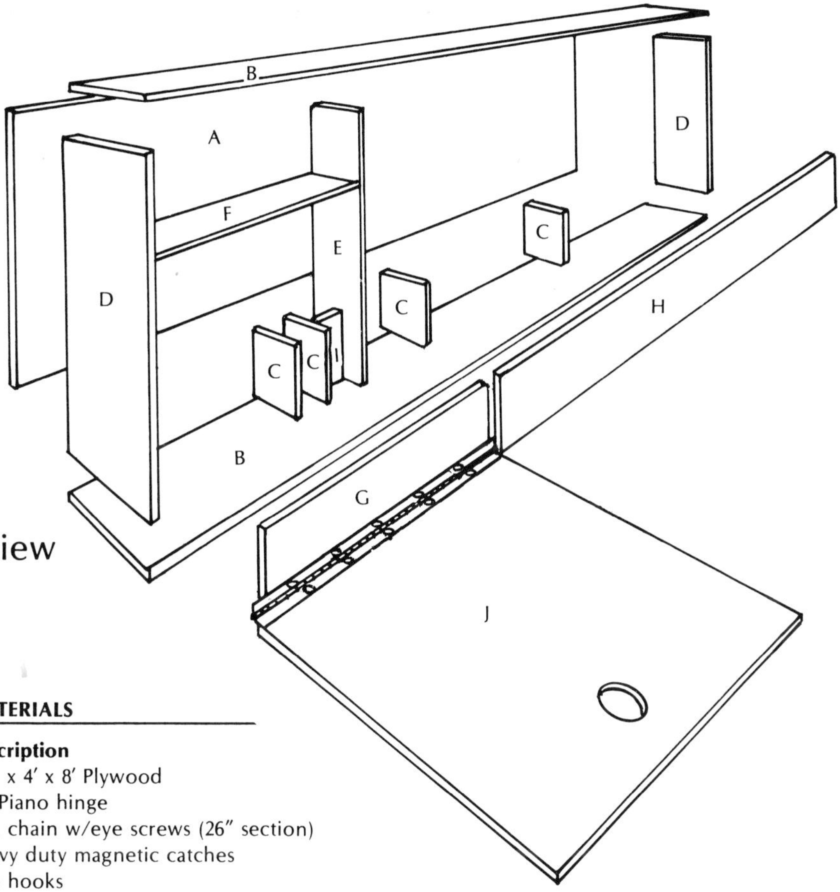

Exploded View

MATERIALS

Quantity	Description
1 panel	1/2″ x 4′ x 8′ Plywood
1	18″ Piano hinge
1	Link chain w/eye screws (26″ section)
2 sets	Heavy duty magnetic catches
14	Cup hooks
2	Cork squares (size — as desired, and to fit space)
—	Wood putty
—	Fine abrasive paper
—	White glue
—	6d Finishing nails
—	Interior semi-gloss enamel paint

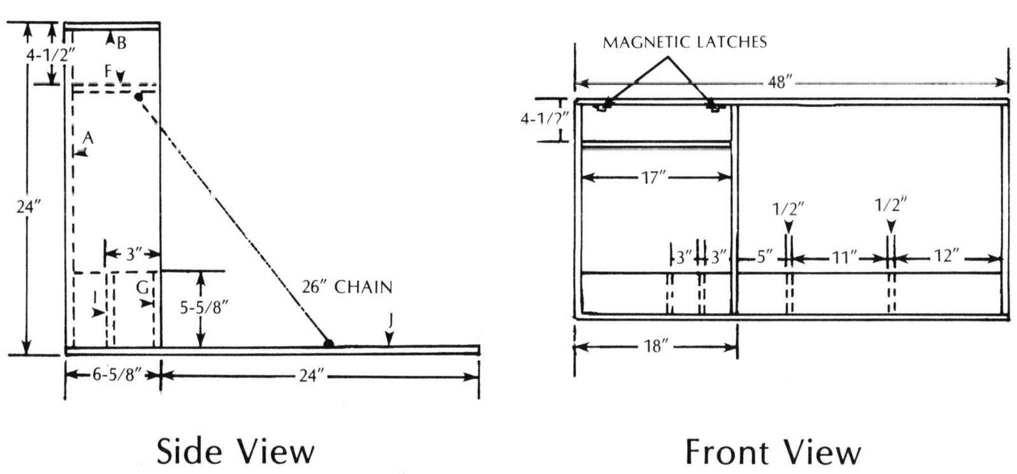

Side View

Front View

BUTCHERBLOCK PLANTER

The core stock of this planter requires no finishing, since it is entirely covered with decorative plastic laminate — in this case, butcherblock maple. The box is easily assembled, using butt joints at the corners as illustrated. The laminate is then veneered around the four sides in rotation. The top surface is done before laminating the sides. The corner diagonals will mark the center. Use a compass to outline the cutout mark which should be sized to suit the flowerpot. But, before starting the project let us first cover some important facts about working with laminate plastics.

Cutting. Always cut the plastic about 1/4″ greater in length and width than the surface to which it will be bonded. If you are using a portable jig saw, remember to mark and saw the panel with the decorative face side *down,* since the blade cuts on the up stroke. With a table saw, the material is cut with the finished side face up. For a neat job, regardless of what tool was used, trimming is always done after bonding.

Applying Adhesives. Generally, it is best to apply the cement to the back side of the laminate first, then the core piece. Since the latter is more absorptive, glue dries faster on it. While the cement may be applied with a paintbrush, a short-nap paint roller does a better job of distributing the glue evenly and takes less time.

Which Surface To Bond First? The order in which to apply various panels is determined by the edge most visible to the eye and subject to abuse. Thus, self-edge strips always go on before the top panel.

Positioning Pieces. Some users advocate keeping cemented surfaces apart by using large sheets of paper, but 3/4″ dowels spaced about 12″ apart are better. Make certain the dowels (or sticks, if used) are absolutely clean and do not transport dust to the cement-coated surfaces.

Applying Pressure. Most contact cements need only momentary pressure after bonding. But do not mistake momentary for light. Do not worry about applying too much pressure.

Trimming. Trim the overhang with a router and a straight cutter. To prevent scorch marks, protect the edge with petroleum jelly. Trimming is completed when you dress the edges using a carbide bevel cutter in the router. Lacking a router, use a fine mill file to get a neat bevel after trimming with a block plane. When filing, hold the file at a 60° angle to the top. Apply the pressure from above and only on the down stroke and against the edge, to avoid chipping and scuffing.

Cleanup. To dissolve contact cement on the surface, use lacquer thinner or contact adhesive solvent and scraps of laminate — *never use metal* — to scrape off heavy globs. Or use naphtha. This solvent dissolves only the resins in the cement and leaves the cement's rubber on the laminate. The rubber can be rolled off with your fingertips or a soft cloth. Use the solvent sparingly at the edges or joints to avoid penetration and possible delamination. Be sure to follow all safety precautions for solvent use and provide adequate ventilation.

MATERIALS

Quantity	Description
4	3/4" x 18" x 24" Plywood (sides)
1	3/4" x 16-1/2" x 16-1/2" Plywood (top)
4	3/4" x 2-1/2" x 23-1/4" Lumber (cleats)
4	18-1/2" x 23-1/2" Plastic laminate (sides)
1	17" x 17" Plastic laminate (top)
—	White glue
—	1-1/4" No. 8 Flathead wood screws
—	Contact cement
—	Adhesive solvent

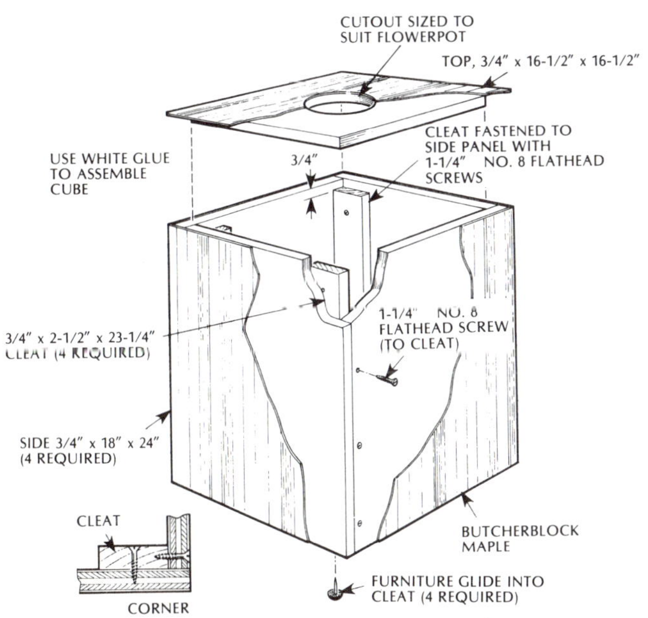

APPLIANCE CART

Now all your kitchen appliances can be at your finger tips in their bright, attractive appliance cart. It combines convenient storage with additional countertop space, a welcome addition to any kitchen.

To assemble the cart, proceed as follows:

1. Carefully measure and drill holes a 1/4" deep for the dowels in pieces (A) and (K).
2. You may wish to paint the pieces before assembling them. Therefore, where needed, fill the edges with plastic wood filler and sand each piece smooth before painting.
3. Glue-nail piece (B) to the base, piece (A).
4. Glue-nail piece (C) to both (A) and (B).
5. Attach piece (D) and (E) to the base (A) and piece (C).
6. Glue-nail the dowels into piece (A). Install the shelves (L), (H), (K) and (J).
7. Attach panels (G) and (F). Install pieces (M), (N), (O) and (P).
8. Attach the casters and the electrical outlet, if desired. Attach the top.

MATERIALS

Quantity	Description
1	3/4" x 4' x 8' Plywood
1	3/4" x 30-3/4" x 34-1/2" Plywood
7 lin. feet	1" x 2" Lumber
13 lin. feet	3/4" dia. Wood dowel
4	2" Spherical casters
2	Screw hooks with square bend
4	1-1/2" x 1-1/2" x 1/2" Metal angles
1	24" x 36" Butcher block
-	6d Finish nails; white or urea-resin glue; wood putty or synthetic filler; fine abrasive paper; top-quality primer and paint.
1	Multiple convenience outlet with extension cord

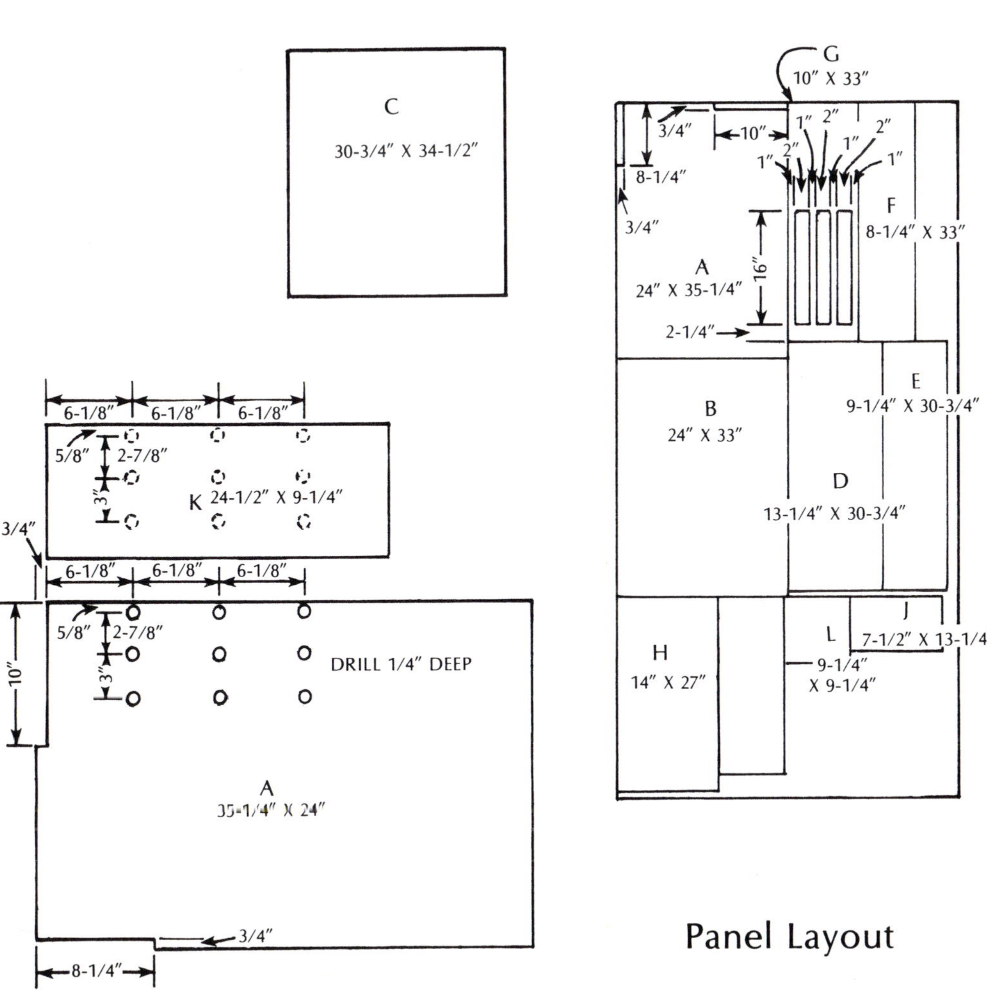

Panel Layout

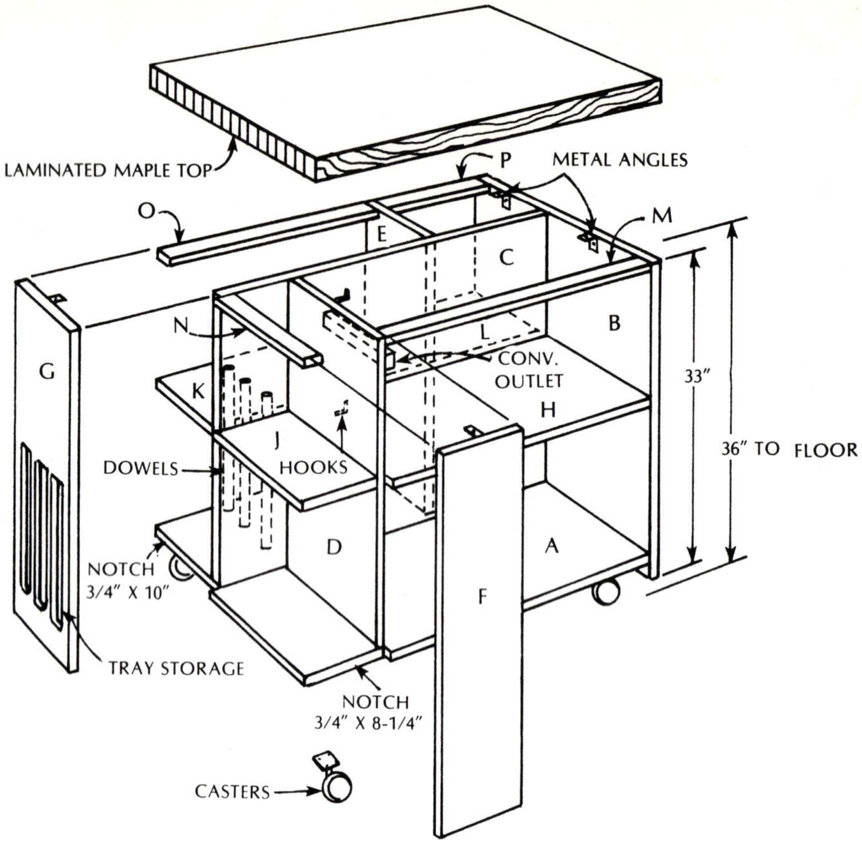

LAMINATED MAPLE TOP
P
METAL ANGLES
O
M
E
C
B
G
N
L
CONV.
OUTLET
33″
K
H
J
36″ TO FLOOR
DOWELS
HOOKS
D
A
NOTCH
3/4″ X 10″
F
TRAY STORAGE
NOTCH
3/4″ X 8-1/4″
CASTERS

Exploded View

2′0″
10″
1′2″
O
LAMINATED
TOP
G
N
C
F
3/4″ DOWELS
BEHIND
K
J
16″
A
3/4″ RAD. TYP.

G End View

3′0″
10″
2′2″
P
O
C
G
B
E
L
K
2′9″
2′7-1/2″
2′10-1/2″
EQ.
EQ.
EQ.
EQ.
A
1-1/2″
(9) 3/4″ DOWEL DIVIDERS

Side View

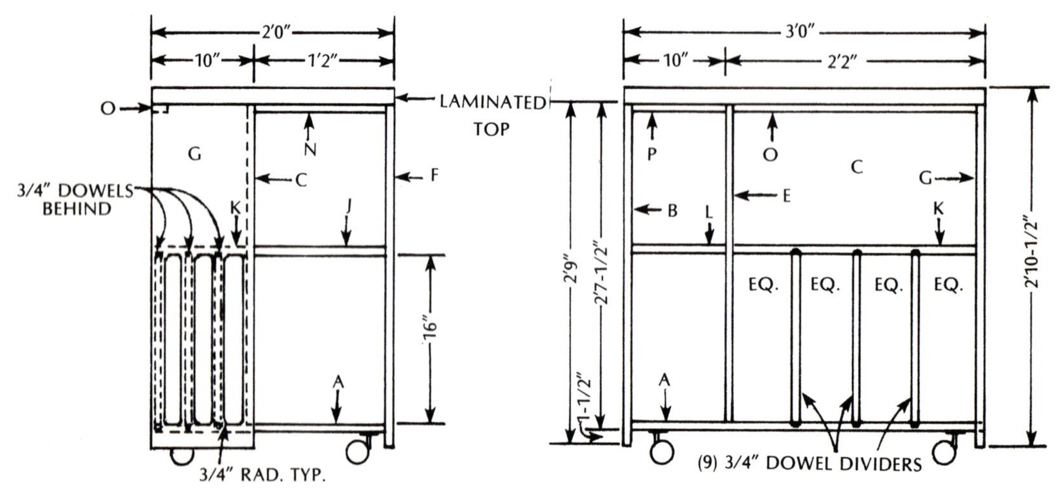

VANITY MIRROR

This vanity mirror can be adapted to a bathroom or bedroom in almost any house. And it is easy to construct, if these steps are carefully followed:

1. Start the construction with the assembly of the outer frame elements. Use 1-1/4″ flathead screws and white glue with a butt joint construction. Set the assembly aside for at least one hour for drying; be sure the screw heads are countersunk flush with the wood surface and all excess white glue is carefully wiped away.

2. Now, begin the construction of the inner frame or mirror surround section. First, cut a 1/4″ by 1/4″ groove in both the vertical elements of the frame structure 3-1/4″ from the top and 3-1/4″ from the bottom to accommodate the rabbeted edges of the horizontal frame members. Next, cut a 1/4″ by 1/4″ rabbet in the edges of the top (8″ by 28-1/2″) and bottom (7-1/4″ by 28-1/2″) elements.

3. Assemble these inner frame members with white glue and 1-1/4″ No. 8 flathead screws. Wipe away any excess white glue and set it aside to dry.

4. Using a router, cut a 1/4″ by 1/4″ rabbet around the inside perimeter of the back edge of the mirror surround or inner frame member.

5. Fasten together the two frame elements, taking care to mount them so that the inside surfaces of the mirror surround (or inner frame) are precisely 4″ from the outside frame members at the top and both sides. Fasten with white glue and 1-1/4″ No. 8 flathead wood screws.

6. Now, fasten the three face panels, using 1-1/4″ 4d nails and white glue. Be sure to set the nail heads and wipe away any excess white glue. Place 3/4″ by 3/4″ by 2-1/2″ cleats at the inside top edge of the inner frame assembly as shown, using white glue and nails.

7. Once the frame is completed, begin the construction of the drawer. First, cut a 1/4″ by 1/4″ groove 1/2″ from the bottom edge of the sides, front, and back panels of the drawer components. Then, cut a 1/4″ by 3/4″ rabbet along the vertical (3-1/4″ height) edge of both the side panels.

8. Assemble the drawer temporarily and test it for proper fit. Then fasten it permanently with 1-1/4″ 4d nails and white glue. Wipe away the excess glue and allow it to dry.

9. Begin the application of the decorative laminate on the vanity mirror assembly. First, apply the laminate to the outside vertical and inside frame members. Rout

flush.

10. Cut and fit the laminate accurately for the bottom shelf and the upper horizontal element of the mirror surround (see page 10 for laminate working details). Rout flush.

11. Apply the laminate to the front face panels of the entire mirror, using one sheet of laminate to cover the entire area. Bevel trim the outside edges; flush rout the top edge. Trim away the laminate from the drawer opening and mirror mounting area, drilling a hole through the laminate to provide access for the router bit. Be sure to radius all inside corners. Do not file a square corner. Rout flush.

12. Now, complete the laminate application by applying the drawer front (the drawer top edges may be laminated or painted) and the vanity mirror top surface. Flush rout the drawer face; bevel rout the top at all laminate-to-laminate joints.

13. When all of the laminate operations have been completed, mark the location of the drawer pull. Use a nail punch to locate the drill bit in the laminate face surface. Then drill the holes necessary for mounting the pull.

14. Determine the location of the vanity lighting (Fig. 2). Mark the center of each socket opening in the laminate with a nail punch. Use a hole saw or drill bit to produce the openings for the lighting. It is advisable to consult an electrician or your electrical supply dealer for the proper techniques for mounting and wiring the lights.

15. Only after all the construction and lighting installation steps have been completed, should the mirror be installed. Fit the mirror in the rabetted cut out at the back edge of the inner frame element (Fig. 3). Install the plywood backing sheet, using 1-1/4" No. 8 flathead wood screws.

MATERIALS

Quantity	Description
2	3/4" x 7-1/4" x 30" Plywood (sides)
2	3/4" x 7-1/4" x 34-1/2" Plywood (top and bottom)
3	3/4" x 8" x 28-1/2" Plywood (vertical and top members)
1	3/4" x 7-1/4" x 28-1/2" Plywood (bottom shelf)
2	3/4" x 3/4" x 2-1/2" Plywood (cleats)
2	3/4" x 4" x 30" Plywood (side panels)
1	3/4" x 4" x 28" Plywood (top panel)
1	3/4" x 3-1/4" 28" Plywood (drawer front)
1	3/4" x 3-1/4" x 27" Plywood (drawer back)
2	3/4" x 3-1/4" x 7-1/4" Plywood (drawer sides)
1	1/4" x 7-3/4" x 27" Plywood (drawer bottom)
1	1/4" x 23" x 29" Plywood (backing)
2	7-3/4" x 30-1/2" Plastic laminate (outer sides)*
1	8-1/2" x 36-1/2" Plastic laminate (top)*
2	8-1/2" x 28" Plastic laminate (horizontal surfaces)*
2	8-1/2" x 22" Plastic laminate (vertical surfaces)*
1	30-1/2" x 36-1/2" Plastic laminate (panel surface)*
1	3-3/4" x 28-1/2" Plastic laminate (drawer front)*
—	White glue
—	1-1/4" 4d Finish nails
—	1-1/4" No. 8 Flathead wood screws
1	Cabinet pull
1	22" x 28" Mirror
—	Lighting components
—	Contact adhesive
—	Adhesive solvent

* *Note:* All the necessary laminate pieces can be cut from one 48" by 72" laminate sheet. Take the time to lay out the vanity mirror part sizes before cutting to assure a proper yield.

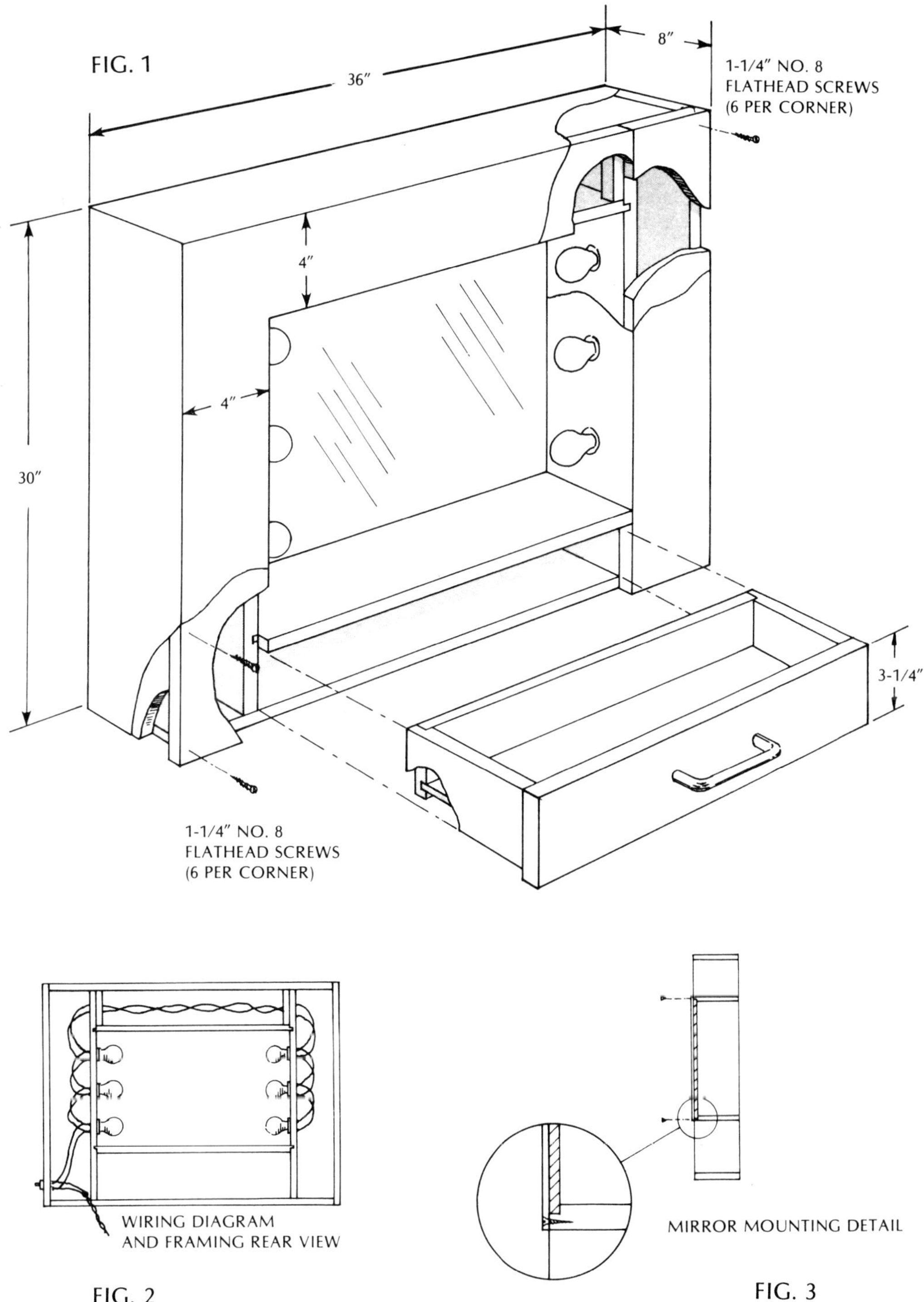
FIG. 1
36″
8″
1-1/4″ NO. 8
FLATHEAD SCREWS
(6 PER CORNER)
4″
4″
30″
3-1/4″
1-1/4″ NO. 8
FLATHEAD SCREWS
(6 PER CORNER)
WIRING DIAGRAM
AND FRAMING REAR VIEW
FIG. 2
MIRROR MOUNTING DETAIL
FIG. 3

COLONIAL SPICE RACK

The fruitwood or Early American finished spice rack lends a touch of antique elegance to your kitchen accessories. It makes a very handsome wall decoration as well as a functional shelf for your everyday kitchen use. The two shelves will hold an ample supply of your favorite spices.

The shelf sides are made of 1/2″ thick maple stock. The 1/4″ stop grooves in the side pieces for the shelf stock are made on the table saw with a dado head (Photo 1). They can also be made with a high speed router fitted with a 1/4″ router bit. Using the squares method, draw an outline of the scrolled shelf side. Tack both side pieces together and cut them at the same time on a scroll saw (Photo 2), band saw, or portable jig saw.

The scrolled shelf guard rails and the back stretcher are made of 3/16″ thick stock and cut on the scroll saw as indicated in the drawing. The top scrolled edge can be rounded off with a three lip cutter (Fig. 2) on a shaper. A router equipped with a similar cutter can also be used (Photo 3).

Complete the project with maple stain followed by two coats of satin effect polyurethane finish. Screw fasten two metal hangers to the back of the rack side pieces as shown in the drawing.

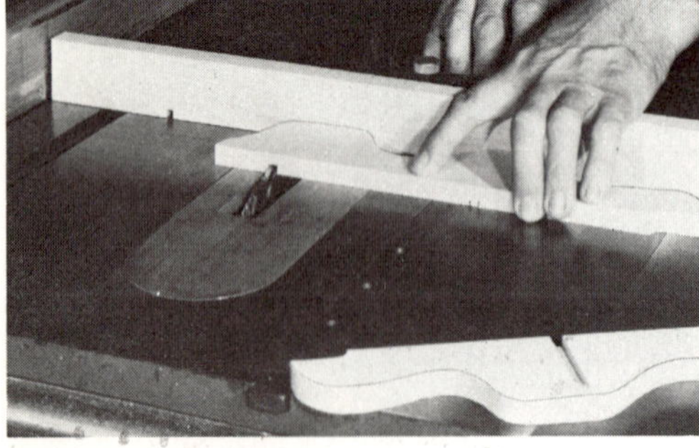

Photo 1: Stop grooves for the shelves are made with a high speed router fitted with a 1/4″ router bit, or on a table saw using two 1/8″ outside cutters of the dado head set. Note: Blade guard removed for clarity.

MATERIALS

Quantity	**Description**
2	1/2″ x 2-1/2″ x 12-1/2″ Lumber (sides)
2	1/4″ x 2-5/8″ x 14-3/4″ Lumber (sides)
2	3/16″ x 1-1/16″ x 15-1/2″ Lumber (stop pieces)
1	1/4″ x 2-5/8″ x 15-3/4″ Lumber (stretcher trim)
2	Metal hangers
—	Screws and/or finishing nails
—	White glue
—	Maple stain
—	Fine abrasive paper
—	Polyurethane finish

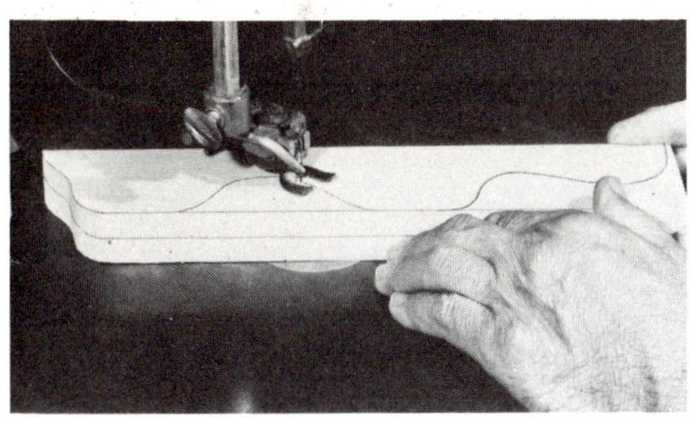

Photo 2: By tacking both side pieces of the rack, they are cut at the same time on the scroll saw using a jeweler's blade.

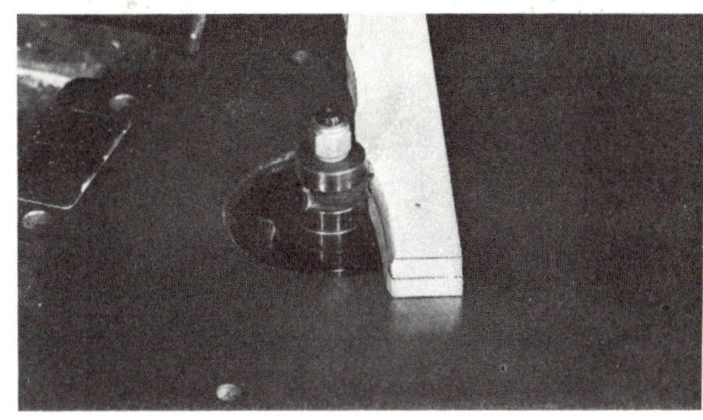

Photo 3: The rounded edges of the shelf guard rails are molded with a router or on a shaper. Note: One piece is used as a template.

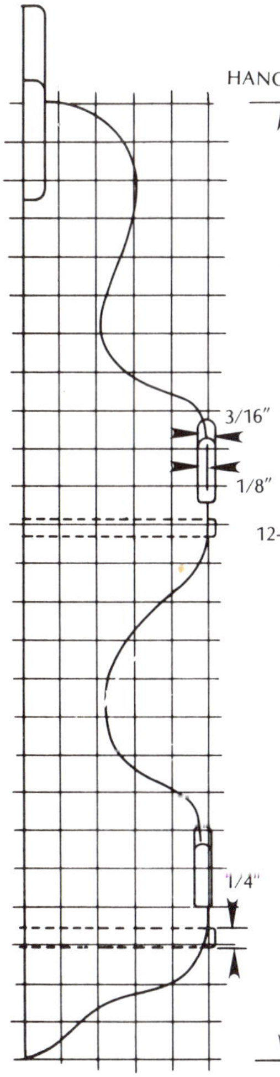

¢

HANGER

2-5/8"

1/2" SQUARES

3/16"

1/8"

12-1/2"

1-1/16"

STOCK

LIP CUTTER

MOLDED EDGE

FIG. 2

1/4"

1/4"

1/2"

15-1/4"

FIG. 1

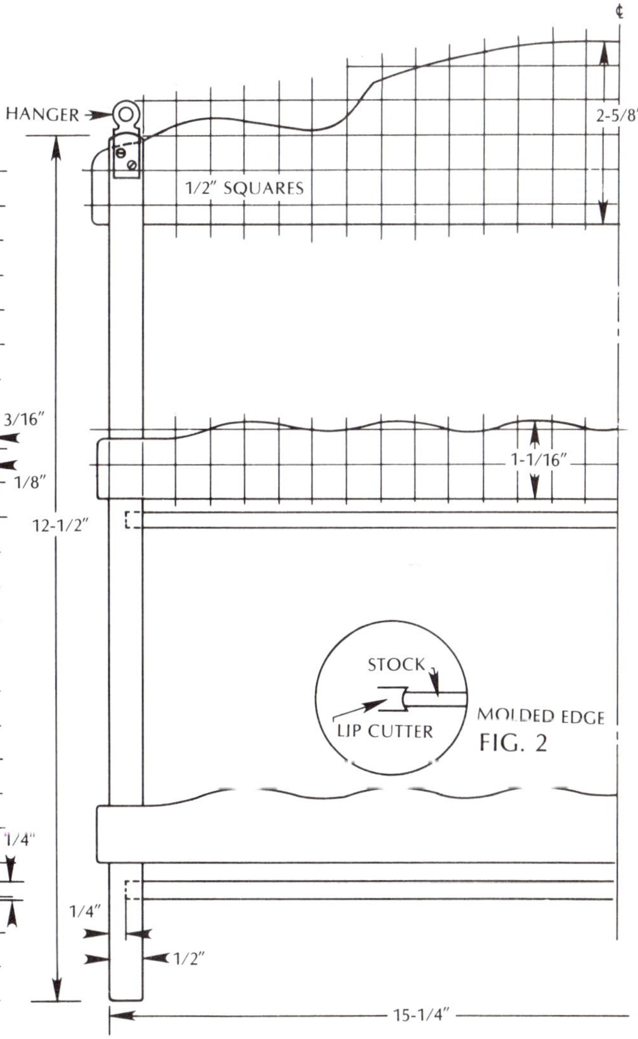

FIG. 3

MEAT CUTTING BLOCK

This sturdy hardwood meat cutting block will take a lot of hard use in any kitchen. The unique feature of this cutting block is the end grain cutting surface. The short tapered legs give it the appearance of the large meat blocks used in old time butcher shops. To prevent the cutting block from sliding over the plastic covered counter top while in use, rubber headed nails are fastened to the tapered feet.

The top is made from 2″ by 6″ hard maple stock cut into 2-3/4″ lengths. Use a stop block on the table saw to prevent the pieces from binding between the blade and the fence (Photo 2). The cut pieces are glued together with waterproof glue. Be sure to stagger the joints the same as you would if you were laying a brick wall (Fig. 1).

After the glue has set for at least twenty-four hours, plane and scrape the top surface, but do not sand. The sanding is omitted to avoid the possibility of imbedding abrasive grit into the cutting surface of the block. Before applying olive oil or mineral oil to the working surface, bore four 3/4″ holes 1-3/4″ from the edges on each corner for the dowel portion of the tapered legs (Fig. 2).

The sides, bottom, and feet are sanded smooth and finished with a sealer and varnished or painted to match the color scheme of the kitchen. Colored decals or painted designs can be added to the block sides.

MATERIALS

Quantity	**Description**
1	2″ x 6″ x 48″ Maple lumber (top)
1	3″ x 3″ x 16″ Maple lumber (legs)
4	3/4″ dia. Rubber headed nails
—	Waterproof glue
—	Olive oil
—	Fine abrasive paper
—	Polyurethane finish

Photo 1: The bottom view shows the four tapered feet with the rubber headed nails in place.

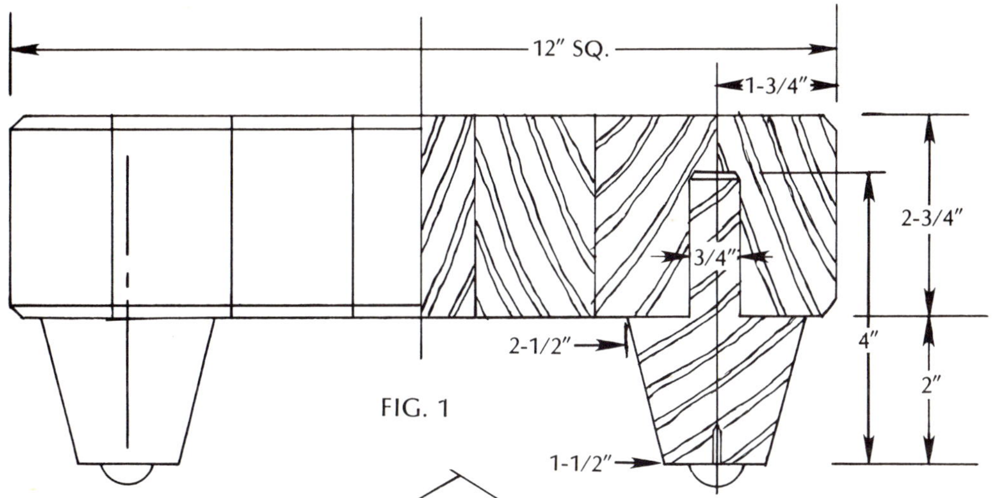

12" SQ.
1-3/4"
2-3/4"
3/4"
2-1/2"
4"
2"
FIG. 1
1-1/2"

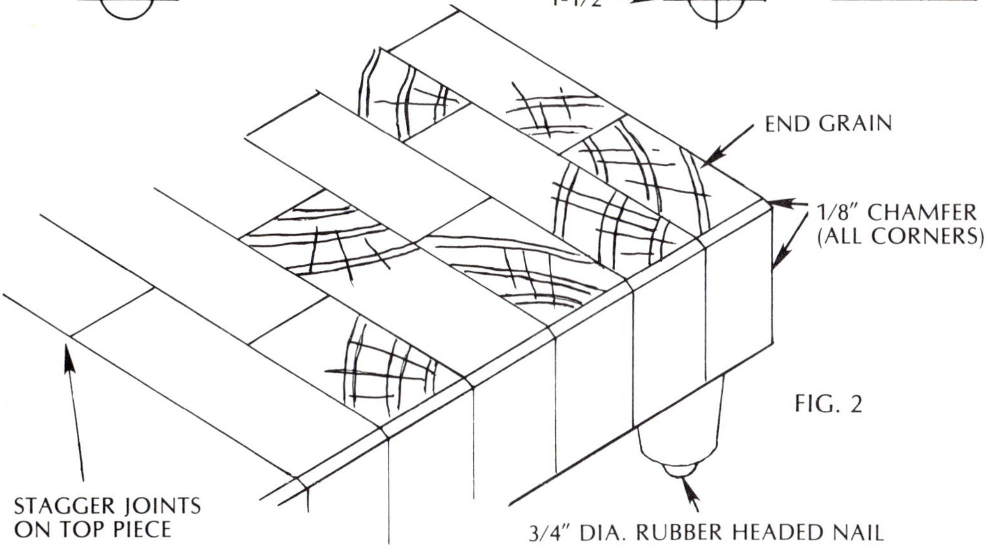

END GRAIN
1/8" CHAMFER
(ALL CORNERS)
FIG. 2
STAGGER JOINTS
ON TOP PIECE
3/4" DIA. RUBBER HEADED NAIL

Photo 2: With a stop block fastened to the rip fence of your table saw, the top stock pieces are safely cut to prevent the pieces from catching between the blade and rip fence. Note: Blade guard removed for clarity.

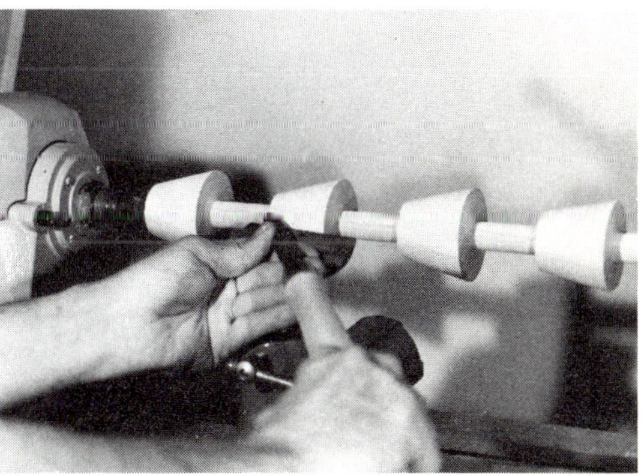

Photo 3: All four legs can be turned at the same time on your lathe.

WALL DESK

If you need a desk but do not have the space for one, build this neat little unit that hangs on the wall. It is ideal for the kitchen, den, or family room; the desk has lots of nooks and crannies, and a desk top that folds up and out of the way when not in use. You can build the unit from a single sheet of A-A or A-B Interior or Medium Density Overlay (MDO) grade-trade-marked plywood. The shelves are nailed and glued in place as detailed in Fig. 1. If you wish more rigidity and have the equipment available, cut 3/8″ grooves for these parts in the sides, top, and bottom with either a router equipped with a straight cutter or a table saw with a dado head.

MATERIALS

Quantity	Description
1	3/4″ x 4′ x 8′ Plywood panel
1 pair	8″ to 12″ Chrome plated lid supports (depending on availability)
1	39″ Chrome or cadmium plated piano hinge
4	3/8″ dia. x 3″ Cadmium plated lag bolts
1	Magnetic catch and strike plate
-	8d Finishing nails
-	Glue (urea resin type recommended)
-	Wood putty
-	Fine abrasive paper
-	Finishing material (paint, antiquing, etc.)
Optional	16″ x 36″ "Suede finish" plastic laminate, with corners rounded to 2″ radius, for desk surface

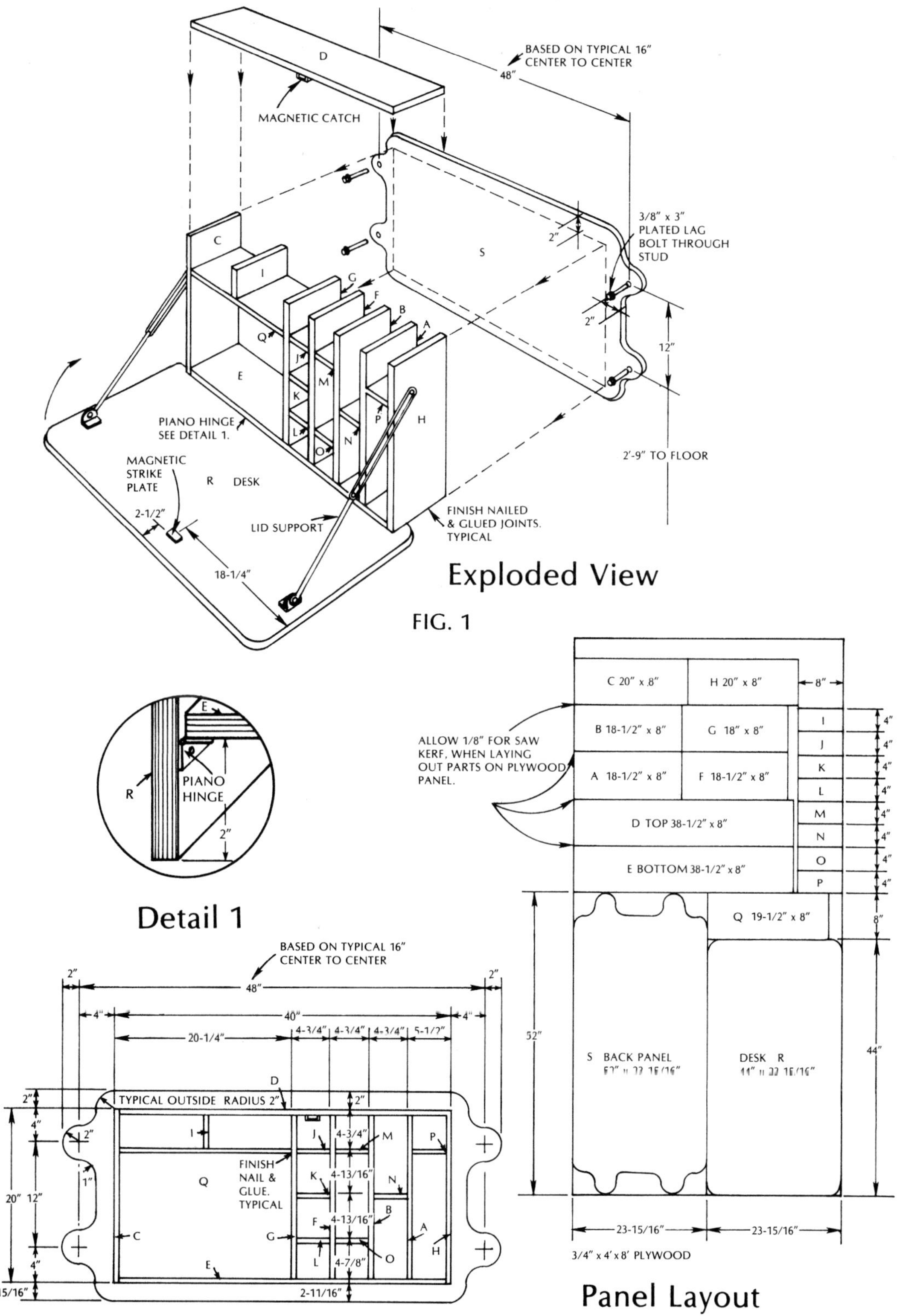

Exploded View

FIG. 1

Detail 1

Panel Layout

BOX KITE

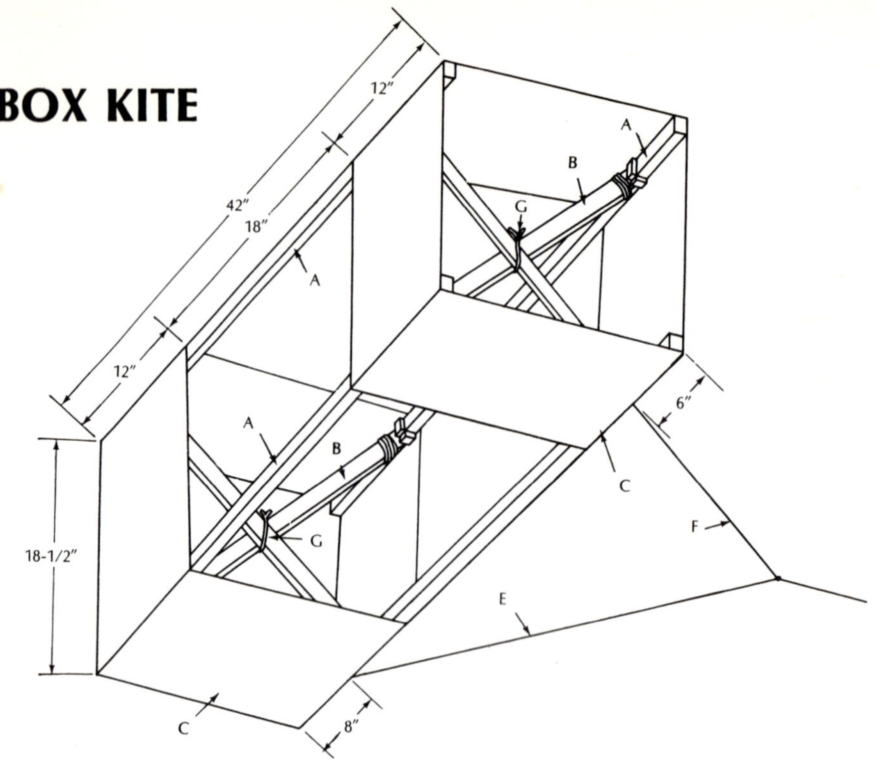

Every kid loves to fly a kite. The sticks of this box kite should be made with straight grain wood: spruce or pine. The corners (A) are 3/8" square. The struts (B) are 1/4" by 1/2", approximately 26" long. The cloth bands are made of lightweight percaline. Adjust the bridle strings (E and F) according to the wind strength.

MATERIALS

Quantity	Description
4	3/8" x 3/8" x 42" Lumber (spines — A)
4	1/4" x 1/2" x 26" Lumber (struts — B)
2	13" x 75 " Lightweight percaline (bands — C)
64	1/4" x 3/8" x 3/8" Lumber (support blocks — D)
-	String (bridle E and F)
-	String or thin wire (strut fasteners — G)
-	White glue

BOWLINE KNOT

SQUARE KNOT

FIG. 1

SPINE (A)

SUPPORT BLOCK (D)

FIG. 2

STRING OR WIRE (G)

STRUT (B)

FIG. 3

SHIPS WHEEL CLOCK

The ships wheel clock described here is well suited for the study, living room, or hall. It can be fitted with a wind movement or with electric movement as desired. You may even want to use it as a barometer case instead of a clock case.

Start the project by cutting the spoke stock from 1/2" by 1/2" mahogany. Cut the lengths of the pieces about 10" long. This will make two spokes at one time on the lathe. If you use the wood turning duplicator attachment on your lathe, a 1/8" hardboard template is required (see Fig. 1 and Photo 1).

The rim and hub are made up of segments which are cut to the dimensions shown in the drawing on page 27. All the segment pieces are cut at an angle with the miter gauge set at 67 1/2°. It is very important that the setting on the miter gauge be set accurately to insure perfect glue joints on the segment pieces. Assemble the 1/2" thick inner pieces of the rim using a 1/2" spacer between each piece as shown in the drawing. When the glue has dried overnight, cut the outside diameter of the rim, and fit it tightly into a wood jig for turning in the lathe (Photo 5). Turn half of the top and half of the bottom diameters; turn the piece around and proceed to turn the other side. The hub segments are glued together and, when dry, the 1/2" mortises are made on the drill press with a 1/2" mortising chisel (Photo 3). After mortising and boring, the outside diameter is rough cut on the band saw and fitted into a wood chuck for finish turning the inside and outside diameters. While in the lathe, make a rabbet cut for the clock dial stock.

Stock for the clock base is screw fastened to a 3" face plate and the outside edge and inside opening are turned to fit the clock mechanism (Photo 6).

First, glue the turned hub to the clock base. When the glue has set, insert the eight spokes into the rim and the hub with dabs of glue on the square portions of the spokes. The spokes can be held in place with small brads on the back of the rim. Drill 1/2" holes 1/4" deep for the mahogany dowels as indicated in Fig. 3 of the drawing. Be sure to remove all glue marks and sand the project thoroughly before proceeding with the finish.

Apply two or three coats of a brush lacquer finish. Use a fine brush for this operation. Be sure to smooth the surface between coats with No. 4/0 steel wool.

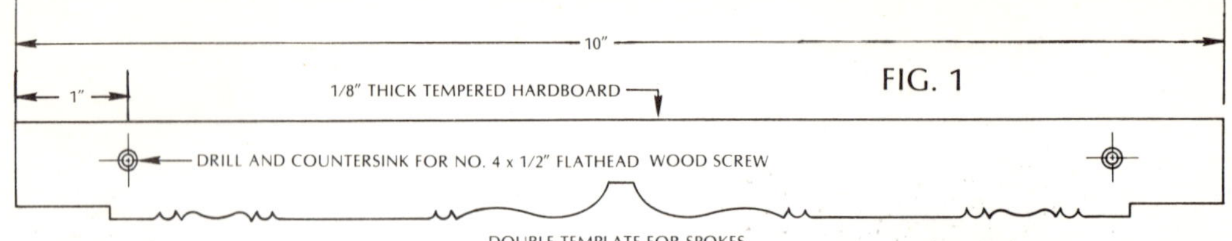

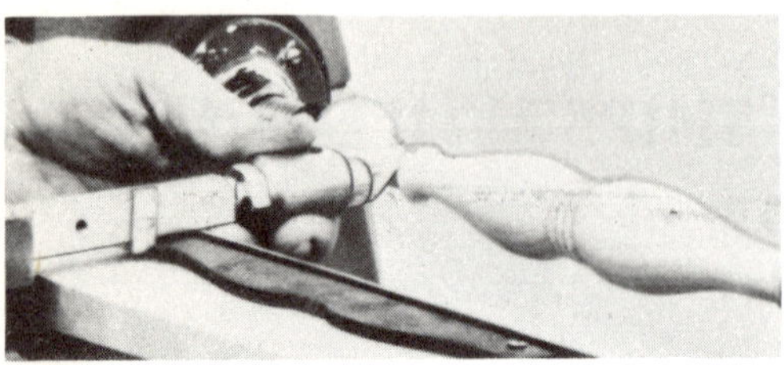

Photo 1: Two spokes are turned at the same time on the lathe using a wood turning duplicator attachment. Note: The template fastened to the duplicator against which the stylus pin follows the same contours as the spoke.

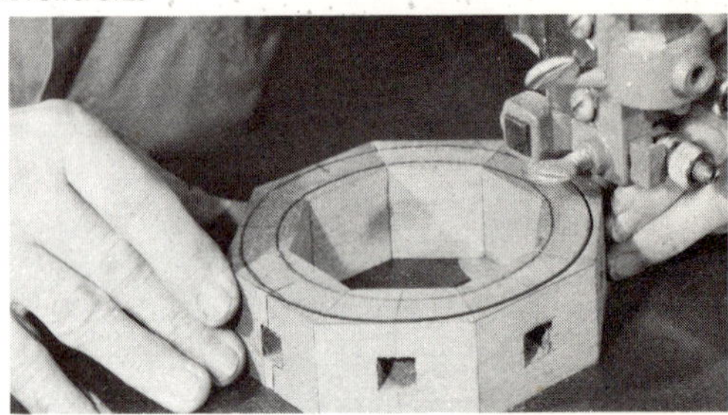

Photo 4: The outside diameter of the hub is cut round on the band saw, for mounting onto a wood chuck for turning both diameters.

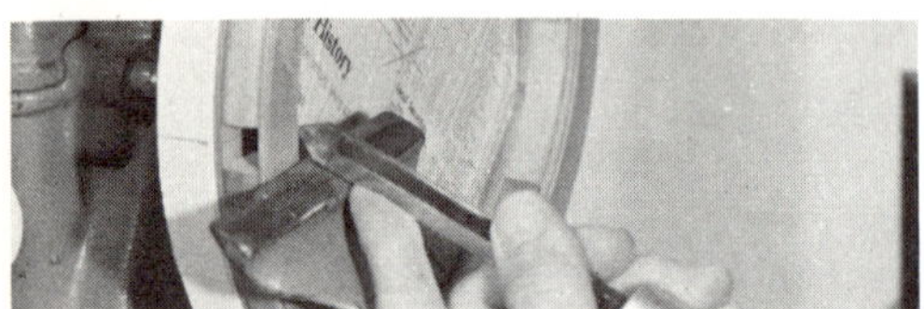

Photo 2: The glued up rim is mounted in a wood jig for turning the molding effect on the top and bottom diameters.

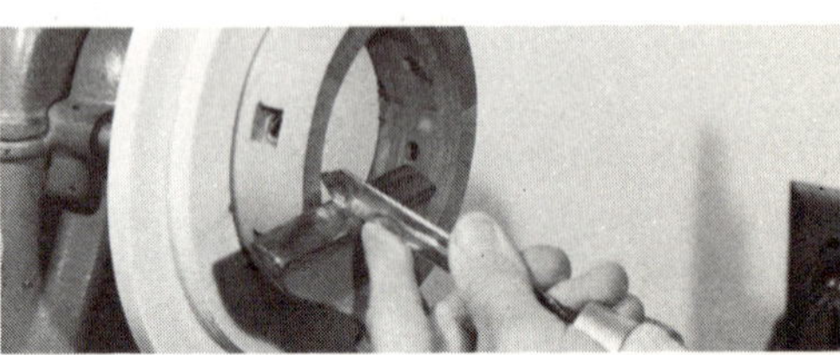

Photo 5: Diameters of the hub are being turned on the lathe using a parting tool.

Photo 3: Before turning the hub, the spoke holes are mortised and bored in the center of each segment. A 1/2" mortising chisel is used for the mortise and a 5/16" drill for the dowel hole.

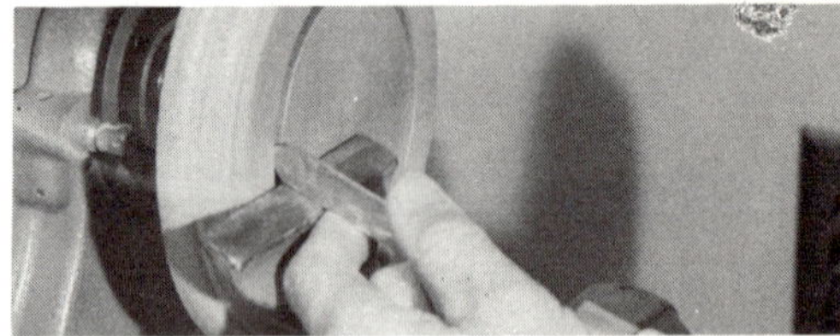

Photo 6: Stock for the base is mounted on a 3" face plate for turning the outside diameter and the inside opening.

Photo 7: Finishing cuts on the mounted dial molding are made on the lathe with a 1/8" parting tool.

MATERIALS

Quantity	Description
8	1/2″ x 1/2″ x 4-5/16″ Lumber (spokes)
8	7/16″ x 1-1/2″ x 3-9/16″ Lumber (wheel segments)
16	1/8″ x 1-1/2″ x 4-1/16″ Lumber (wheel segments)
8	7/8″ x 1-5/8″ x 2-3/16″ Lumber (hub segments)
1	1″ x 6-1/2″ x 6-1/2″ Lumber (base)
1	1/4″ x 4-13/16″ x 4-13/16″ Lumber (dial mounting)
1	Metal wall hanger
1	Clock movement (approx. 4″ dia.)
1	1/2″ No. 4 Flathead wood screw
—	Glue
—	Small brads
—	Brush lacquer
—	No. 4/0 Steel wool

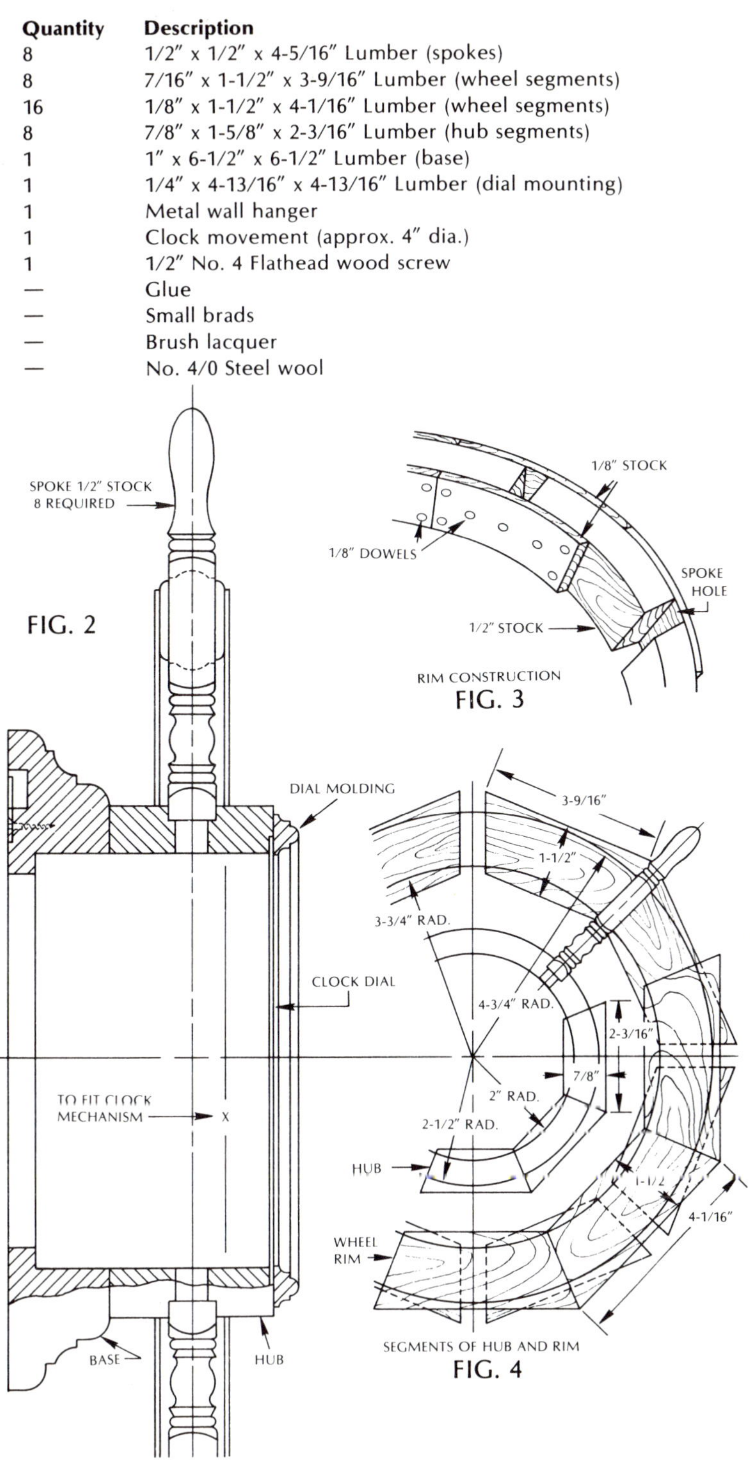

FIG. 2

RIM CONSTRUCTION
FIG. 3

SEGMENTS OF HUB AND RIM
FIG. 4

EARLY AMERICAN WALL PLANTER

The uses for this attractive wall shelf are limitless—it can be hung in practically any downstairs room and used to hold anything from an ivy plant to your fancy condiment containers.

It is made entirely of 3/8" thick solid cherry (except for the 1/8" hardboard drawer bottoms) and is an easy project to build. A band saw (or scroll saw), and a table saw are the only power tools needed. After laying out one side piece, drawing the curves with a compass (Fig. 2), tack the other side piece to it and cut both simultaneously. Separate the pieces and dado each one in three places with a 3/8" wide by 1/8" deep groove. The same size groove is also made in the center of the two lower crossmembers.

The drawers have conventional tongue and groove joint construction: the sizes are indicated in Fig. 1A. All of the curves can be sanded smooth with a carbide-coated sanding drum. Assemble the project with glue and either 1-1/4" brads or No. 4 by 1" flathead wood screws. Finish with polyurethane finish. Highly polished 1/2" brass knobs add the final touch.

Photo 2: Dado the side pieces on the table saw using one 1/8" outside and one 1/8" inside cutter.

Photo 1: By tacking the boards together, the two side pieces can be cut simultaneously on a scroll saw or band saw.

Photo 3: Sanding curved edges is an easy matter with a small sanding drum that will fit into either the scroll saw or a drill press.

MATERIALS

Quantity	Description
2	3/8" x 6-1/2" x 13-1/2" Lumber (sides)
3	3/8" x 6-1/2" x 7-1/2" Lumber (shelf boards)
1	3/8" x 6-1/2" x 2-1/4" Lumber (separator)
1	3/8" x 8" x 15-5/8" Lumber (back)
2	3/8" x 2" x 3-7/16" Lumber (drawer fronts)
4	3/8" x 2" x 6-3/8" Lumber (drawer sides)
2	3/8" x 1-1/2" x 3-1/16" Lumber (drawer backs)
2	1/8" x 3-1/16" x 6-5/16" Hardboard (drawer bottoms)
2	1/2" dia. Brass drawer knobs
-	White glue
-	1-1/4" Brads and/or No. 4 x 1" flathead wood screws
-	Fine abrasive paper
-	Polyurethane finish

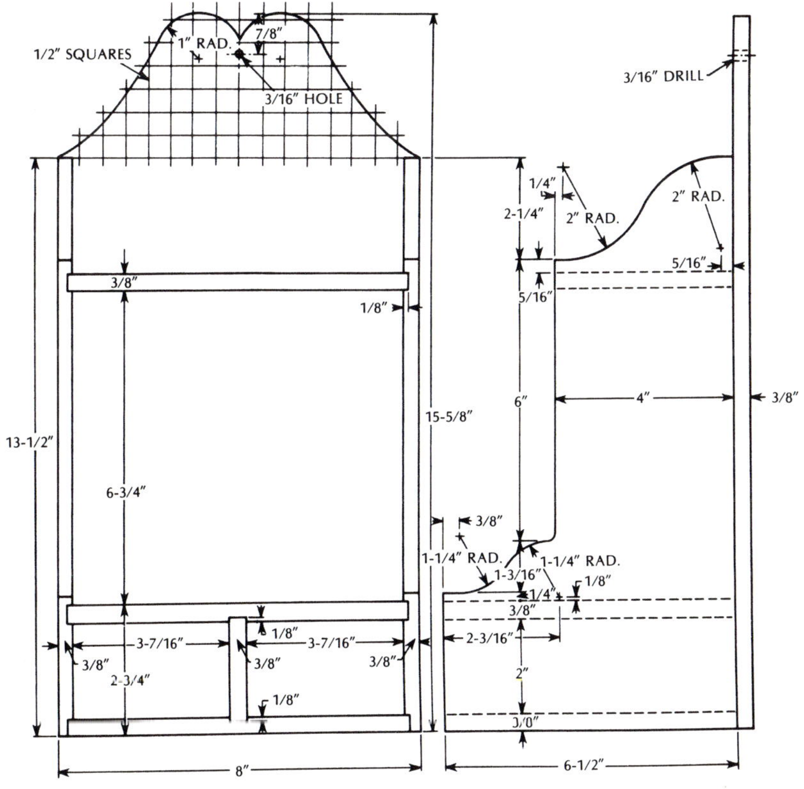

FIG. 1A FIG. 2

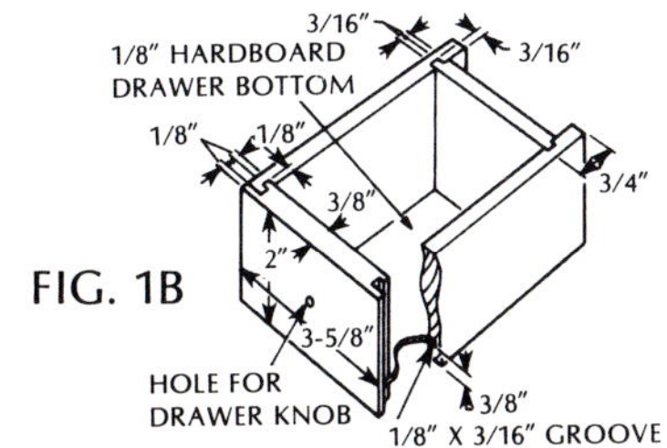

FIG. 1B

TRIVET TRAY

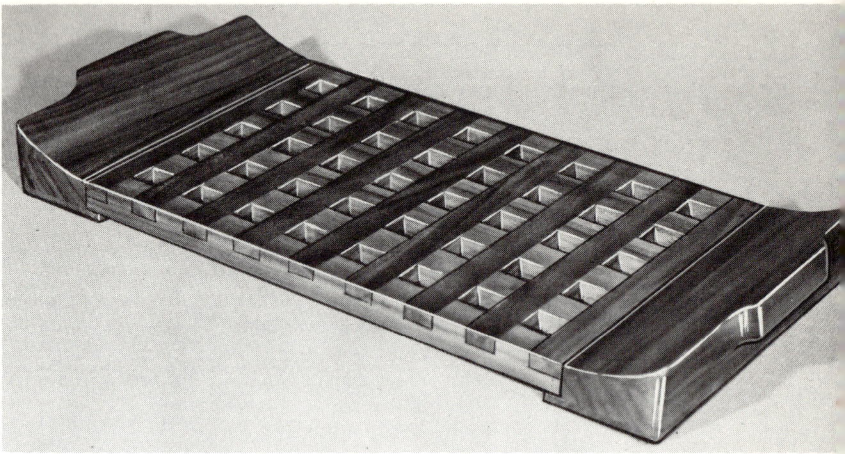

Functionalism and beauty are neatly combined in this wooden trivet tray. It will keep hot dishes from scorching your dining room table, and it can be used after dinner as a decorative centerpiece for the table.

The tray, made of walnut or mahogany, is a pattern of cross-lap joints of 3/4" strips spaced 3/4" apart. The 3/8" deep dadoes for the cross-lap joints are cut at one time in a solid piece of stock which is then cut into strips. They can also be cut one at a time in individual strips. Either way, a spacing jig is most helpful. After the dadoes are made, rip the stock into 3/4" strips. Cut them to lengths of 12-3/4" for the lengthwise sections and 8-1/4" for the cross members. When assembling, it is only necessary to glue the outside, or perimeter, crosslap joints.

The tray handles are coped simultaneously from one solid piece of stock 1-3/4" thick (or two glued together pieces) by 5-3/8" wide by 8-3/8" long, which is then cut in half, lengthwise, to give two symmetrical handles. Set the auxiliary fence (Photo 1) at an angle 39-1/2° to the miter gauge slot for a 10" blade. Make the cope cut in a series of light passes until you reach the desired 1" depth. The finger grip is also molded, before the piece is cut into the two handles, with molding cutters. (A 1/2" cove and 5/16" quarter round cutters were employed in the making of this tray as shown in Fig. 4.) The handles are cut to final shape on the band saw and are sanded with a 1-1/2" drum sander on the drill press. A 1/4" base strip is glued to the bottom of the tray. This strip should have a felt covering on its undersection.

Sand the entire project with medium to fine abrasive paper. Be sure to break all of the sharp edges. Finish natural with two coats of satin or flat polyurethane, sanding between the applications with very fine paper.

MATERIALS

Quantity	Description
1	3/4" x 7" x 22" Lumber (tray)
1	1-3/4" x 5-3/8" x 8-3/8" Lumber (tray)
—	Abrasive paper
—	Glue
—	Satin or flat polyurethane finish

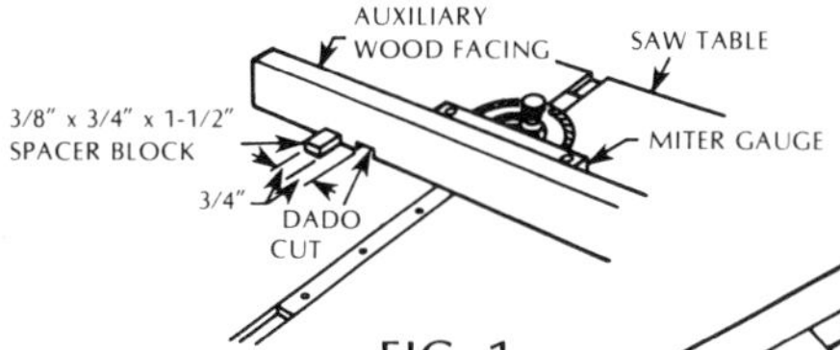

AUXILIARY WOOD FACING
SAW TABLE
3/8" x 3/4" x 1-1/2" SPACER BLOCK
MITER GAUGE
3/4"
DADO CUT

FIG. 1

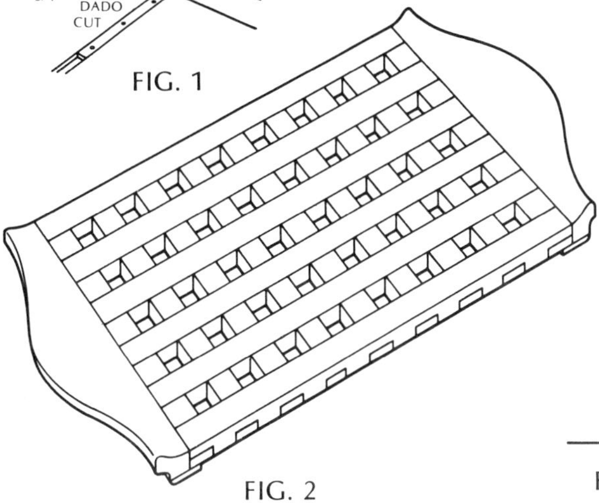

FIG. 2

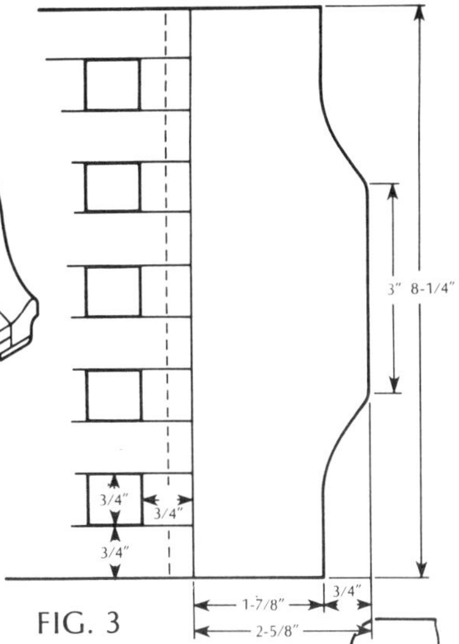

3" 8-1/4"
3/4"
3/4"
3/4"
1-7/8"
3/4"
2-5/8"

FIG. 3

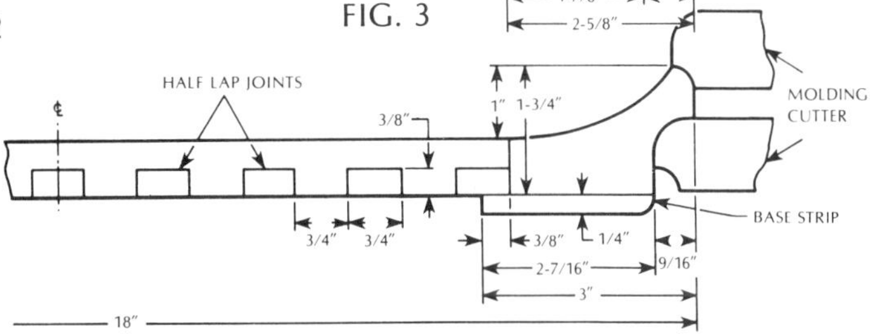

HALF LAP JOINTS
℄
3/8"
1" 1-3/4"
MOLDING CUTTER
BASE STRIP
3/4" 3/4"
3/8" 1/4"
2-7/16"
9/16"
3"
18"

FIG. 4

Photo 1: An auxiliary wood fence is C-clamped to the saw table to guide the stock that is being cope-cut. The blade is raised a fraction for each pass. This piece of stock, cut in half, makes the two handles. Note: Blade guard is removed for clarity.

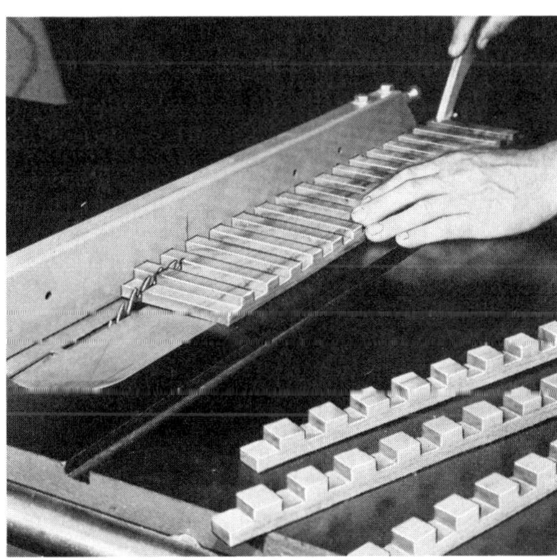

Photo 2: Cutting the grooved board into 3/4" strips. These strips are set into each other to form the pattern of half-lap joints. Note: Blade guard is removed for clarity.

KITCHEN ISLAND

This attractive, useful kitchen island is built beginning with the end panels. Build the 2″ end panels by sandwiching a frame constructed of 1/2″ pine between two pieces of 3/4″ plywood. Cut all the pieces for both end panels and assemble them using white glue and 1-1/4″ ringed nails. Wipe away any glue squeezed out before it dries with a damp cloth. Fill any voids in the plywood edges, sand smooth, dust, and set the panels aside until the white glue dries (about one hour). When dry, bond the laminate to the *inside surfaces of the end panels only* and set the panels aside temporarily.

Next, cut the plywood stretcher panel to the exact size. Notice the 5-1/4″ by 6-1/4″ notch at the upper right hand corner of this panel to allow for the full length cutting drawer. Laminate both sides of the stretcher panel and trim all overhang. Then, cut all the parts and assemble the pair of shelves. Laminate and trim the shelves. Do the front edges first, then the top surfaces. Details on laminating and trimming can be found on page 10.

Now, assemble the end panels, stretcher, and shelves as shown. Start by fastening the end panels to the stretcher using 2-1/2″ No. 10 flathead screws through the end panels and into the stretcher. Use at least four screws on each end (along with the white glue). Pilot drill holes should be made through the end panel's laminated surface. To install the shelves, clamp temporary cleats on the end panels at a height that puts the shelves at the desired location. Permanently fasten the shelves by installing 1-1/4″ No. 8 flathead wood screws through the shelf's permanent cleats into both the end panels. When the shelves are secured, remove the clamps and temporary cleats.

With the unit's base assembled, you can now go to work on the framing for the drawers — i.e., the divider rails — and the drawers themselves. On this unit, the two roomy, functional center drawers are built the same size for ease of construction. At one end of the island, a long narrow drawer serves to catch vegetable cuttings and the like. Once this drawer is made, you can add a sheetmetal liner for sanitary reasons. Whether you have the liner fashioned by a local sheetmetal shop, or you elect to do it yourself, use solder at the corners so there is no chance of liquid leakage.

With the base assembled and the rails and dividers in place, take the measurements for — and start building — the drawers. Temporarily assemble each drawer as you make it — test each for fit in the unit to make certain the drawers slide the way you want them to. When satisfied, take the drawers apart and permanently reassemble them using glue, screws, and small finishing nails. Laminate the drawer fronts with the appropriate laminate and set the drawers aside.

Build the top as shown. Before cutting the pieces, check the dimensions of your base and make sure the top fits, as shown in the drawing and photo. The top consists of three parts —the plywood top proper — and two 3/4" by 1-1/4" strips installed to create a thickened edge. Use white glue and 1-1/4" ringed nails to attach the strips to the underside of the countertop.

To create the knife slot in the top, draw in the slot's outline in its exact location on the top. Then bore through a 3/16" dia-

MATERIALS

Quantity	Description
4	3/4" x 24" x 37-1/4" Plywood (end panels)
1	3/4" x 37-1/4" x 44" Plywood (stretcher)
2	3/4" x 11-5/8" x 44" Plywood (shelves)
1	3/4" x 24" x 48" Plywood (top)
1	3/4" Plywood needed for drawer fronts, rails etc. — see drawing.
2	1/4" x 12" x 28" Plywood (drawer bottoms)
1	1/4" x 4" x 23" Plywood (drawer bottom)
20'	1/2" x 2" Pine lumber (filler strips)
19'	3/4" x 1-1/4" Pine lumber (shelf cleats and top edging)
4	1/2" x 4" x 10-3/4" Pine lumber (drawer sides)
2	1/2" x 3" x 28" Pine lumber (drawer backs)
1	1/2" x 3" x 3-1/2" Pine lumber (cutting drawer)
2	1/2" x 4" x 22-1/2" Pine lumber (cutting drawer)
15'	1/2" x 1/2" Aluminum angle
—	White glue
—	Assorted screws (see drawer)
4	Furniture glides
—	Contact cement
—	Adhesive solvent
	WOODGRAIN PLASTIC LAMINATE*
1	25" x 49" — Top
2	25" x 38" — Outer surfaces
2	2-1/2" x 48-1/2" — Top
4	2-1/2" x 40" — Verticals
	SOLID COLOR PLASTIC LAMINATE*
2	38" x 45" — Stretchers
2	12" x 45" — Shelves
2	1-3/4" x 45" — Shelf edging
2	24-1/2" x 48" — End panels
2	5" x 49" — Drawer fronts

* Two laminate patterns were used on the kitchen island illustrated: Maple woodgrain and solid white. Other designs may be substituted. All necessary pieces of the woodgrain laminate can be cut from one 60" by 96" sheet. All necessary pieces of the solid color can be cut from one 60" by 96" and one 60" by 60" laminate sheet. Take the time to lay out the island part sizes to assure a proper yield.

meter hole at both ends of the slot, to provide the entry holes for a jig saw blade: insert a fine-tooth blade in your saw and cut out the lines between the two bored holes. Repeat these steps to create the larger slot (for cuttings) at the other end of the island. For this slot, however, before you laminate the top, you are well advised to cover the slot sides for sanitary reasons. To do it, first add the 3/4" by 1-1/4" strips of pine to thicken the cutout edge (see drawing), cut two pieces of laminate to exactly fit both ends of the slot, and apply contact cement to the ends of the slot and the mating laminate pieces. Bond the pieces in place. Repeat these steps to cover the sides of the slot.

Assemble the top to the base using white glue and 1-1/4" No. 8 flathead screws through the top and into the end panels. Also, install several screws through the top and into the drawer-divider sections. The top should rest perfectly flat on the base (i.e., no rocking motion).

Apply the laminate to the 2" wide horizontal and vertical surfaces of both sides and trim. (*Note:* Use a miter cut at the top where the vertical strips meet the horizontal self-edging.) Finally, apply the laminate to the top surface and trim as necessary.

Taking care to protect the laminate surfaces, flop the unit on one side, and bore the holes for the four casters. Right the unit. Install the furniture glides and the drawers. Clean up the laminate surfaces, using contact cement solvent recommended on the label instructions. Be sure to follow all safety precautions for solvent use and provide adequate ventilation.

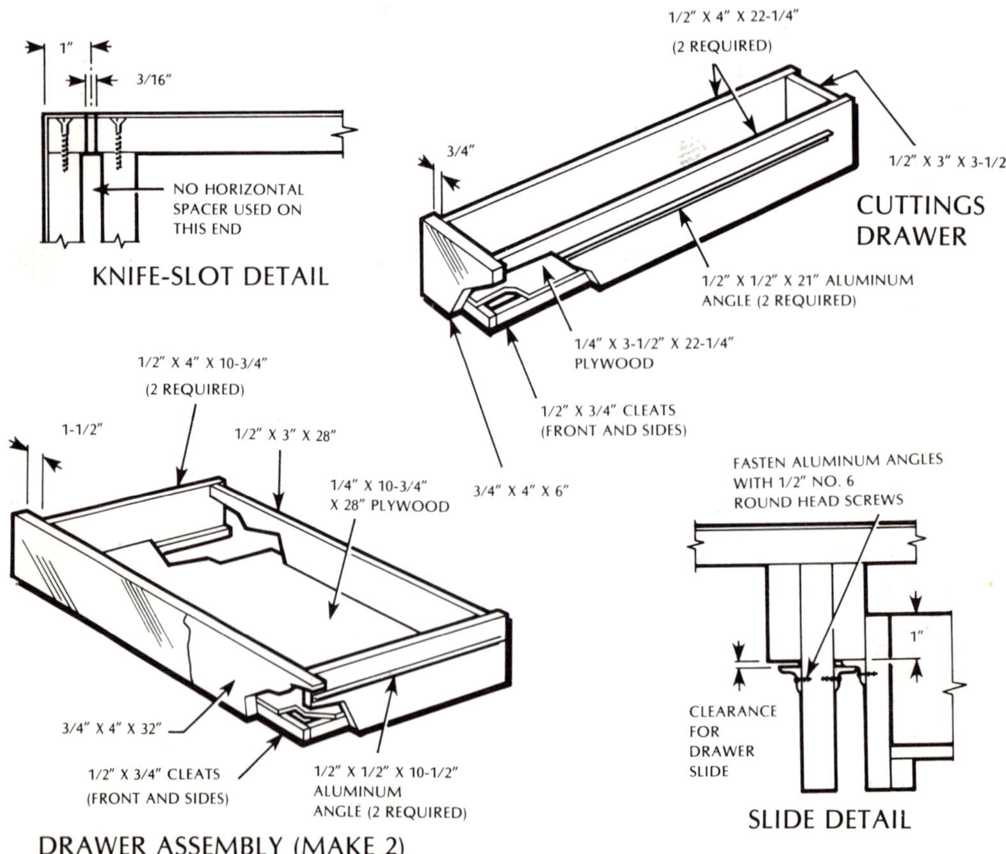

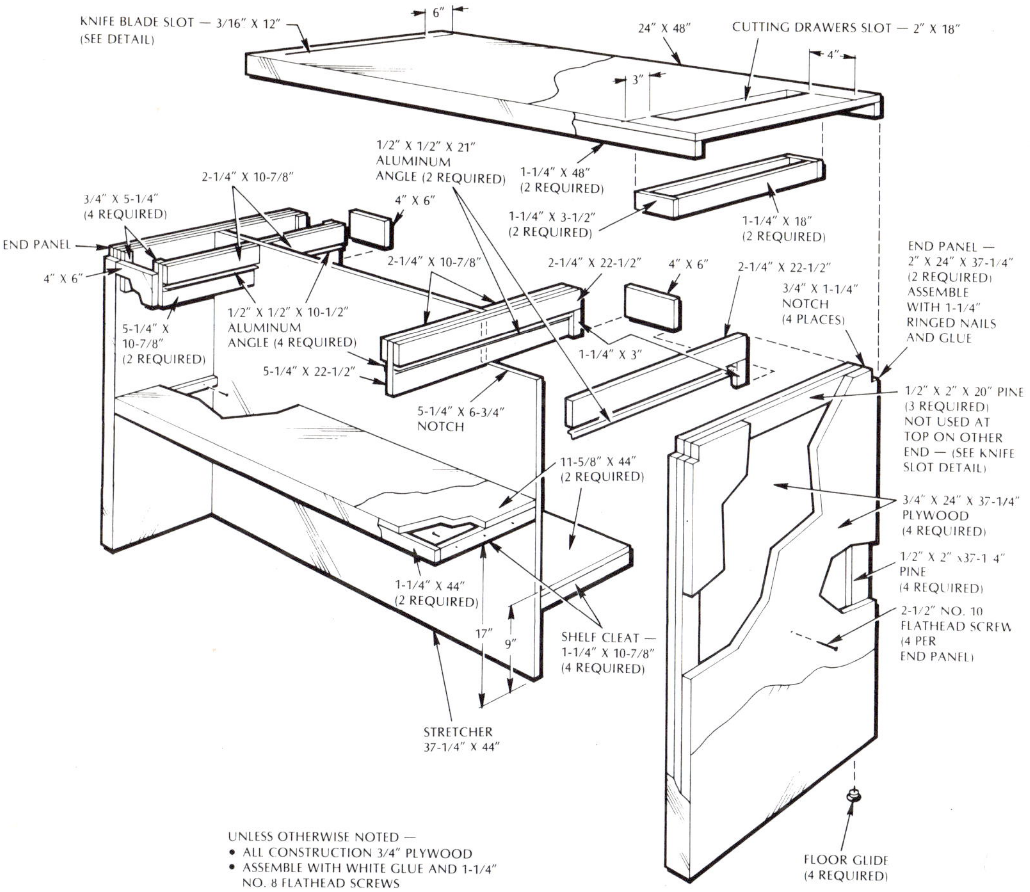

KNIFE BLADE SLOT — 3/16" X 12"
(SEE DETAIL)

6"

24" X 48"

CUTTING DRAWERS SLOT — 2" X 18"

4"

3"

1/2" X 1/2" X 21"
ALUMINUM
ANGLE (2 REQUIRED)

1-1/4" X 48"
(2 REQUIRED)

2-1/4" X 10-7/8"

3/4" X 5-1/4"
(4 REQUIRED)

4" X 6"

1-1/4" X 3-1/2"
(2 REQUIRED)

1-1/4" X 18"
(2 REQUIRED)

END PANEL

4" X 6"

2-1/4" X 10-7/8"

2-1/4" X 22-1/2"

4" X 6"

2-1/4" X 22-1/2"

END PANEL —
2" X 24" X 37-1/4"
(2 REQUIRED)
ASSEMBLE
WITH 1-1/4"
RINGED NAILS
AND GLUE

3/4" X 1-1/4"
NOTCH
(4 PLACES)

5-1/4" X
10-7/8"
(2 REQUIRED)

1/2" X 1/2" X 10-1/2"
ALUMINUM
ANGLE (4 REQUIRED)

5-1/4" X 22-1/2"

1-1/4" X 3"

1/2" X 2" X 20" PINE
(3 REQUIRED)
NOT USED AT
TOP ON OTHER
END — (SEE KNIFE
SLOT DETAIL)

5-1/4" X 6-3/4"
NOTCH

11-5/8" X 44"
(2 REQUIRED)

3/4" X 24" X 37-1/4"
PLYWOOD
(4 REQUIRED)

1/2" X 2" X 37-1/4"
PINE
(4 REQUIRED)

1-1/4" X 44"
(2 REQUIRED)

2-1/2" NO. 10
FLATHEAD SCREW
(4 PER
END PANEL)

17"

9"

SHELF CLEAT —
1-1/4" X 10-7/8"
(4 REQUIRED)

STRETCHER
37-1/4" X 44"

UNLESS OTHERWISE NOTED —
- ALL CONSTRUCTION 3/4" PLYWOOD
- ASSEMBLE WITH WHITE GLUE AND 1-1/4" NO. 8 FLATHEAD SCREWS

FLOOR GLIDE
(4 REQUIRED)

Photo 1: The surface is ready for bonding when the adhesive does not adhere to clean kraft paper. Lay 3/4" dowel sticks on the surface to prevent premature bonding between it and the laminate sheet.

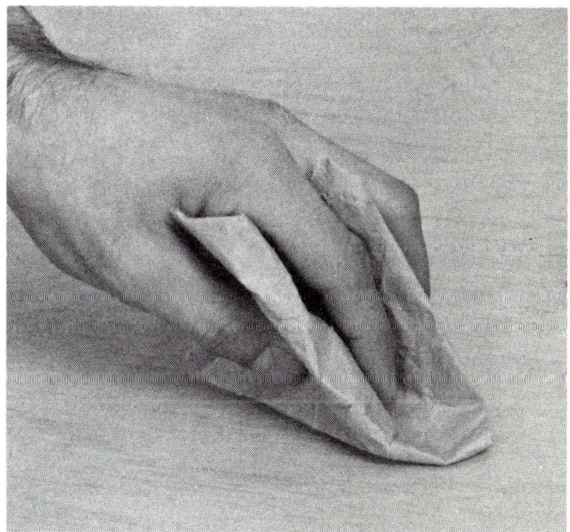

Photo 2: As the dowel sticks are pulled, the laminate will be bonded to the surface. Immediately apply pressure over the entire surface. Give extra attention to the joint at the edges. Glue lines must be tight.

CARVING BOARD & FOOD SERVER

Here is a unique carving board that is also used as a food server. The center carrying section holds a ham, roast, or any fowl where all the juices are collected in the corner wells. The corner leaves are hinged to the server with a roomy well in each for holding various vegetables and garnishes.

The entire project is made from 1-1/4" thick hardwood, either birch or maple. The serving block is 12" square. Make a corner design of the carved tree and well using the squares method. Lay out the design onto a 1/8" tempered hardboard and cut it out on a scroll saw (Photo 1) or a portable jig saw. This is used as a template for making the carved trees and wells with a router. A template guide on the center follows the cutout template. The 5" diameter wells in the corner leaves are routed out using a template with a template guide mounted in a router fitted with a 3/8" router bit. The gain for the continuous hinge is cut out on the table saw in one operation (Photo 2 and Fig. 6).

Eight ball feet are turned on the lathe from brass or a matching hardwood as shown in Fig. 2. Screw studs for fastening the ball feet to the serving board can be made from a 1-1/2" No. 8 ordinary wood screw by sawing off the head and threading the screw shank with an 8-32 thread (Fig. 3).

Sand all parts with a fine and very fine abrasive paper, breaking sharp corners. Do not apply any finish to the well surfaces of the server except to the edges and undersides which should be sealed with two coats of polyurethane finish. Apply vegetable shortening or olive oil to the serving portion of the tray and leaves.

Photo 1: Templates for the routing operations are made of 1/8" thick tempered hardboard and cut out on the scroll saw using a jeweler's blade. The cut can also be made with a jig saw.

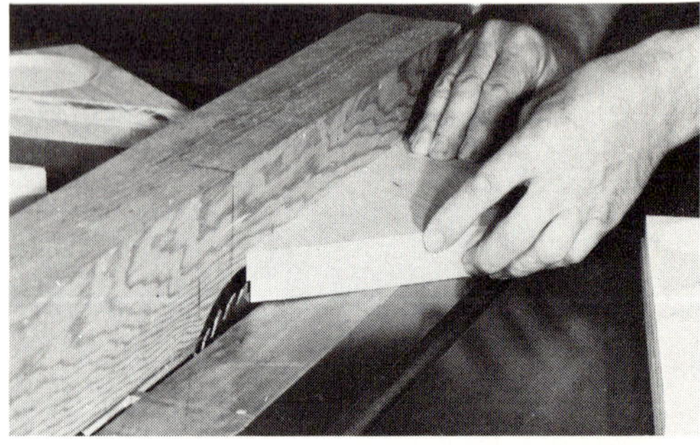

Photo 2: Gaining for the continuous hinges is done on the table saw with the stock lying flat. Note the auxiliary wood fence fastened to the rip fence of the saw to prevent the blade from striking the metal fence.

Photo 3: The design is cut with a router using the template as a guide.

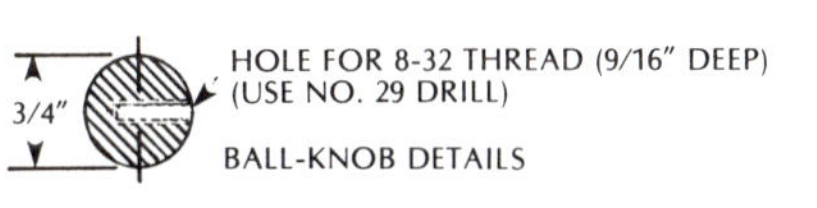

FIG. 2

FIG. 3

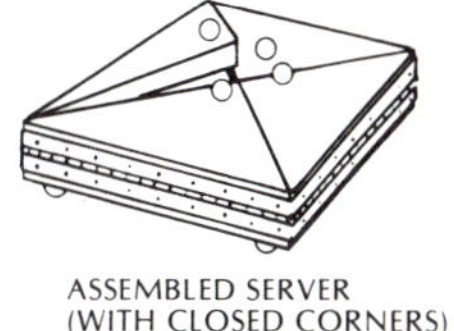

FIG. 4

17-1/4"
12"
2-1/4"
2-1/2" DIA.
17-1/4" SQ.
1/2" SQUARES
CONTINUOUS
HINGE
2-1/2"
4" DIA.
1"
1"
TOP VIEW

FIG. 1

CONTINUOUS
HINGE
GAIN
FOR HINGE
CENTER
BOARD
LEAF
HINGE MOUNTING

FIG. 6

2-1/2"
1-1/4" 1-1/4"
CHROME
PLATED
CONTINUOUS
HINGE
(1-1/2" x 12")
END VIEW (FOLDED)

FIG. 5

BUCKIN' BURRO GLIDER

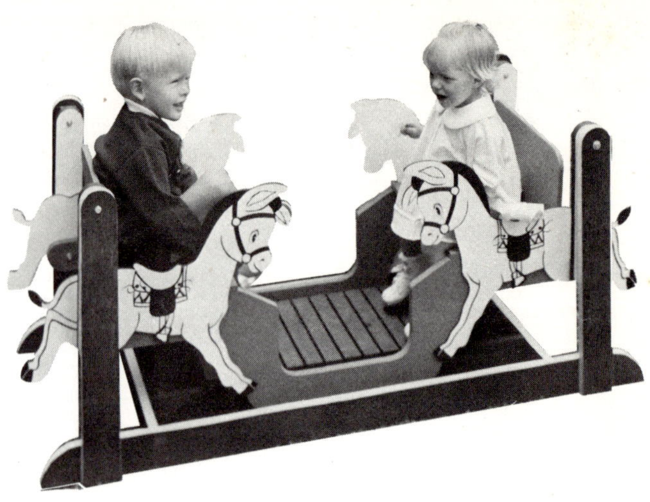

This project is bound to be a hit with the kids. The glider is designed so that even the smallest child can sit in it and glide back and forth without fear of falling out.

The glider frame and base, as well as the floor assembly, are made of 3/4" A-A, A-B, or B-B grade marked exterior plywood. The seat boards and seat backs are made of 1/2" exterior plywood. The four burro designs are cut from 3/8" exterior plywood.

Lay out the burro design on a piece of wrapping paper or directly onto one of the pieces of plywood, using the squares method. By tacking all four pieces (A) together, they can be cut at one time on either the band saw or scroll saw (Photo 1). *Note*: Scroll saw cut-outs (X) on the foot spur and tail do not necessarily have to be made. As a matter of fact, the tail cut-out would have a tendency to weaken the outline, causing it to break off if it is handled roughly. Pipe bushings in spacer blocks (F) are used as the pivot points for mounting the burro cut-outs to the glider frame sides (L), see Figs. 7 and 8 of drawing.

The glider frame sides (L) are assembled together with the cleats (M), the seat, and the seat backs (J) and (K), Figs. 6 and 7. The position of the burro is indicated in Fig. 7.

All the necessary details of the glider base are shown in detail in Figs. 2, 3, 3A and 9.

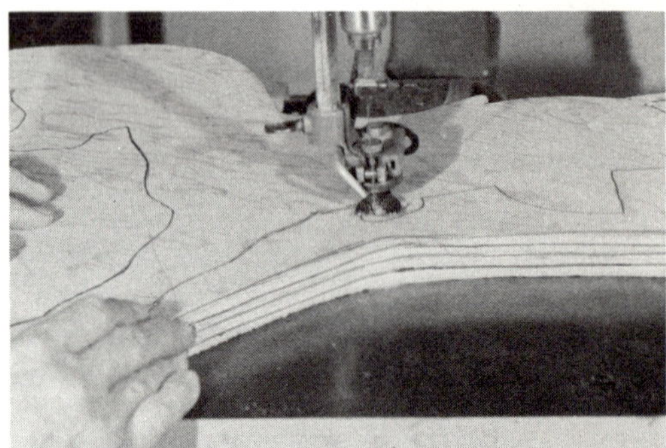

Photo 1: Tack all four burro pieces together with light brads and cut the outlines on either the band saw or scroll saw. A jeweler's blade is best for this operation. Run the saw about 1725 rpm.

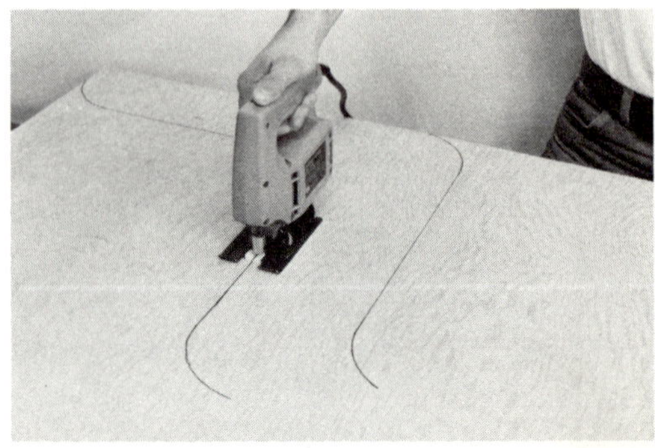

Photo 2: Because the pieces of the glider frame are too large to handle on the scroll saw or band saw, a portable jig saw is excellent for this purpose.

The floor assembly is screw fastened to the base frame sides with No. 8 x 1-3/4″ flathead brass wood screws.

Break all the sharp corners with a fine abrasive paper to prevent splinters. The glider frame assembly should be treated with a wood preservative followed with an outside undercoat and enamel. The burro should be painted with a lighter enamel with feature lines in black or brown.

MATERIALS

Quantity	Description
4	3/8″ x 18″ x 20-1/2″ Plywood (burro sides — A)
4	3/4″ x 2-7/8″ x 23-3/8″ Plywood (posts — B)
2	3/4″ x 3-1/2″ x 54″ Plywood (base sides — C)
2	3/4″ x 3-1/2″ x 19-1/2″ Plywood (base ends — D)
4	3/4″ x 3″ x 14-3/8″ Plywood (glider arms — E)
8	3/4″ x 1-1/2″ x 1-1/2″ Plywood (spacers — F)
8	2-5/16″ Pipe bushings (for 1/4″ carriage bolts — G)
2	3/4″ x 3-1/2″ x 34-3/4″ Plywood (floor cleats — H)
12	3/4″ x 1-3/4″ x 34-3/4″ Plywood (floor slats — I)
2	1/2″ x 10-1/4″ x 15-1/4″ Plywood (seats — J)
2	1/2″ x 11-3/8″ x 15-1/4″ Plywood (backs — K)
2	3/4″ x 10-1/2″ x 47-1/2″ Plywood (frame sides — L)
2	3/4″ x 2-3/4″ x 13-3/4″ Plywood (frame cleats — M)
8	1/4″ x 2-1/2″ Carriage bolts and nuts
-	No. 8 x 1-3/4″ Flathead wood screws
-	Resorcinol-type waterproof glue
-	Wood putty
-	Fine abrasive paper
-	Wood preservative
-	Exterior undercoat and enamel

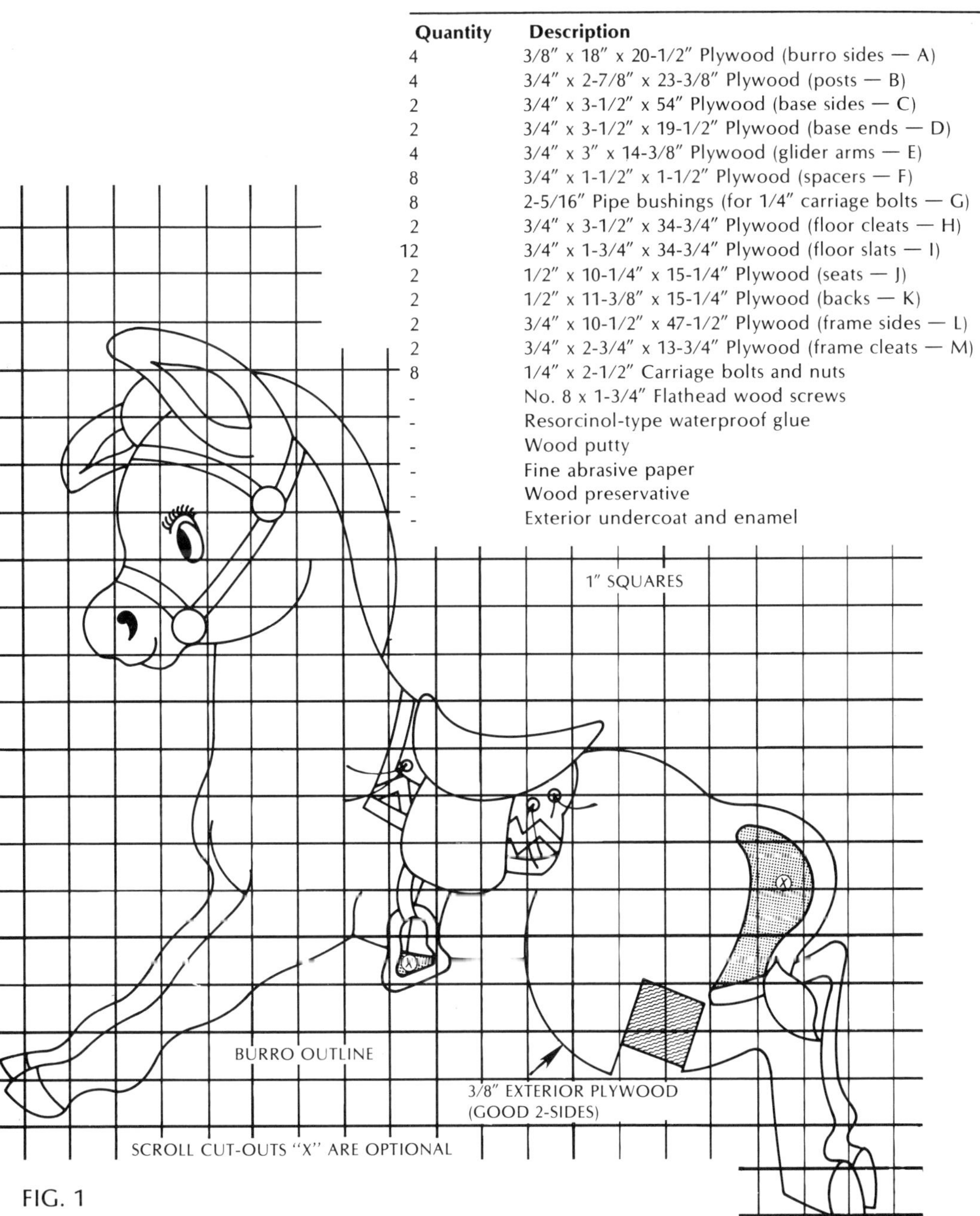

FIG. 1

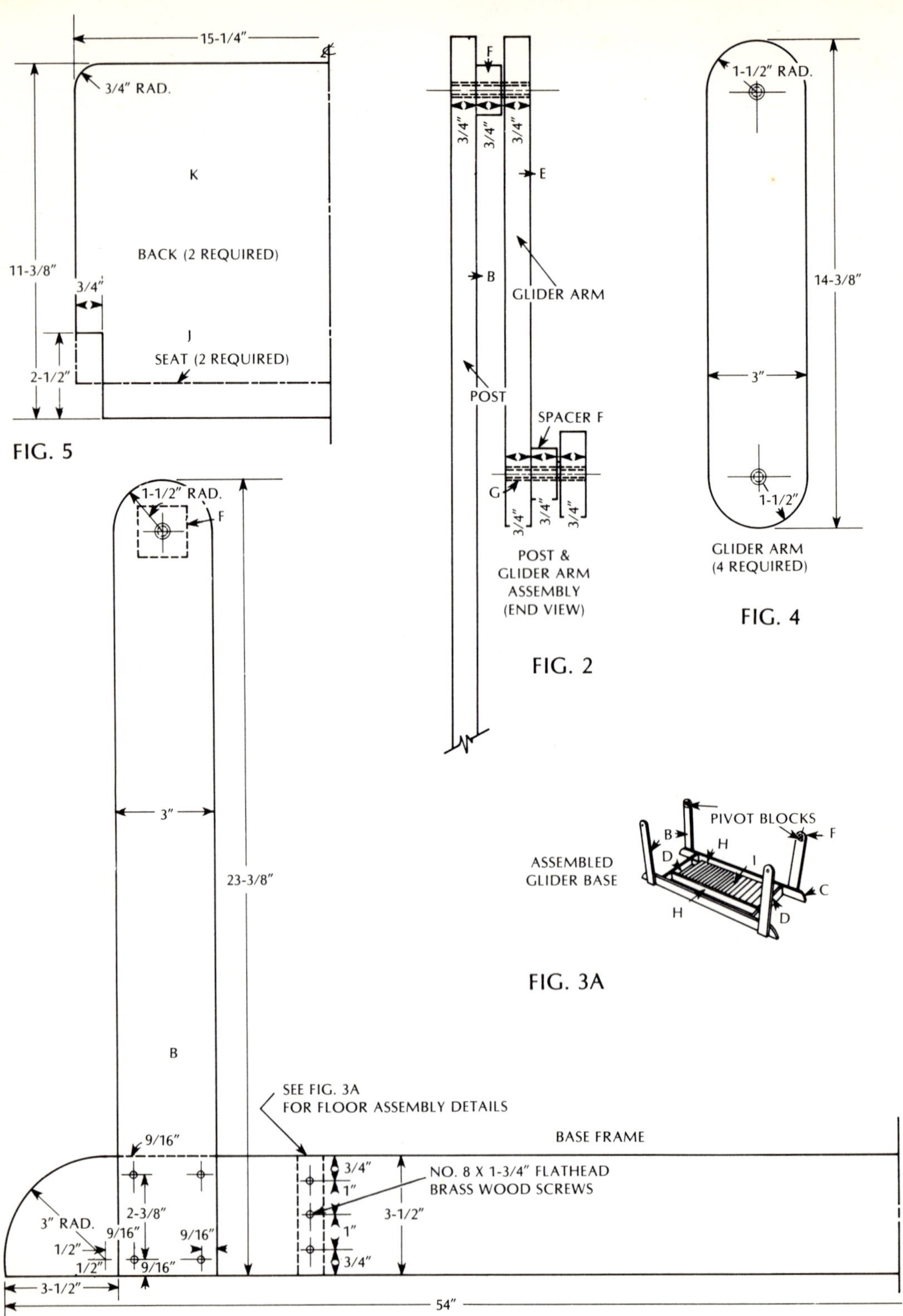
15-1/4"
3/4" RAD.
11-3/8"
K
BACK (2 REQUIRED)
3/4"
J
SEAT (2 REQUIRED)
2-1/2"
FIG. 5
F
3/4"
3/4"
3/4"
E
B
GLIDER ARM
POST
SPACER F
G
3/4"
3/4"
3/4"
POST &
GLIDER ARM
ASSEMBLY
(END VIEW)
FIG. 2
1-1/2" RAD.
14-3/8"
3"
1-1/2"
GLIDER ARM
(4 REQUIRED)
FIG. 4
1-1/2" RAD.
F
3"
23-3/8"
PIVOT BLOCKS
B
H
F
D
I
ASSEMBLED
GLIDER BASE
C
H
D
FIG. 3A
B
SEE FIG. 3A
FOR FLOOR ASSEMBLY DETAILS
BASE FRAME
9/16"
3/4"
1"
1"
3/4"
NO. 8 X 1-3/4" FLATHEAD
BRASS WOOD SCREWS
3-1/2"
2-3/8"
3" RAD.
9/16"
9/16"
1/2"
1/2"
9/16"
3-1/2"
54"

FIG. 3

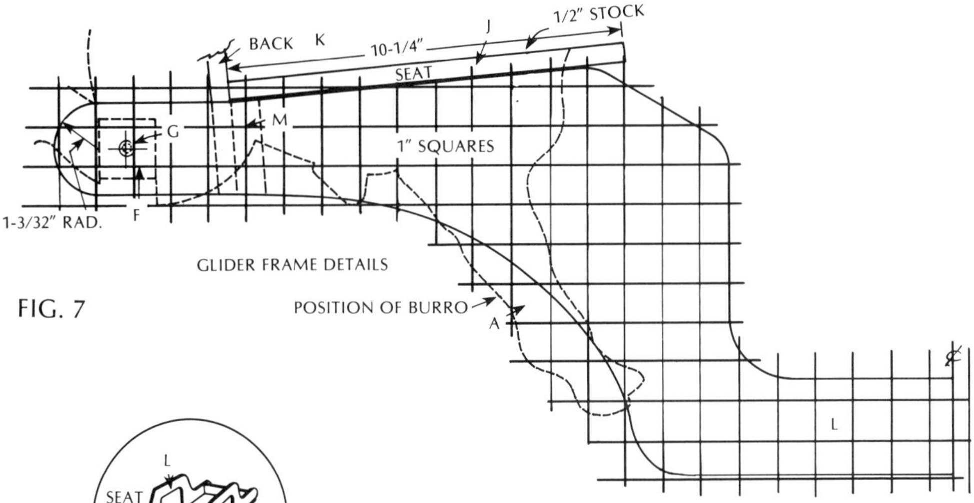

BACK
K
10-1/4"
J
1/2" STOCK
SEAT
M
G
1" SQUARES
1-3/32" RAD.
F
POSITION OF BURRO
A
L
GLIDER FRAME DETAILS

FIG. 7

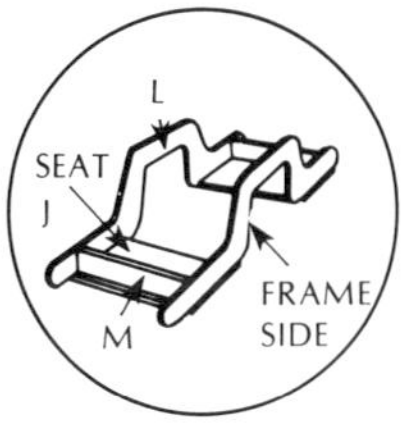

L
SEAT
J
FRAME
SIDE
M
GLIDER FRAME ASSEMBLY BOTTOM VIEW

FIG. 6

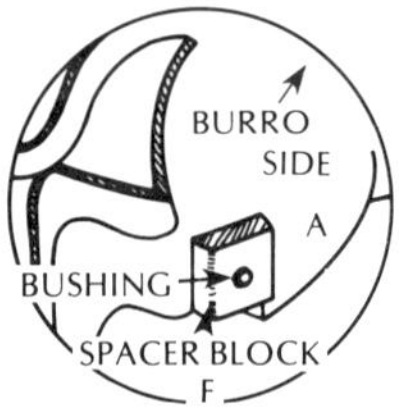

BURRO
SIDE
A
BUSHING
SPACER BLOCK
F
BURRO ATTACHED TO GLIDER

FIG. 8

D
4"
H
11-1/2"
19-1/2"
H
4"
1-3/4"
1/4" APART
3/4"
3/4"
36"
FLOOR ASSEMBLY

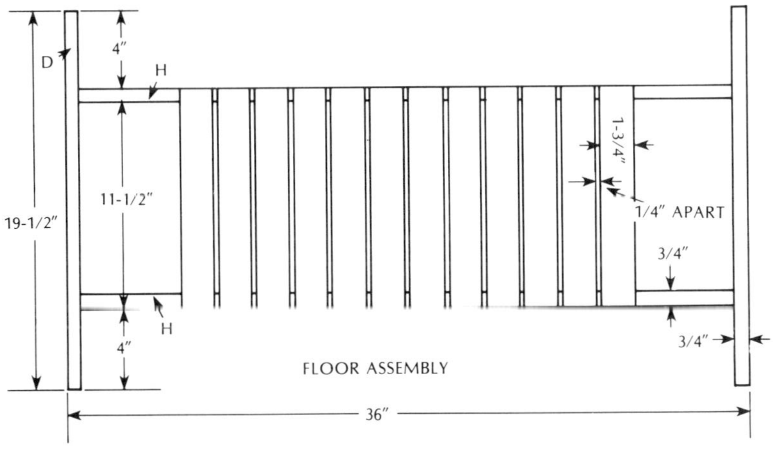

FIG. 9

BATHROOM CABINET

Keep towels and toiletries conveniently at hand in this simply styled cabinet. It is sure to dress up a bathroom wall and provide extra storage for bath items.

Because of dampness present in a bathroom, it is wise to use A-C Exterior or Medium Density Overlaid (MDO) grade-trademarked plywood. For the inside cuts required for Part A, start a hole with a drill, then use a coping or keyhole saw. Or, if available, you may use a portable jig saw or a stationary scroll saw. In any case, be sure the blade enters the good face of the panel.

When assembling the bathroom cabinet, keep these building hints in mind:

1. Fasten the shelves to the side panels by gluing the shelf ends and nailing through the side panels.

2. Glue-nail the front and back panels to the shelves and side panels.

MDO plywood needs no preparation and is finished with conventional paints for an exceptionally smooth and durable surface. Sanded panels require very little preparation, primarily "touch sanding" (in direction of grain only) to smooth any filler or putty applied to minor openings in the panel face or to remove blemishes. Do not paint over dust, spots of oil, or glue. Any knots or pitch streaks should be touched up with sealer or shellac before painting.

MATERIALS

Quantity	Description
1	3/4″ x 4′ x 8′ Plywood panel
—	Fine abrasive paper
—	White glue
—	8d Finishing nails
—	Wood putty
—	Interior semi-gloss enamel paint

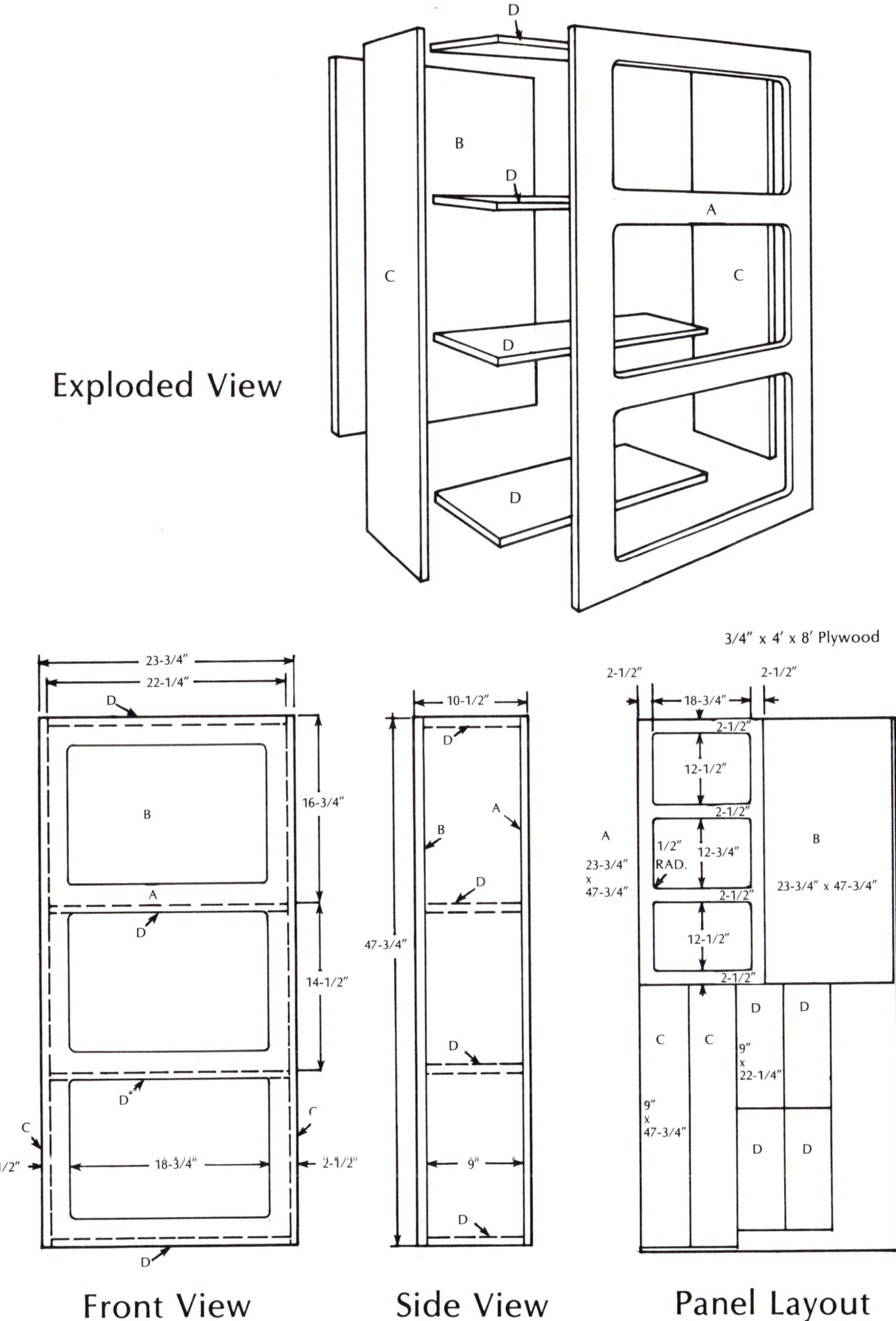
Exploded View
A
B
C
C
D
D
D
D
3/4" x 4' x 8' Plywood
23-3/4"
22-1/4"
16-3/4"
14-1/2"
18-3/4"
2-1/2"
2-1/2"
Front View
10-1/2"
47-3/4"
9"
Side View
2-1/2"
2-1/2"
18-3/4"
2-1/2"
12-1/2"
2-1/2"
1/2" RAD.
12-3/4"
2-1/2"
12-1/2"
2-1/2"
A
23-3/4" x 47-3/4"
B
23-3/4" x 47-3/4"
C
C
9" x 47-3/4"
D
D
9" x 22-1/4"
D
D
Panel Layout

MAGAZINE CUBE

The dimensions may be varied to accommodate various size magazines or other articles to be stored in this handy and easy-to-make rack. But, whatever the size, the basic construction remains the same. That is, start by cutting the plywood to your specifications or to the proper sizes shown in Fig. 1. Then before assembling any components, laminate all the inside surfaces of the magazine rack—the sides, ends, and bottom (see page 10 for details). Rout all the edges flush.

Now, begin the assembly. Using No. 8 by 1-1/4″ flathead screws, fasten the side and end components into the box structure, using simple butt joints. Drill pilot holes through the laminate. Be sure that all the laminate-clad surfaces are on the inside of the box. Then, fasten the bottom member. Be certain that the screws are countersunk flush with the wood surface. After filling any voids, sand the surface smooth and dust it thoroughly.

Next, fasten together the 1-1/2″ by 6-1/2″ components to make a pair of solid casters for the rack. Laminate the edges, starting with the ends on each small piece and rout flush. Laminate the other sides and bevel the edges. The top and bottom surfaces are *not* to be laminated.

Continue to laminate the exterior surfaces of the rack, starting with the ends, and rout flush. Then apply the side surfaces, bevel routing at the laminate-to-laminate side/end joints, flush routing the

MATERIALS

Quantity	Description
2	3/4″ x 7-1/4″ x 7-1/4″ Plywood (ends)
2	3/4″ x 7-1/4″ x 13-1/4″ Plywood (sides)
1	3/4″ x 8″ x 14″ Plywood (bottom)
4	3/4″ x 1-1/2″ x 6-1/2″ Plywood (caster strips)
4	8-1/2″ x 8-1/2″ Plastic laminate*
6	8-1/2″ x 14-1/2″ Plastic laminate*
4	2″ x 7″ Plastic laminate*
—	White glue
—	Fine abrasive paper
—	No. 8 by 1-1/4″ Flathead wood screws
2	Solid casters
—	Contact adhesive
—	Adhesive solvent

*Note: All the necessary laminate pieces can be cut from one 30″ by 48″ laminate sheet. Take the time to lay out the magazine rack part sizes to assure the proper yield.

top and bottom edges. Now, laminate the one full 8-1/2" by 14-1/2" laminate piece to the top edges of the assembly. Carefully drill a hole through the laminate to start the router edge finishing of the inside edges. Rout the inside edges flush, taking care to radius all the inside corners slightly. The outside edges should be bevel routed.

To complete the magazine rack project, lay the rack on its top edges carefully and fasten the two solid casters to the bottom surface, using white glue. After the white glue has been allowed to dry for at least one hour, apply cork, felt or urethane bumpers to the bottom for a smooth, scratch-free surface.

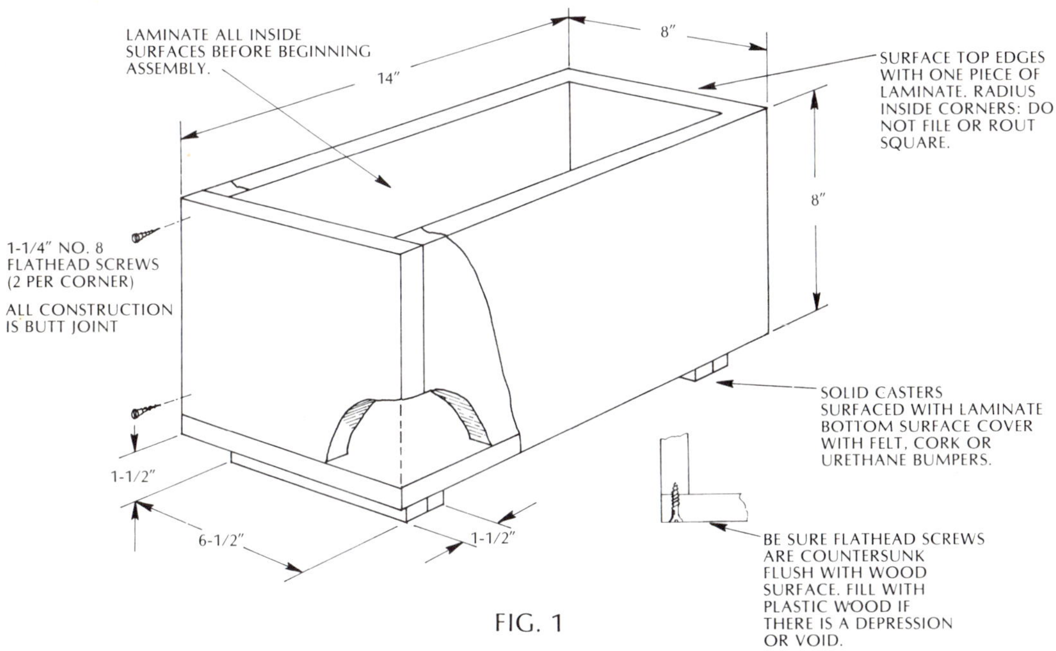

FIG. 1

Photo 1: Trimming the laminate is done first with a straight cutter, then by a bevel carbide bit.

Photo 2: The laminate trimmer uses one cutter; it is adjustable for straight and bevel cutting.

TOY WHEELBARROW

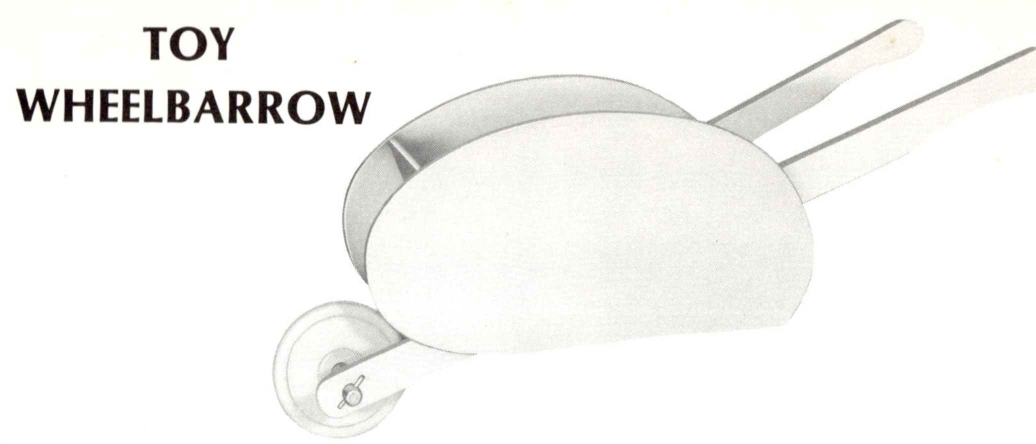

This is the type of toy that will give the little ones endless hours of pleasure throughout the year. They will use this wheelbarrow to store toys, give the pets a ride and dozens of other activities. To make it a personalized toy, the child's name can be painted on the wheelbarrow sides.

The project should be made of a hard wood to withstand hard wear. The sides, back and bottom of the wheelbarrow box are made of 3/8" A-A or A-B Exterior plywood. Draw the curved shape of the box sides onto some paper using the squares method indicated in Fig. 3. Tack both sides together and cut to shape on the band saw (Photo 1). For added strength on the box assembly, glue and nail a piece of 1/2" quarter round molding on the two inside corners (Fig. 2 and 3).

Handles are made of 3/4" by 1-3/8" by 27-1/4" hardwood stock, either birch or maple. Bore the axle dowel holes 1" from the end of the handle stock (Photo 3). Round off the handle ends as well as the underside of the handle portion for easier gripping. The assembled wheelbarrow box is fastened to the handle stock with glue and nails.

The wheel is turned on the lathe with the stock mounted between centers (Photo 2). If you decide on inserting a bushing, bore out the hole to suit the outside size of the bushing stock. To prevent the wheel from riding back and forth on the axle, place pipe bushings between the wheel hub and handle stock. The 1/8" dowel pins hold the axle in place (Figs. 1 and 2).

Sand all the parts to break all sharp corners and seal with an enamel undercoat. Two coats of enamel should put a hard finish to the project.

Photo 1: By tacking the side pieces of the wheelbarrow together, the two pieces are cut at the same time on the band saw using a 1/4" skip tooth blade. They could also be cut with a portable jig saw.

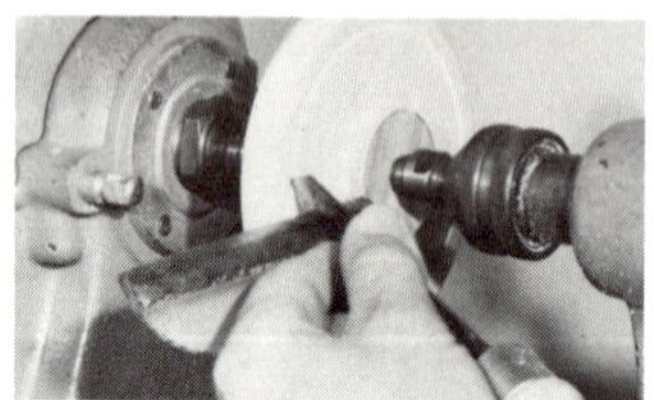

Photo 2: The wheelbarrow wheel is turned on the lathe between centers. Note: The 1/4" plywood disk on the tailstock end helps to hold the wheel steady while being turned.

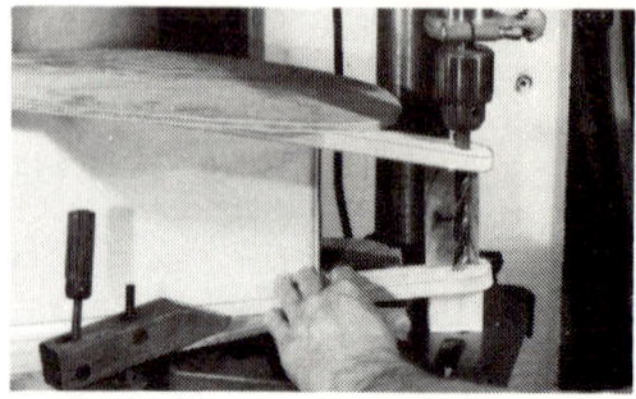

Photo 3: Holes for the wheel axle on the handle stock are bored on the drill press using a 1/2" bit. Note: The scrap blocks are to prevent the stock from tearing and also to support the stock.

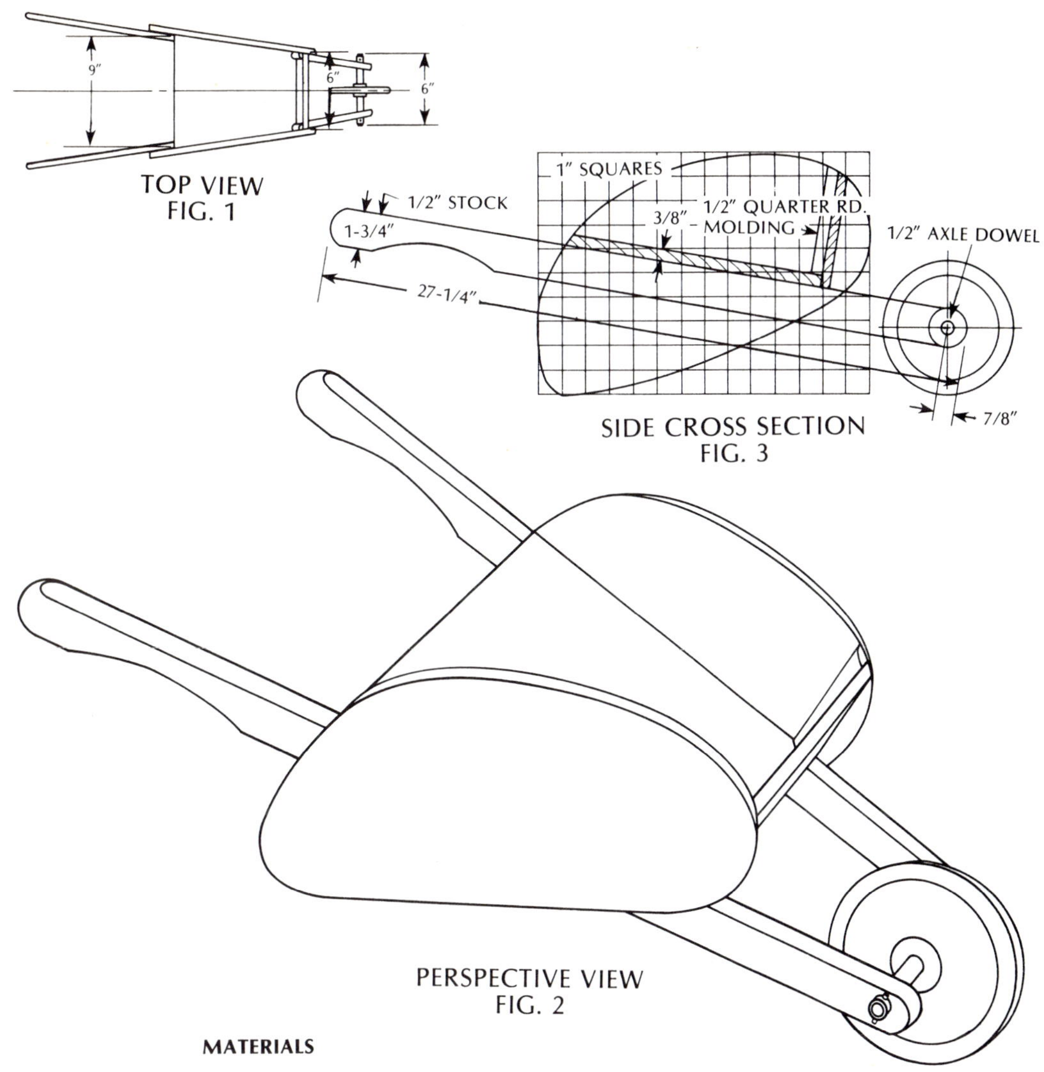

TOP VIEW
FIG. 1

SIDE CROSS SECTION
FIG. 3

PERSPECTIVE VIEW
FIG. 2

MATERIALS

Quantity	**Description**
2	3/8" x 10" x 14" Plywood (sides)
2	3/4" x 1-3/8" x 27-1/4" Lumber (handles)
1	3/8" x 9" x 10-3/4" Plywood (bottom)
1	3/8" x 4-1/4" x 6" Plywood (end)
1	3/4" x 5" dia. Lumber (wheel)
2	1/2" x 4-1/2" Quarter round molding
1	1/2" dia. x 6" Dowel (axle)
2	1/8" dia. x 7/8" Dowel (axle pins)
1	1/2" I.D. x 3/4" Brass bushing (optional)
-	White glue
-	Finishing nails
-	Fine abrasive paper
-	Wood putty
-	Enamel undercoat
-	Enamel

5/8"
5/8"
3/4"
BRASS
BUSHING
(OPTIONAL)
1/2"
5" DIA.

WHEEL DETAILS
FIG. 4

MUSICAL MOTIF WALL PLAQUES

In addition to producing beautiful sounds, musical instruments also lend themselves quite easily to fascinating designs. These musical motif walnut wall plaques make handsome conversation pieces for any home.

Lay out the sounding box and head block using the squares method as indicated in Figs. 1 and 3. Mortise both the sounding box and head block to accept the fingerboard. See Figs. 1, 2, 3, 4 and Photo 1. Cut the 2″ hole (Fig. 3) on the scroll saw, as shown in Photo 2. Drill 1/2″ holes in the head block for the keys, (Photo 3). Rough cut the sounding box and head block on the band saw. The outer edge of the sounding box is finished to a 2″ radius.

The keys, bridge and string holder are cut to size as indicated in Figs. 1 and 3. Note, the key end which fits into the head

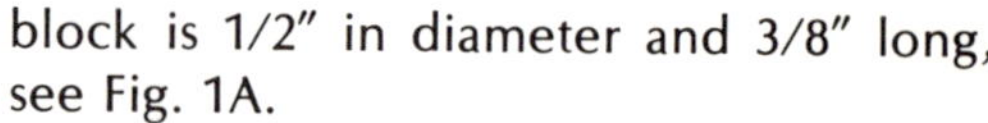

block is 1/2″ in diameter and 3/8″ long, see Fig. 1A.

Assemble all pieces with glue, and sand with fine, or very fine, sandpaper. For a satin effect, use a penetrating resin finish.

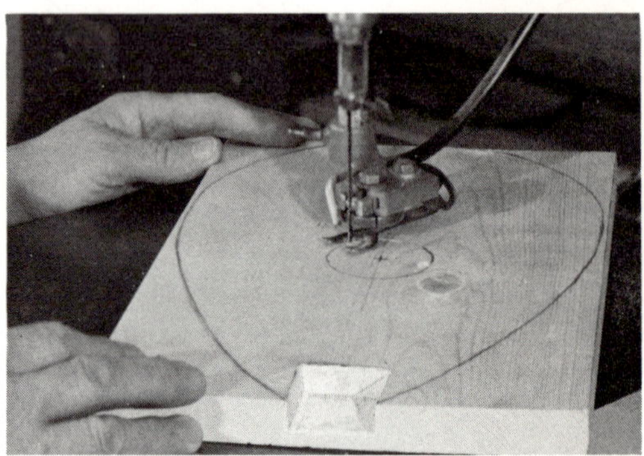

Photo 2: If a 2″ hole-saw is not available, the hole can be cut on the scroll saw using a jeweler's blade or on a portable power jig saw.

Photo 1: The square groove in the sounding box is made on the drill press by making a series of 1/2″ mortises on the drill press fitted with a 1/2″ mortise chisel and bit.

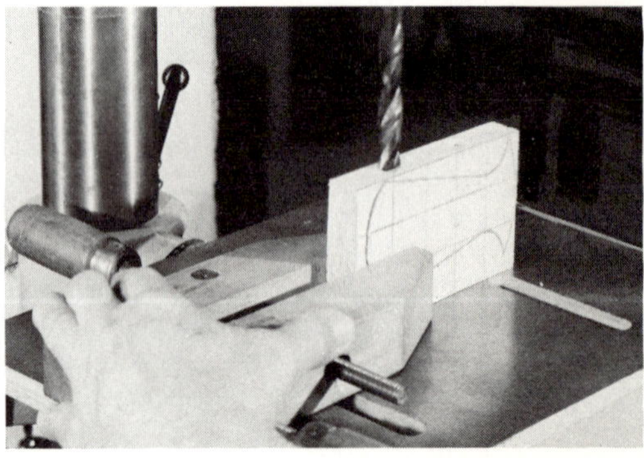

Photo 3. Holes for the turn keys on the head blocks are bored on the drill press with a 1/2″ machine spur bit. All holes are drilled to the same depth.

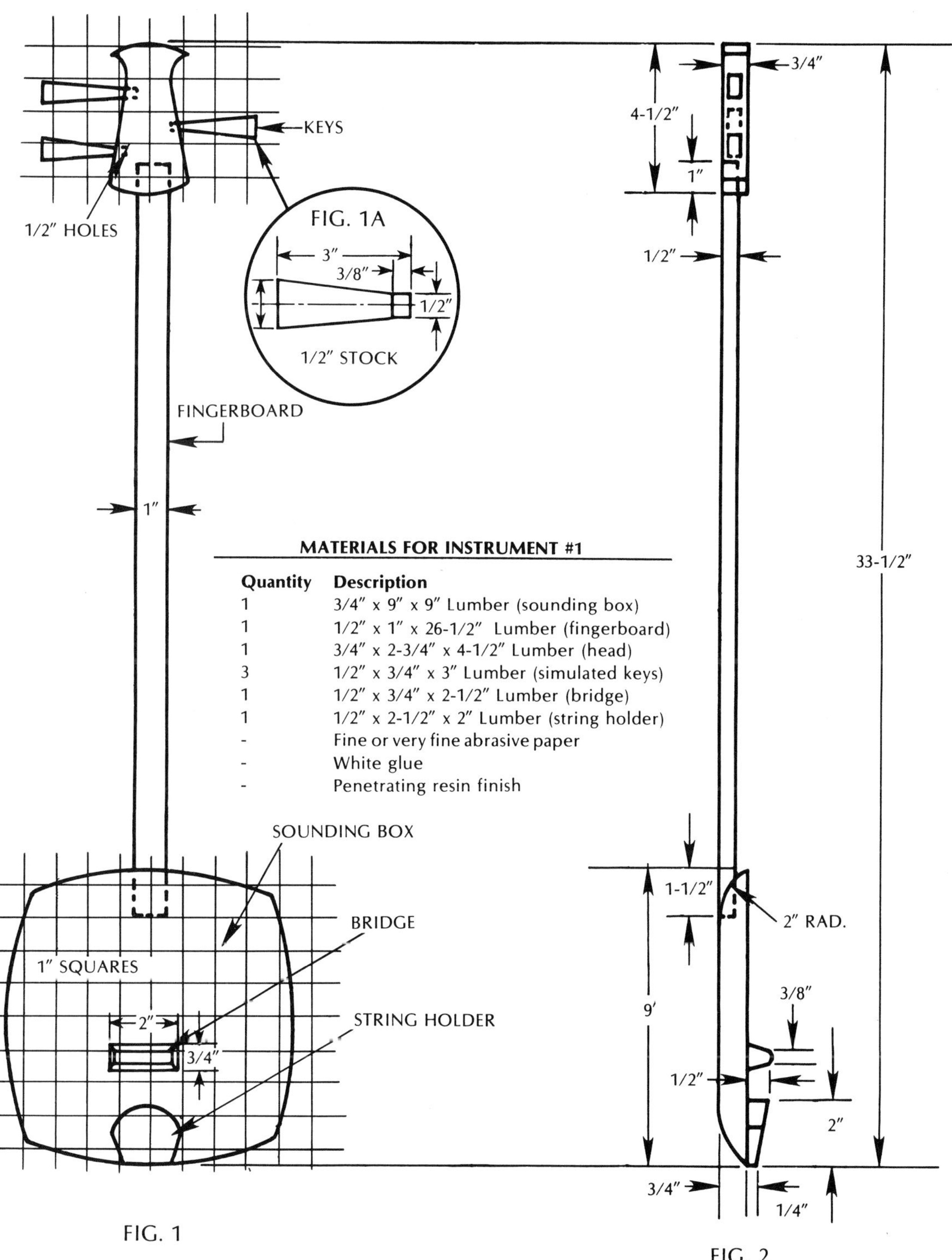

MATERIALS FOR INSTRUMENT #1

Quantity	Description
1	3/4" x 9" x 9" Lumber (sounding box)
1	1/2" x 1" x 26-1/2" Lumber (fingerboard)
1	3/4" x 2-3/4" x 4-1/2" Lumber (head)
3	1/2" x 3/4" x 3" Lumber (simulated keys)
1	1/2" x 3/4" x 2-1/2" Lumber (bridge)
1	1/2" x 2-1/2" x 2" Lumber (string holder)
-	Fine or very fine abrasive paper
-	White glue
-	Penetrating resin finish

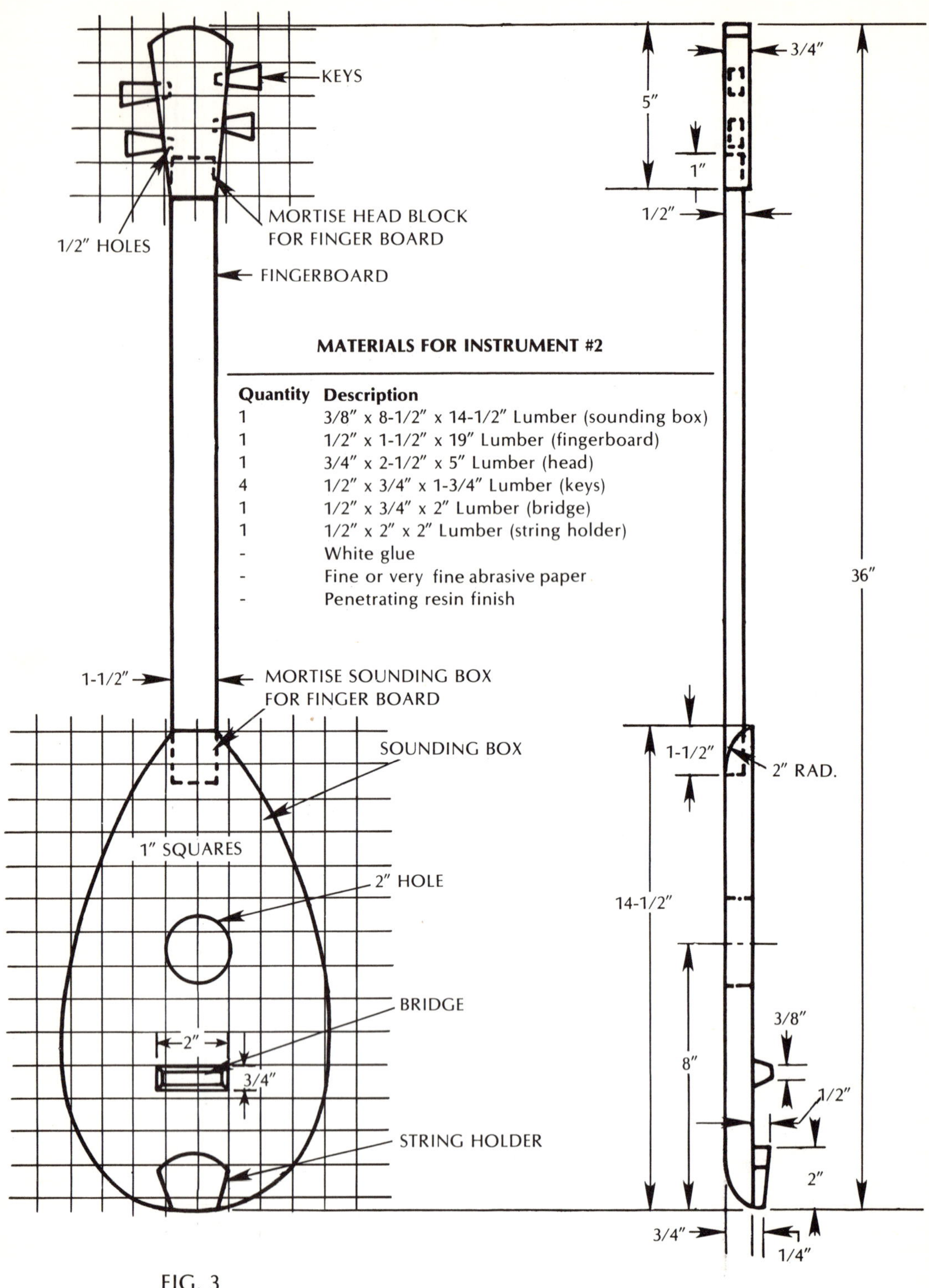

MATERIALS FOR INSTRUMENT #2

Quantity	Description
1	3/8″ x 8-1/2″ x 14-1/2″ Lumber (sounding box)
1	1/2″ x 1-1/2″ x 19″ Lumber (fingerboard)
1	3/4″ x 2-1/2″ x 5″ Lumber (head)
4	1/2″ x 3/4″ x 1-3/4″ Lumber (keys)
1	1/2″ x 3/4″ x 2″ Lumber (bridge)
1	1/2″ x 2″ x 2″ Lumber (string holder)
-	White glue
-	Fine or very fine abrasive paper
-	Penetrating resin finish

FIG. 3

FIG. 4

DISPLAY CABINET

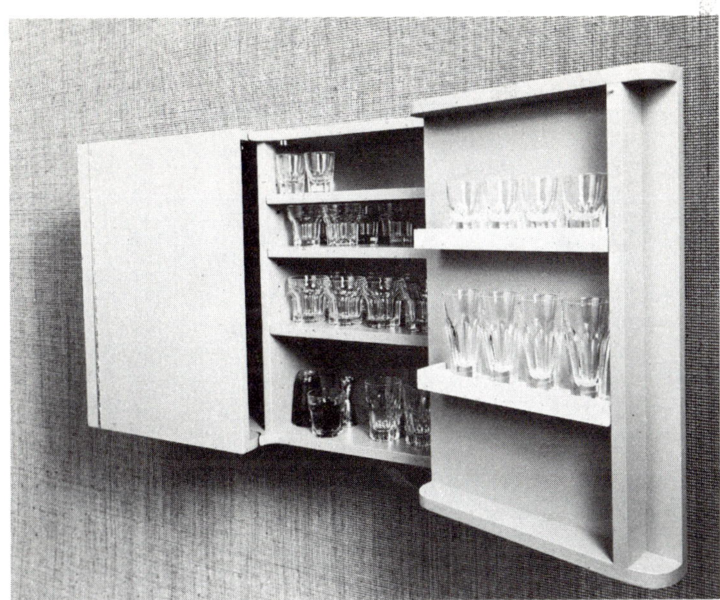

This wall-mounted display cabinet can be used in almost any room in the house — in the kitchen or dining room for glassware; the bathroom for toiletries; the den or workshop for craft supplies.

Following the panel layout (Fig. 1), draw all parts on the plywood panels using a straightedge and a carpenter's square for accuracy. Use a compass to draw corner radii. Be sure to allow for the saw kerfs when plotting the dimensions; if in doubt, check the width of your saw cut.

For strong joints, use a combination of glue and nails (or screws); to nail-glue, check for a good fit by holding the pieces together. The pieces should make contact at all points for lasting strength. Mark the nail locations along the edge of the piece to be nailed. In careful work where nails must be very close to an edge, you may wish to predrill using a drill bit slightly smaller than the nail size. Always predrill for screws.

Other construction tips are:

1. Drill the shelf support holes for parts (D) and (E) according to the shelf placement you desire.
2. Assemble and glue-nail the elements of each cabinet door.
3. Assemble and glue-nail the remainder of the cabinet. Attach the cabinet doors to the cabinet with piano hinges.
4. Paint.
5. Attach the cabinet to the wall with molly type bolts, or screw it directly into the wall studs.

MATERIALS

Quantity	Description
1	3/4″ x 4′ x 8′ Plywood panel
2	24″ Piano hinges (cut to fit)
2 pair	Cabinet catches or magnetic catches
—	Adjustable shelf supports
—	8d Finishing nails
—	Wood screws or molly bolts
—	White glue
—	Wood putty
—	Fine abrasive paper
—	Interior semi-gloss enamel paint

Exploded View

FIG. 2

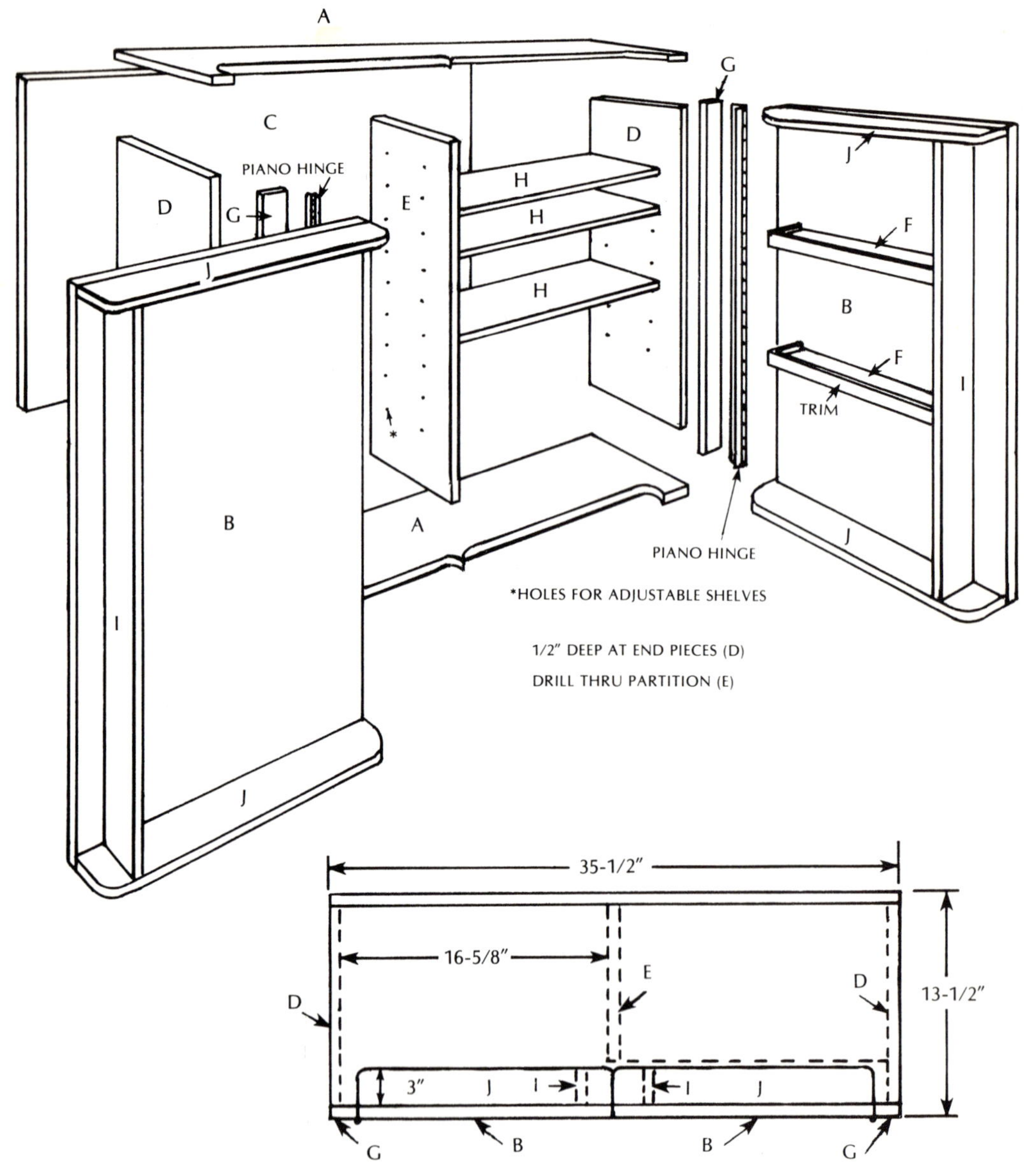

Top View

FIG. 3

Panel Layout

FIG. 1

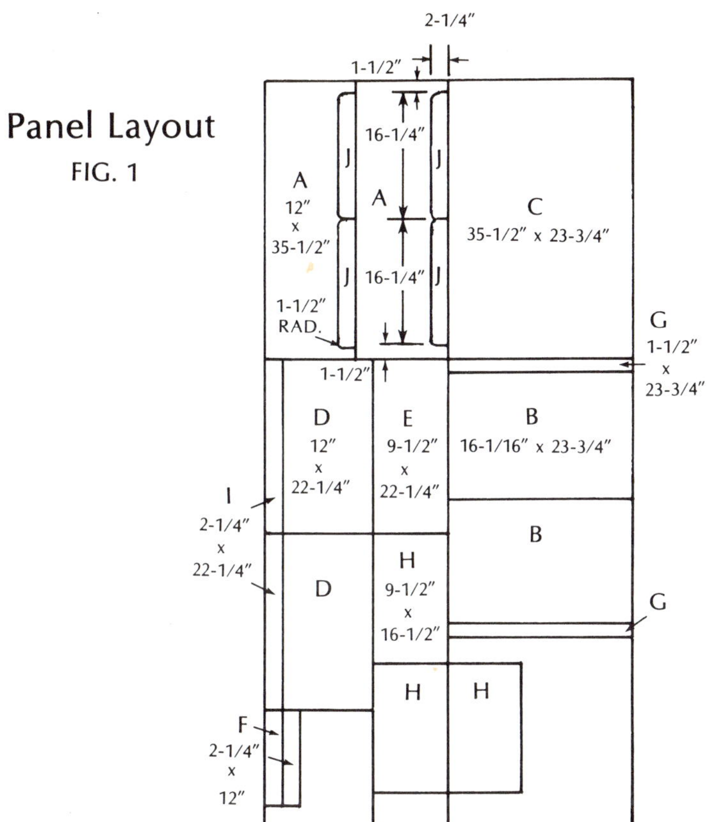

3/4″ x 4′ x 8′ PLYWOOD

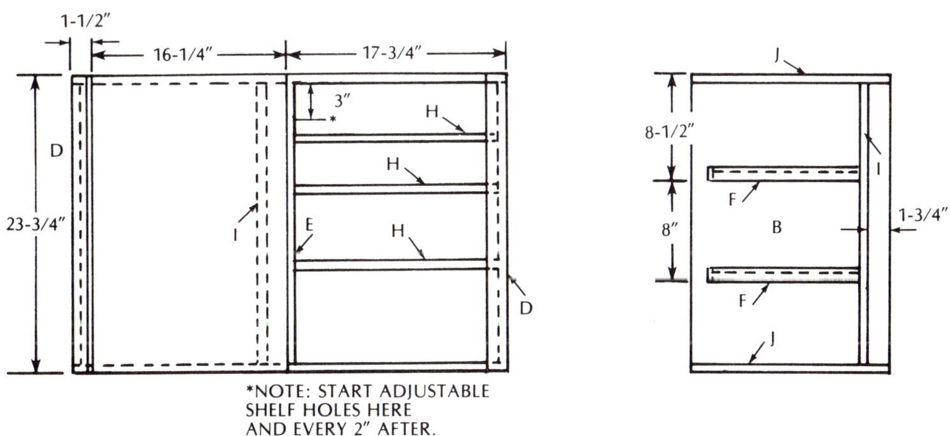

Door

Front View

FIG. 4

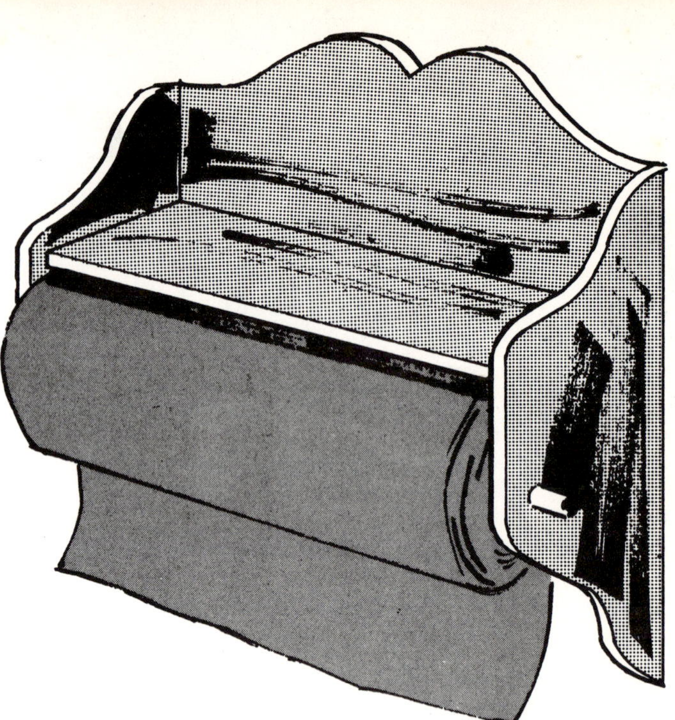

COLONIAL TOWEL RACK

This paper roll towel rack in a honeytone or maple finish will go well with the extra utility shelf in the kitchen. It can also be used in the bathroom, den, game room, or above the work-bench. It would make a very practical addition near the barbecue pit during the summer months.

Birch wood would be most suitable for this project since it will take on various shades of stain to produce an authentic reproduction. The entire shelf is made of 1/2″ thick material, except for the 3/4″ diameter dowel used to hold the paper roll toweling.

By tacking both side pieces together with small brads and gluing the drawn design to the tacked pieces with rubber cement, they can be cut at the same time on the band saw, scroll saw, or portable jig saw (Photo 1). After cutting, the edges are sanded on the drill press with a 3″ sanding drum (Photo 2). While the pieces are still tacked together, a 3/4″ hole is bored at a center point, 3-1/4″ from the bottom and 2-1/2″ from the back edge for the towel support dowel (Fig. 2). The stop grooves in the sides for the shelf and the stop rabbet for the back crosspiece can be made with a portable router using a 1/2″ router bit.

For a Colonial finish, apply a maple stain followed by two coats of satin polyurethane varnish, sanding lightly between coats with extra fine abrasive paper. A penetrating resin-oil finish may also be employed. To hang the shelf on the wall, bore two holes in the back crosspiece for round head wood screws, or use two hanger plates fastened to the shelf back.

MATERIALS

Quantity	Description
2	1/2″ x 4″ x 9″ Sides
1	1/2″ x 4-1/2″ x 13-1/8″ Back
1	1/2″ x 3-5/8″ x 13″ Shelf
1	3/4″ dia. x 14-1/2″ Wood dowel
-	Small brads
-	White glue
-	Wood putty
-	Fine and extra fine abrasive paper
-	Finishing material

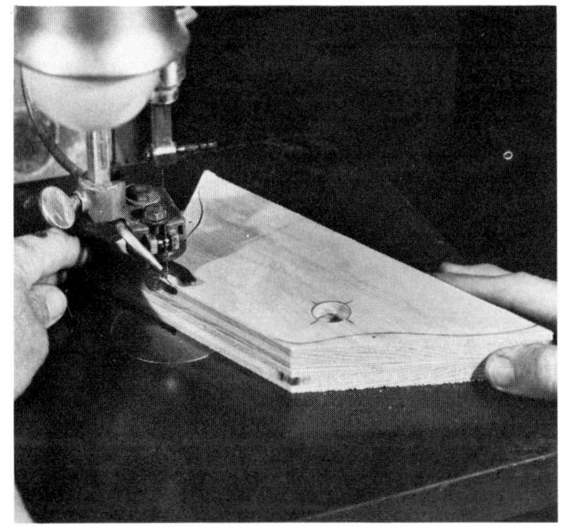

Photo 1: Tack the stock for the towel rack sides together with brads and cut the outline on a scroll saw, band saw, or portable jig saw.

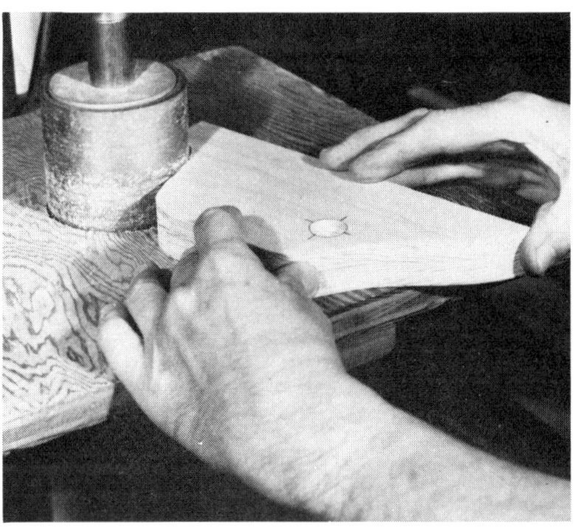

Photo 2: After cutting the sides to shape, sand the curved edges on a drill press fitted with a 3″ drum. The drum can also be used to break the edges.

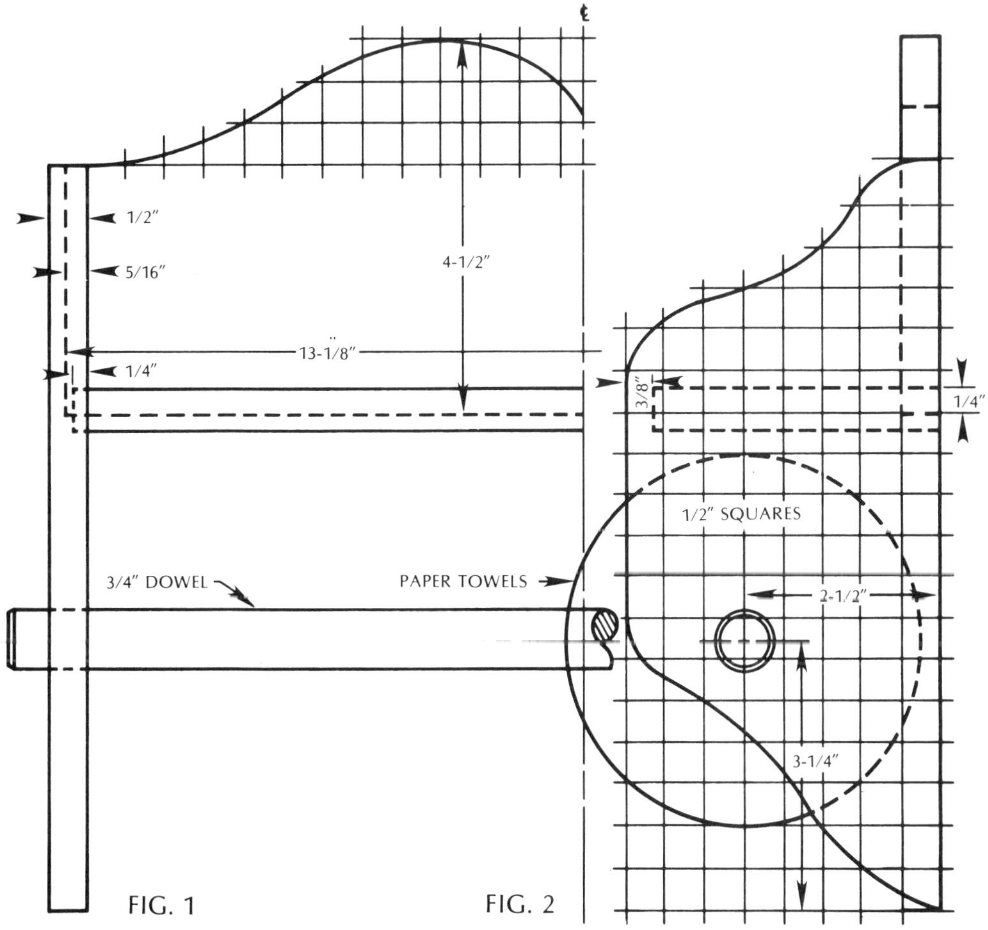

1/2″
5/16″
4-1/2″
13-1/8″
1/4″
3/8″
1/4″
1/2″ SQUARES
3/4″ DOWEL
PAPER TOWELS
2-1/2″
3-1/4″

FIG. 1

FIG. 2

SHOP BELLOWS

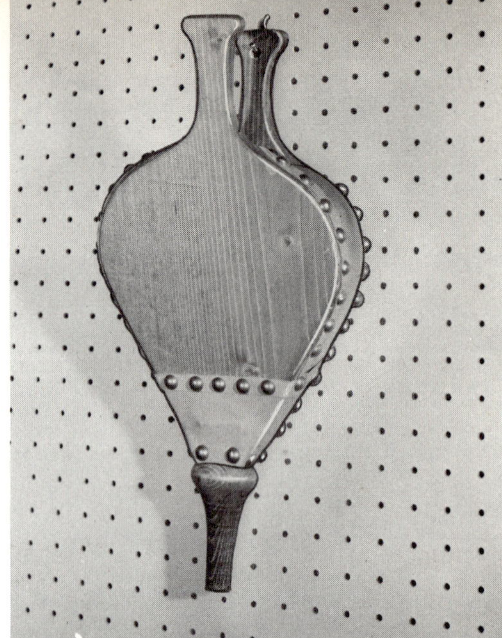

You will find this bellows very useful around the shop for cleaning sawdust and chips off of your tools and workbench. It will come in handy by the fireplace, too, in helping you start a good fire.

The sides on this bellows are made of 5/8" pine and cut to shape using the squares method as indicated in the line drawing (Fig. 3). One inch of the nose end on the top half of the bellows is cut off and glued to the bottom half with a 1/4" spacer in between (Fig. 4). After the glue has set, the nose is bored on the drill press with a 7/8" drill for the shank of the wood spout (Photo 1). A 1-1/4" breather hole is bored in the bottom piece with a 2-1/4" by 2-1/4" piece of leather (B) tacked in place.

The wood spout is turned from a piece of hard maple 2" in diameter by 4-1/4" long (Photo 2). The 1/2" spout hole is bored on the drill press with a machine spur bit. Stain and varnish the wood parts before applying the leather. Cut the bellows side leather (D) and the hinge cover leather (C) as indicated in Figs. 1 and 2 in the drawing. Glue and tack the leather in place with No. 3 tacks. For a more decorative effect, tack brass furniture nails on the edges and the hinge cover leather pieces.

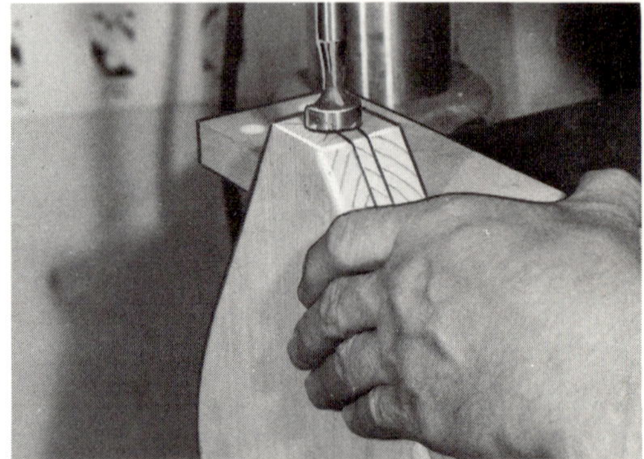

Photo 1: A 7/8" hole is bored in the assembled top nose end, spacer, and bottom half of the bellows using a 7/8" multi-spur bit.

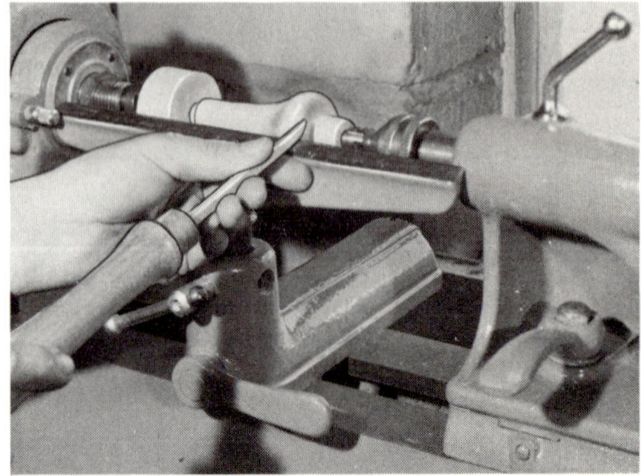

Photo 2: The spout for the shop bellows is turned on the lathe using a 1/4" round nose turning chisel.

MATERIALS

Quantity	Description
2	5/8" x 7-1/2" x 12-1/2" Lumber (sides)
1	2" x 2" x 4-1/4" Lumber (spout)
1	1/4" x 1" x 3" Plywood (spacer)
1	1" x 1" x 3" Tight pin hinge
1	2-1/4" x 2-1/4" Leather (B)
1	3" x 7" Leather (C)
1	6" x 21" Leather (D)
70	No. 3 Carpet tacks
56	1/2" Small brass head furniture nails
—	White glue
—	Fine abrasive paper
—	Wood stain
—	Polyurethane finish

FIG. 1

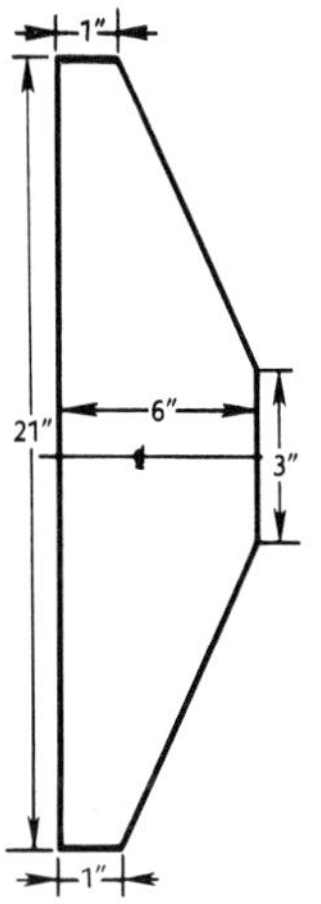

BELLOW SIDE LEATHER D

TOP LEATHER C

FIG. 2

TOP OF BELLOWS

FIG. 3

CROSS SECTION OF BELLOW SPOUT

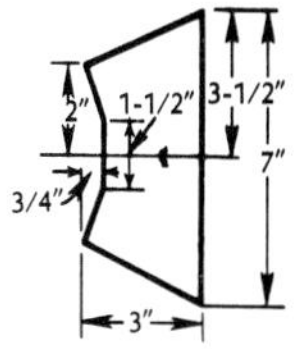

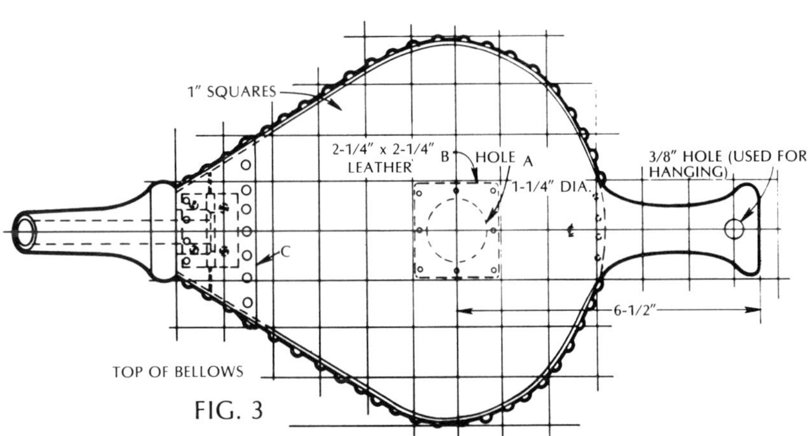

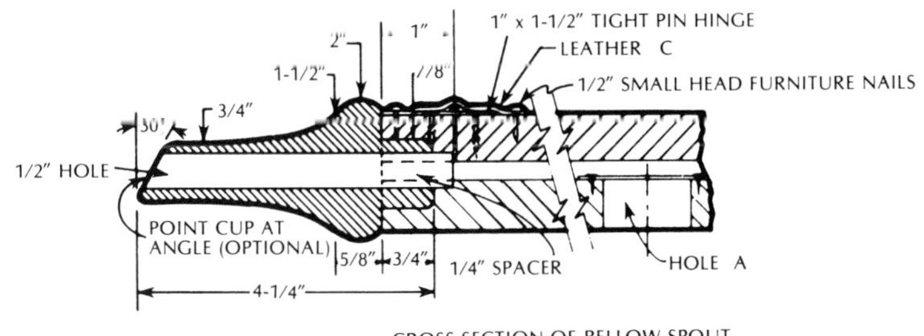

FIG. 4

HALL MIRROR

This attractive hall mirror is easy to build. Begin the carpentry by assembling the shelf unit, using 1-1/4″ No. 8 flathead wood screws and white glue. Build the box frame, using butt joints, checking for squareness before installing the 6-1/2″ by 30″ top member. Be sure all screws are countersunk flush and any adhesive excess removed. Set the assembly aside and allow the glue to dry. Fill the voids in the edges and seams, and sand smooth after the glue has dried.

Next, begin assembling the mirror frame: Cut a 3/4″ by 2″ notch into the top inside edge of the 48″ vertical frame members. Fit the 26-1/2″ frame top member into the notch and fasten it with a 2″ No. 8 flathead wood screw and white glue. Measure 40″ down each side of the vertical frame member from the bottom edge of the mirror frame element and cut a 3/4″ by 2″ notch at the inside of the framing. Fasten the second 26-1/2″ frame crosspiece with a 2″ No. 8 flathead screw and white glue. Lay the frame element flat on the work surface and attach the 1/2″ plywood face frame elements, using white glue and 1″ 4d finish nails. Set the entire assembly aside and allow it to dry. After drying, fill any voids in the edges or seams and sand it smooth.

Now before assembling the frame and shelf components, laminate all the edges of the mirror frame (see page 10 for laminating details), and the mirror return. Rout flush. Then, laminate the mirror face, using the 30-1/2″ by 8-1/2″ piece, bevel routing the edges and the inside opening. Take care to curve the radius at all the inside corners of the mirror frame.

Begin laminating the assembled shelf unit; first complete the two sides and rout flush at all the edges. Then, face the front edge; rout flush. Apply the laminate to the shelf top. Rout flush at the back edge and bevel rout all the laminate-to-laminate surfaced edges.

After the laminate operations are completed, lay the mirror frame on its back and join the frame and shelf units, using two 1-1/4″ No. 8 flathead screws at each end and two in the middle of the 30″ wide shelf back edge.

Size the hardboard for a precise fit to the inside of the mirror frame, insert the mirror and the hardboard backing and secure it with glazier points at the corners and the middle of each side.

MATERIALS

Quantity	Description
1	1/2″ x 6-1/2″ x 30″ Plywood (bottom member)
1	1/2″ x 2-1/2″ x 30″ Plywood (top member)
2	1/2″ x 2-1/2″ x 39″ Plywood (side members)
1	1/2″ x 3-1/2″ x 30″ Plywood (shelf member)
1	1/2″ x 3-1/2″ x 29″ Plywood (shelf member)
2	1/2″ x 3-1/2″ x 6″ Plywood (frame members)
1	1/2″ x 1/2″ x 30″ Plywood (shelf top)
1	1/8″ x 26″ x 40″ Hardboard
2	1″ x 2″ x 48″ Pine lumber (side members)
2	1″ x 2″ x 26-1/2″ Pine lumber (top and bottom)
1	7″ x 30-1/2″ Plastic laminate (shelf top)*
2	4-1/2″ x 6-1/2″ Plastic laminate (side edges)*
1	4-1/2″ x 30-1/2″ Plastic laminate (front edge)*
1	30-1/2″ x 48-1/2″ Plastic laminate (frame face)*
2	1-3/4″ x 48-1/2″ Plastic laminate (side edges)*
1	1-3/4″ x 30-1/2″ Plastic laminate (top edge)*
1	3/4″ x 132″ Plastic laminate strip (reveal)*
—	White glue
—	1-1/4″ No. 8 Flathead wood screws
—	2″ No. 8 Flathead wood screws
—	1″ 4d Finish nails
8	Glazier's points
1	26″ x 40″ mirror
—	Contact adhesive
—	Adhesive solvent

* *Note:* All necessary laminate pieces can be cut from one 48″ by 60″ laminate sheet. Take the time to lay out the hall mirror to assure the proper yield.

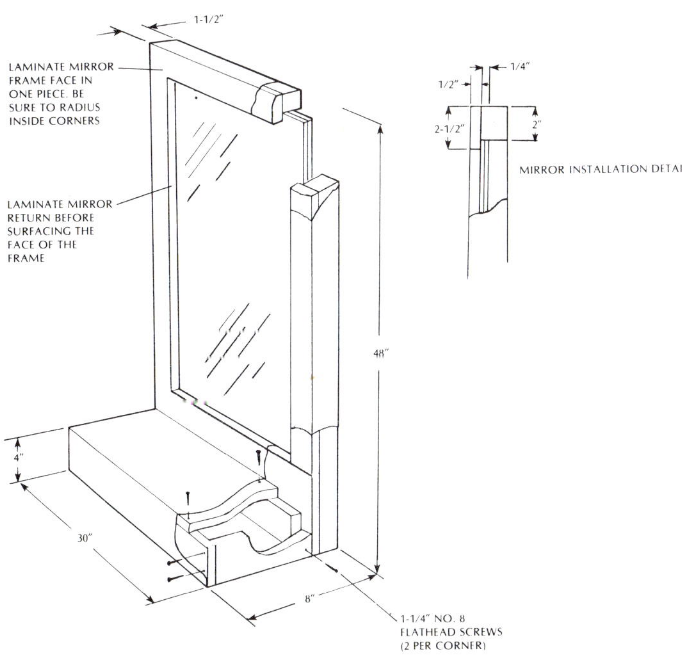

CANDLESTICK BASE

This attractive fluted candlestick would be welcomed and appreciated by any homemaker. The drawing is full size, having a 1/4″ grid suitable for enlarging or reducing the size of the candlestick.

Glue enough stock to form a block 4-3/8″ thick by 5-1/4″ square. In Photo 2 the X's indicate end grain. Make sure the end grain faces the same direction on all pieces. The straight lines indicate an attempt to have the grain pattern flow from piece to piece as if this block were a single piece of wood rather than several pieces glued together. It takes time to do, but is well worth the extra effort.

Cut the block to a 5-1/8″ diameter cylinder on the band saw. Sand the bottom until it is flat. Locate and drill the pilot hole in the bottom, in preparation for mounting in the lathe with a screw center. The complete lathe set-up, using the tailstock to support the turning, is shown in Photo 3. Turn the work to a round cylinder and transfer the lines that extend to the edge of the page, (Fig. 1) to the cylinder. This saves measuring. Turn the work to the various diameters, making the shoulder cuts last and doing the final shaping by eye.

Lay out the 12 equally spaced flutes by using dividers, or the lathe indexing head if your lathe is so equipped. The flutes are spaced five holes apart and are laid out as shown in Photo 4. Take the turning to a vice and cut the flutes by hand, using a 1/4″ outside ground gouge and a mallet as shown in Photo 5. Return the work to the lathe, shape the concave top end and sand the turning. Bore the hole for the candlepin slightly undersize, using a drill chuck mounted in the tailstock as shown in Photo 6 or, do it later on the drill press.

PIN

The candlepin can be made from a brass rod, a drill rod or a nail 3/16″ diameter by 2-3/4″ long. It can be mounted on the lathe in a drill chuck, filed to a point as seen in Photo 7 (or shaped on the grinder) and polished to a high shine using fine silicon carbide finishing paper and steel wool. Drive the pin into the candlestick after the finish has been applied.

FINISH

Our candlestick was made from cherry stock and stained twice. The first application was a light overall color (butternut). The second was a dark color (dark oak) applied only to the fluting and the shoulder cuts to highlight and emphasize the turning. For a finish we used a spray lacquer. All of the finishing materials were applied while the candle stick was mounted on the screw center, so the rubbing and polishing of the finish could be done on the lathe. Cover the bottom with felt or fill the screw hole with wood putty and finish it the same as the other surfaces.

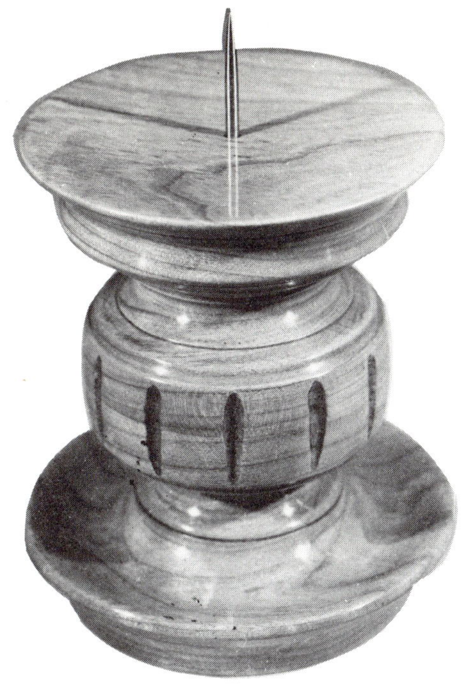

Photo 1: The completed candlestick.

Photo 2: Gluing the discs together.

Photo 3: The "set-up" for turning.

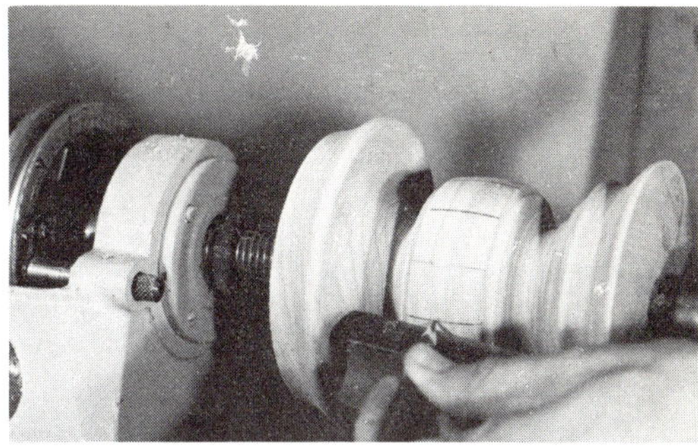

Photo 4: The flute spacing.

Photo 5: Carving the flutes.

Photo 6: Boring the candlepin hole.

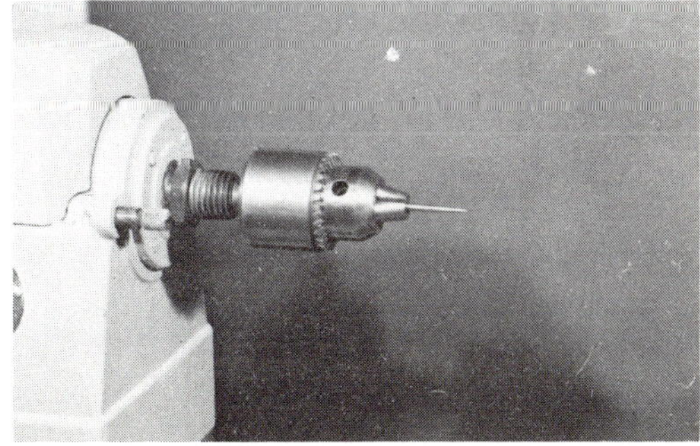

Photo 7: Shaping the candlepin.

MATERIALS

Quantity	Description
1	4-3/8" x 5-1/4" x 15-1/4" Wood block (formed as described in text)
1	3/16" dia. x 2-1/4" Brass rod or nail
—	Steel wool
—	Fine silicon carbide abrasive paper
—	Fine abrasive paper
—	Wood putty
—	Lacquer finish
—	Glue

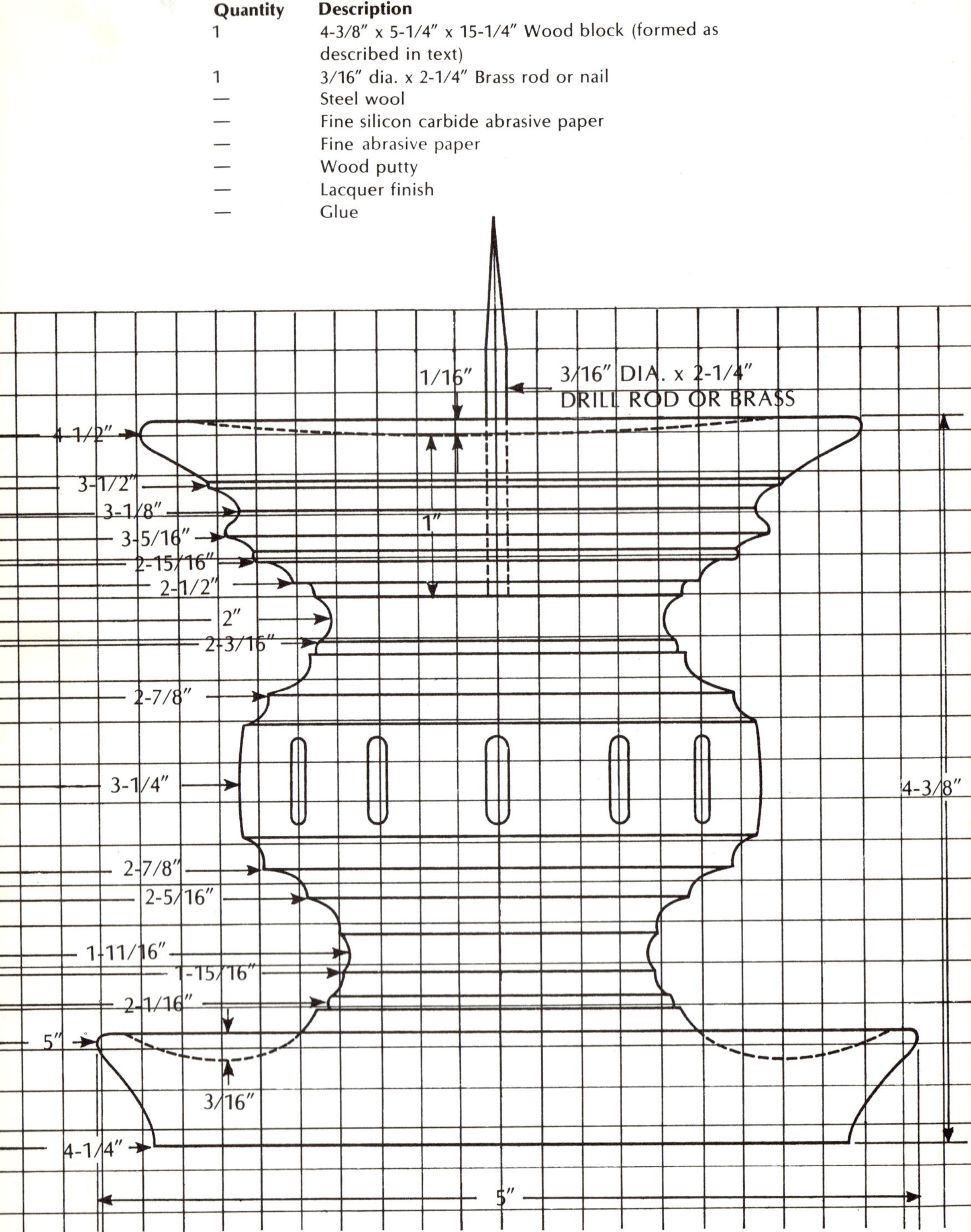

FIG. 1

POCKET CHESSBOARD

School children love to play chess and checkers, and this game board was designed to meet their need. It also makes a good excuse for adults to spend some time in the shop. You can quickly make several to give away as gifts. Follow these instructions and you will have enough glued stock to make five game boards.

To make the chessboard, cut four strips of a dark wood (walnut) from 13/16″ stock and four strips of a light colored wood (maple), 5/8″ x 13/16″ x 46″. Surface plane both 13/16″ faces of all eight strips to exact ly 1/2″ thickness. Glue these 13/16″ faces together, alternating the dark and light wood (Photo 1). Try to have the grain of each strip running the same direction to prevent tearing while surfacing. After the glue is dry, run the glued stock through the surface planer again. Surface both faces to exactly 1/2″ thickness. Cut this piece into eight lengths of 5″ each. Re-glue these pieces, again alternating the dark and light wood (Photo 2). Make sure these pieces do not slip out of alignment during the gluing process.

Square the end of this glued block on the band saw and 6″ stationary belt sander, using a coarse grit belt (Photo 3). Saw a 1″ piece from this block on the band saw using a 3/8″ to 1/2″ wide blade (Photo 4). Sand the face flat as shown in Photo 3. Make the layout for the drawer slot. Set up the table saw using both the miter gauge and rip fence. Tilt the blade 10° and raise it to cut 5/8″ deep. Cut out the remaining portion of the drawer slot with the blade at 90° and reset it to cut 5/8″ deep (Photo 5). Sand the inner surface flat and smooth (Photo 6). Drill holes for the checkers or chessmen.

The drawer pieces are cut to size as shown in Fig 1. Assemble with glue and 1/2″ by No. 20 brads. Set the nails and fill the holes with plastic wood. *(Note:* By making the drawer 1/32″ oversize in length and width, you are assured of a perfect fit, with a little trimming.) Sand the top and bottom of the drawer flat. Glue on a piece of walnut veneer for the drawer bottom (a tablet back or railroad board will do). Trim the bottom and fit the drawer. Use a 5/8″ long rivet or nail for the locking pin. Bore the locking pin hole for a friction fit.

Use your imagination for the chess/checker men. Try 12 round and flathead rivets, use tiny 1/8″ dowel rods painted or stained, common nails with the tops enameled in colors, heavy wire cut to length, or whatever strikes your fancy. The checker kings would be extra pieces of a longer length or with a white dot painted on their tops. Adapt the board for chess by making six different head shaped pieces and bore a hole in every square of the board.

Sand all surfaces smooth using various grades of finishing paper concluding with fine grit paper. Use a can of spray lacquer on the board and drawer; glue felt on the bottom and inside of the drawer.

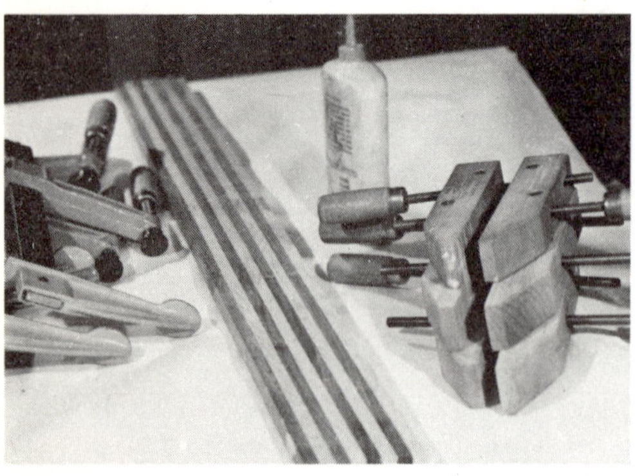

Photo 1: Gluing the 8 strips together.

Photo 2: Gluing the 8 strips together in a block.

Photo 3: Squaring the end using a miter gauge on a belt sander.

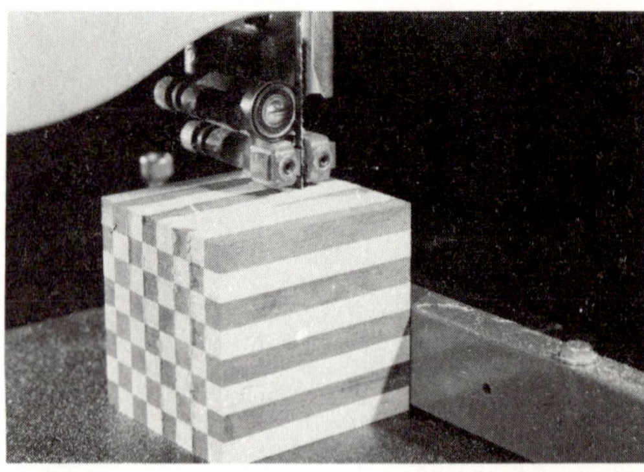

Photo 4: Sawing the boards to thickness on a band saw.

Photo 5: Cutting the drawer slot. Note: Blade guard removed for clarity.

Photo 6: Sanding the inner surface of the drawer slot on a sander/grinder.

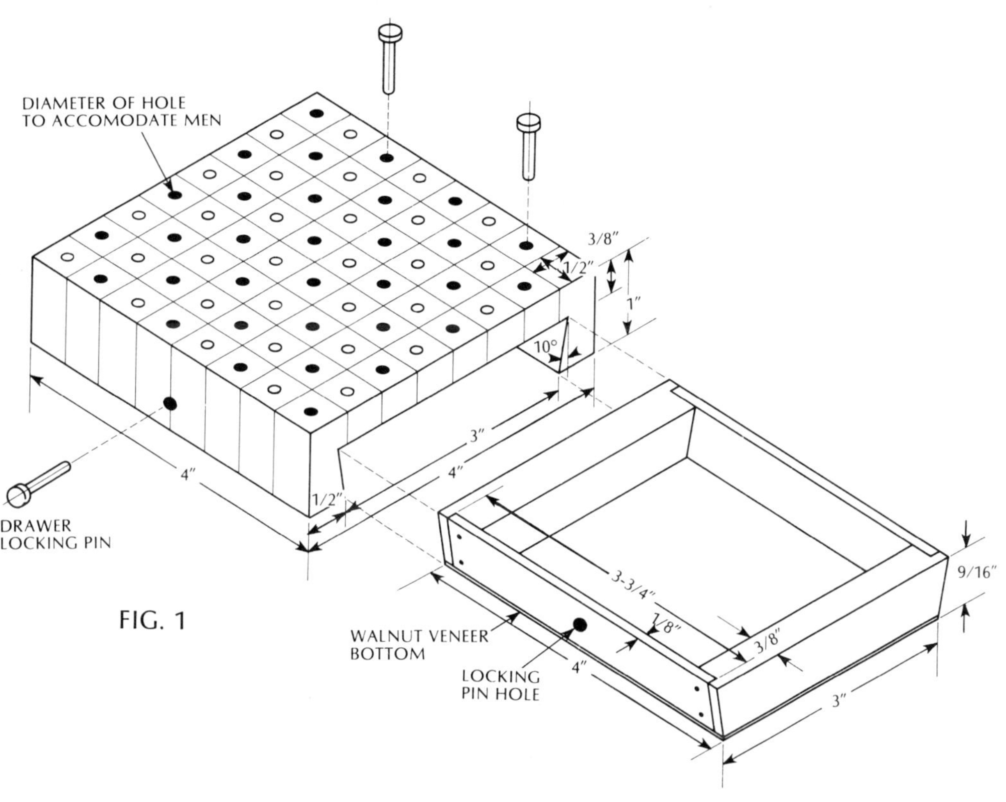

FIG. 1

MATERIALS
(For Five Game Boards)

Quantity	Description
4	5/8″ x 13/16″ x 46″ Walnut lumber (board)
4	5/8″ x 13/16″ x 46″ Maple lumber (board)
1	3/8″ x 9/16″ x 35″ Walnut lumber (drawer)
1	1/8″ x 5/8″ x 40″ Walnut lumber (drawer)
5	1/28″ x 4″ x 3″ Walnut veneer (drawer)
1	Drawer locking pin
-	White glue
-	No. 20 x 1/2″ Brads
-	Various grades of abrasive paper
-	Spray lacquer

Checker Pieces — Optional and to suit:
24 Checkers — 8 Kings — 32 Men
Chess Pieces — 6 Head shapes

TURNED COASTERS

These attractive coasters will make real conversation pieces when you display your favorite photos with descriptive information appearing on the opposite side. The coasters in the feature photo were used to display hex signs commonly found in the eastern section of Pennsylvania. A description of each hex sign is given on the opposite side of the hex design when used with this double glass coaster.

Two pieces of stock are required for each coaster. The main frame is made from material 3/4″ thick by 4-11/16″ in diameter. After cutting the piece to make a rough circle about 4-7/8″ in diameter, mount it on a 3″ face plate and proceed to turn the outside diameter and back side as shown in the drawing and Photo 1. Remove the stock from the face plate and mount it into a wood chuck for turning the face side of the coaster (Photo 2). *Note:* Make sure the stock fits tightly into the wood chuck. The outside bead and rabbet for the glass are turned and finish sanded while mounted

Various designs of hex signs, common in eastern Pennsylvania. Some coasters can be used for other purposes such as coin or stamp displays.

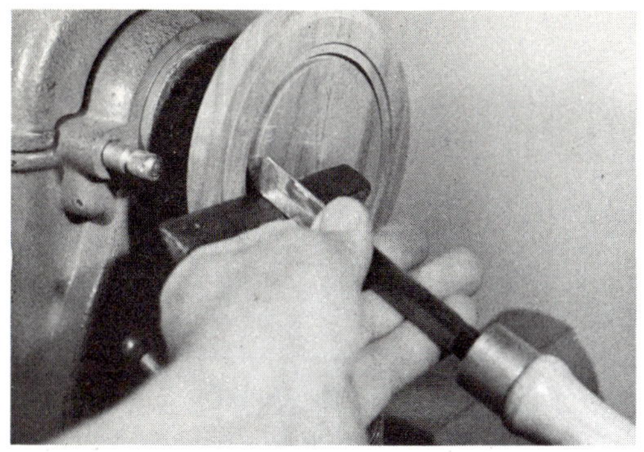

Photo 1: With the coaster stock mounted on a 3″ face plate, the outside diameter and back are turned on the lathe.

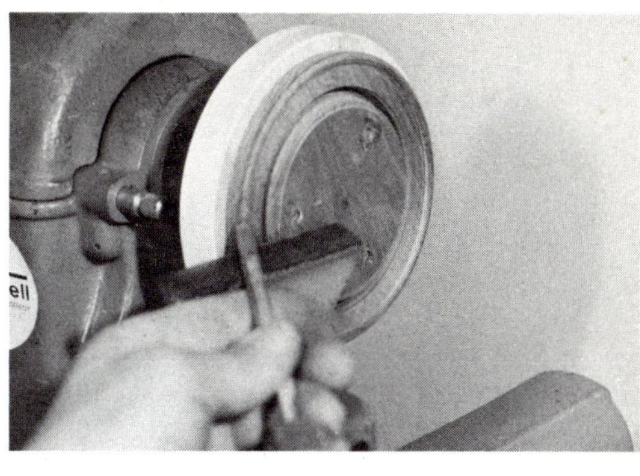

Photo 2: The front of the coaster is turned while being held in a wood chuck. The outside bead and rabbet for the glass are turned at this point of the operation.

Photo 3: After the outer edge of the inside ring is turned down to the proper size it is mounted in a wood chuck for turning the inner edge and removing the waste stock.

in the wood chuck.

The beaded ring that holds the glass and picture in the coaster is next turned by first mounting the stock on a 3″ face plate. The outside diameter of the ring is turned down so it will fit tightly into the rabbet cut of the large coaster ring. The inside portion of the small ring is turned in a wood chuck as shown in Photo 3. While the parts are still in the wood chuck, sand them thoroughly with paper.

To bring out the natural beauty of the material you use, apply several coats of the new type of lacquer finishes now on the market. Most of these finishes can be applied with a soft cloth. Full directions are given on the container.

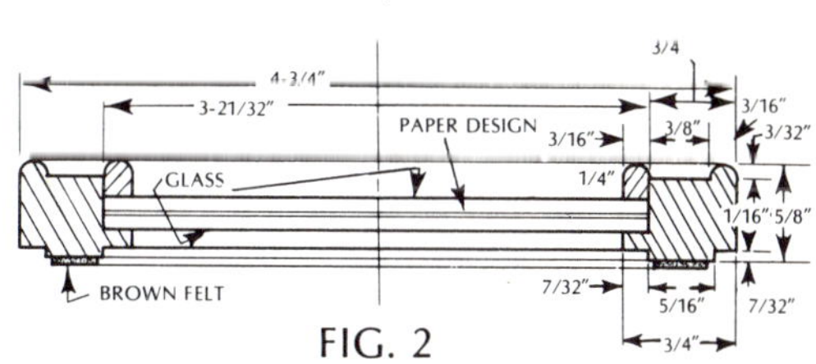

FIG. 2

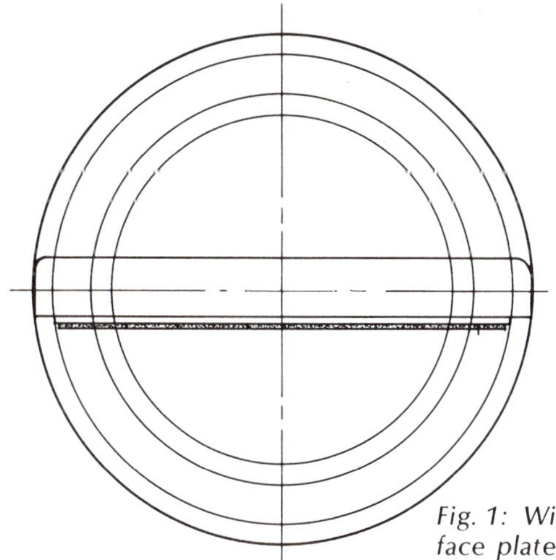

Fig. 1: With the coaster stock mounted on a 3″ face plate, the outside diameter and back are turned on the lathe.

MYSTERY CUBE

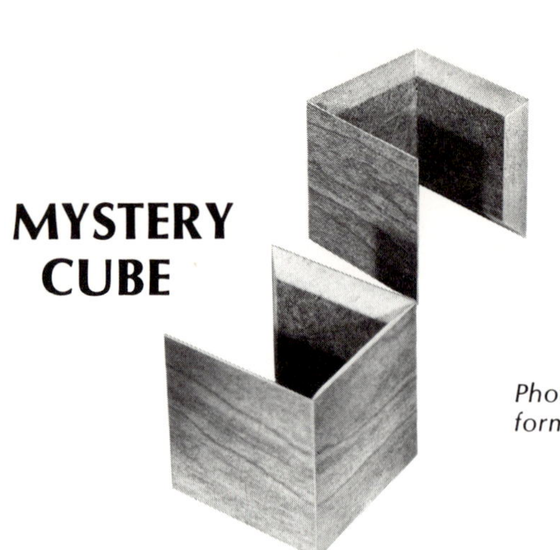

Photo 1: The two sections in position for fitting together.

Photo 2. Sections partially closed.

Photo 3: When sections are assembled they form a perfect cube.

MATERIALS

Quantity	Description
6	1/4" x 2" x 2" Plywood or hardboard pieces
	White glue

Here is a little gadget that will amuse both the young and the old. Scrap pieces of prefinished 1/4" plywood or textured woodgrain hardboard are used for this project. Six, 2" by 2" square pieces (larger pieces could be used) are required for each cube. We suggest cutting enough squares to make several cubes at one time as give-away gifts.

Begin by cutting the stock in 2" wide strips. The first bevel cut is made with the table saw's blade set at 45° and the rip fence adjusted to make the 2" strips. The size of the pieces and the angle cuts are very important. Be sure to check both pieces to insure a perfect fitting cube. The second miter cut on the strip is made with the same setting on both the blade tilt and the fence. In fact, keep the rip fence at the same setting for all remaining cuts. With the fence used as a gauge, proceed to make the third bevel cut. Make the final bevel cut by turning the piece end for end. The best blade for cutting these miters is the panel cutting blade, because of the fine teeth it will give you a smooth cut and no sanding will be required.

Glue three pieces together with the wood grain running in the same direction, see Photo 1. When gluing the sections together, be careful not to get any glue on the outside or exposed bevel surfaces. Wipe off any excess glue with a damp cloth and hold the glued sections together with your fingers for a minute or two for the glue to set.

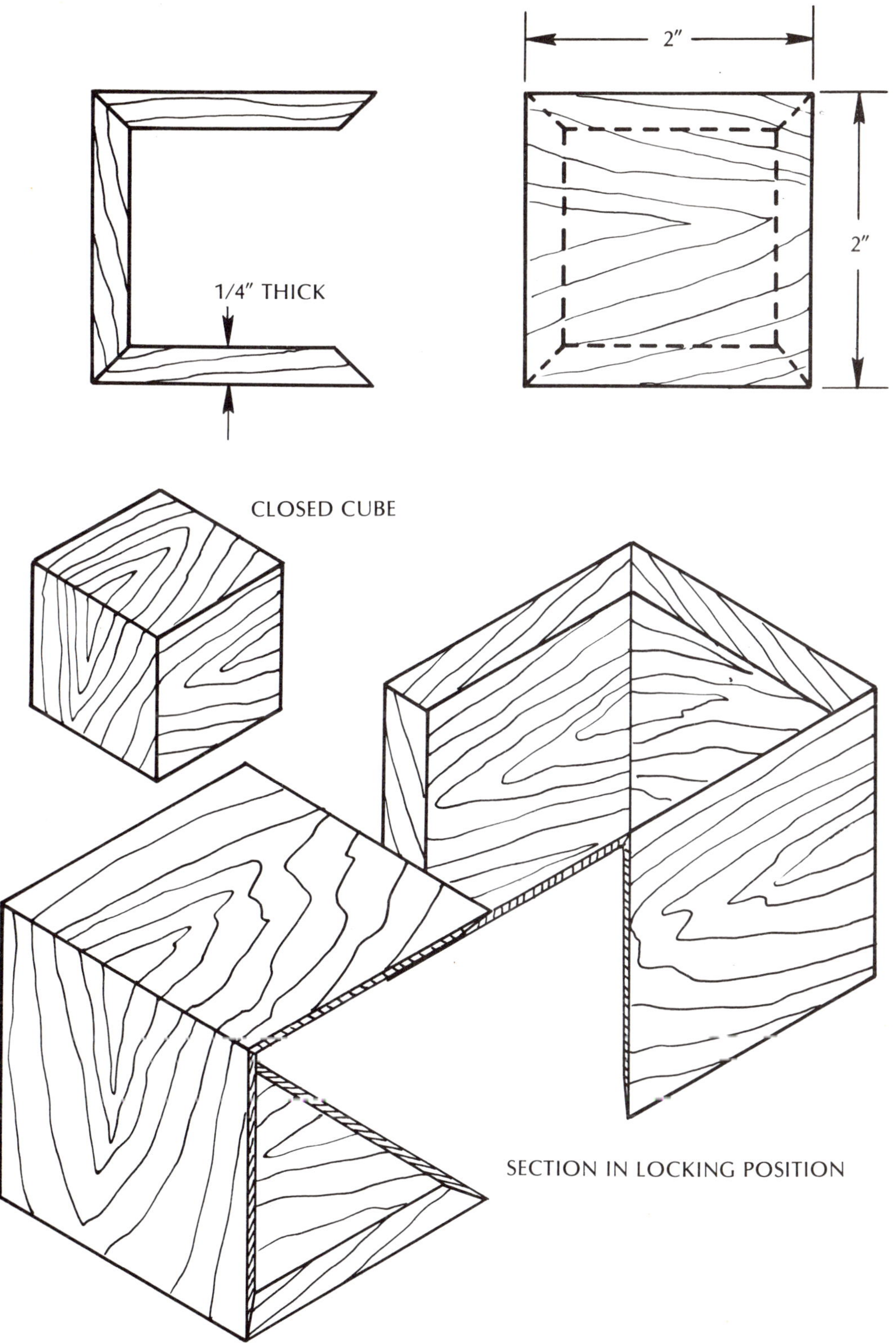
2″
2″
1/4″ THICK
CLOSED CUBE
SECTION IN LOCKING POSITION

TURNED TABLE LAMP

This heavy type lamp gives a feeling of massiveness when used on a living room end table. To make the setting complete, a pair of these will be required, one on each side of the davenport. These projects will be quite handsome if they are made of walnut or mahogany, however, pine or bass wood can also be used for a more rustic look.

To economize on material, make the base in five sections. This will not only save on stock, but will make it easier for drilling the three holes for the 1/8" pipe (Photo 2). If the pipe groove is made on the two inside pieces, cut a groove with a half round molding cutter or dado head for the 1/8" pipe (Photo 3). After the grooves have been made, glue the two halves together and cut in sections to be turned; mount the stock on a lathe. A dovetailed groove can be turned on the bottom to allow for a lead weight which will prevent the lamp from tipping over.

The stem portion between the base turning and the shade harp can be turned from wood, or a brass pipe or tube could be substituted. Counterbore a 7/8" hole, 1-1/8" deep at the bottom of the base for a 1/8" pipe lock nut. A 1/4" hole is bored from the edge of the base to the counterbored hole for a two wire electric lamp cord.

If making a rustic type of lamp from pine or bass wood, a rustic effect can be simulated by making grooves and gauges with hand carving tools and rasps. The original lamp was painted with yellow, brown, and black to simulate a worn out lamp base. A piece of green or brown felt glued to the base will prevent any scratching of table tops.

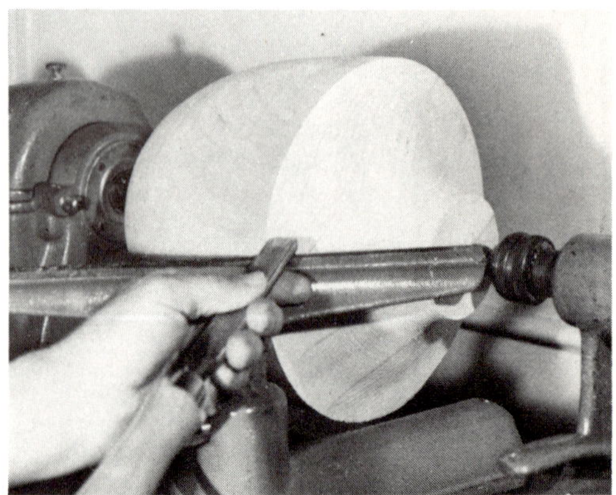

Photo 1: The lamp can be turned in three or four sections for easier handling and saving of materials.

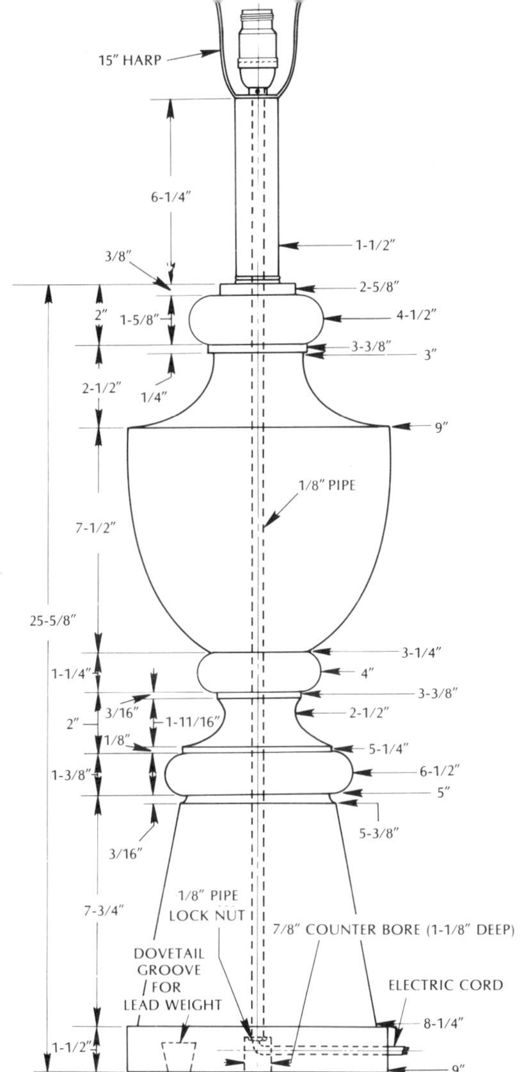

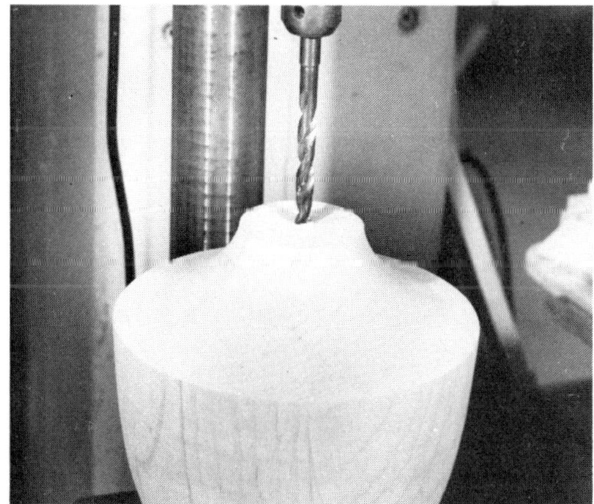

Photo 2: After turning, each section is bored with a 7/16" bit drilling from both ends.

Photo 3: If the lamp is made in one length, each half is grooved with a molding cutter or dado head using two 1/8" outside cutters and one 1/4" inside cutter.

MAGAZINE RACK

Photo 1: An easy-to-make magazine rack.

This magazine rack (Photo 1) is easy to make, modern in design, and will fit into almost any decor. It can be completed in one evening—a quick job for a rainy day.

The magazine rack can be made of mahogany or any other wood that blends into your decor. It fits easily into any part of a room because of its tilting design and 18″ by 18″ size (Fig. 1).

The top front angle cut (Fig. 2) on the rack sides is made on a table saw, using a tapering jig (Photo 2). The bottom front angle cut (Fig. 2) is easier to make on a band or scroll saw. The 1/4″ by 1-3/4″ dadoes in the sides of the rack for the top and bottom crosspieces are best cut on the table saw with three passes of a dado head.

The holes for the nylon twine (Fig. 1) should be drilled in the top and bottom crosspieces before assembly.

Use glue to join the seven component parts of the magazine rack.

For a natural finish, use a matching colored wood filler, followed by two coats of satin effect polyurethane finish or one coat of penetrating resin finish. String the nylon twine to complete the project.

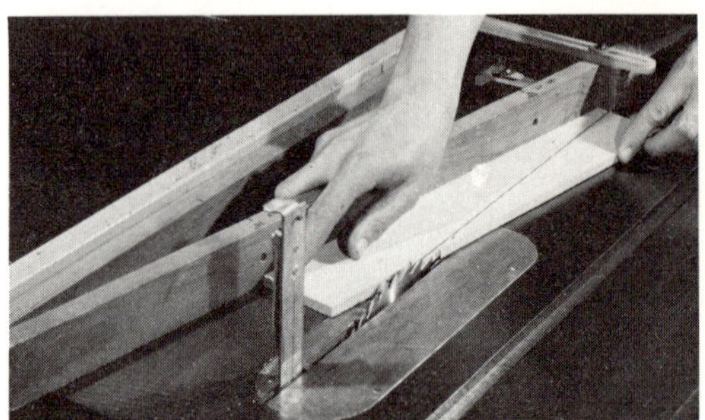

Photo 2: Using a tapering jig on a table saw to cut the top front angle on the rack sides. Note: The blade guard is removed for clarity.

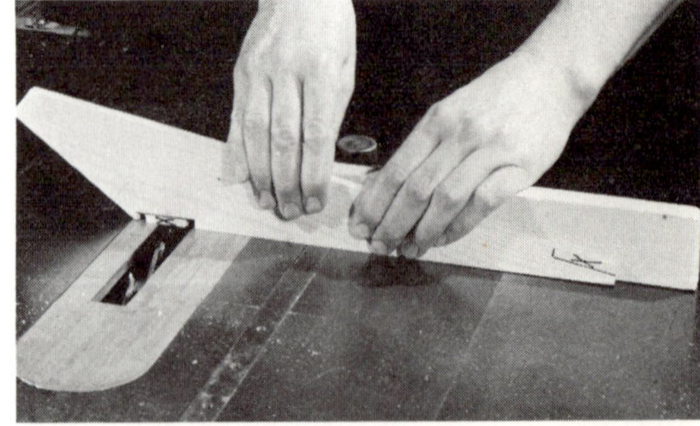

Photo 3: Cutting 1/4″ by 1-3/4″ dadoes in the rack sides for the top and bottom crosspieces. The cuts are made on a table saw with three passes of a dado head.

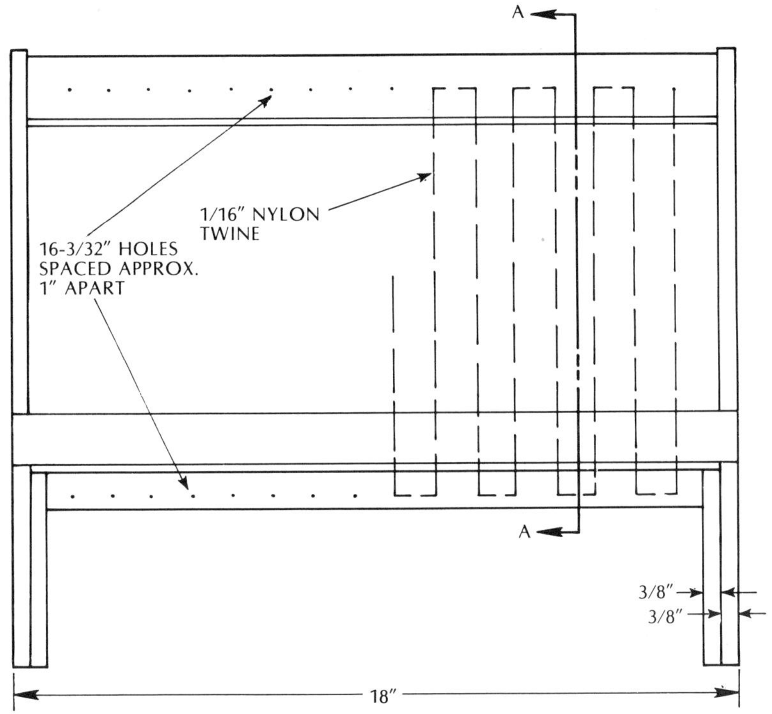

Fig. 1: Front view of the magazine rack.

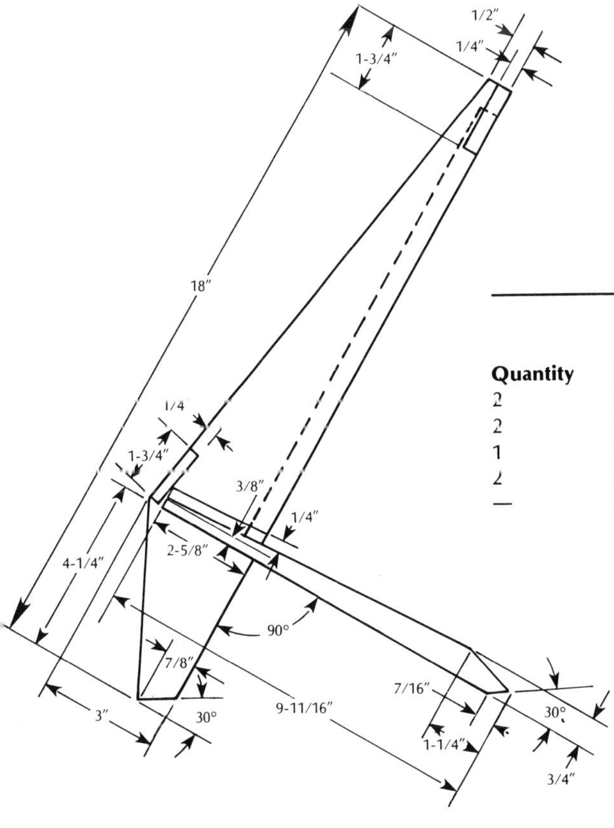

MATERIALS

Quantity	Description
2	3/8" x 3" x 18" Sides
2	1/4" x 1 3/4" x 18" Top and bottom crosspieces
1	1/4" x 2-5/8" x 17-1/4" Bottom
2	3/8" x 3/4" x 9-11/16" Legs
—	Approximately 20' of 1/16" dia. Nylon twine

Fig. 2: Details for the magazine rack sides and legs.

SIMPLE PICTURE FRAMES

Photo 1: A frame using molding A.

Here are two beveled type frames that can be made quickly on a table saw. Tilt the blade at 15° for the face cuts on the frames. The rabbets are made in two cuts of the saw blade. If using a dado head, the rabbets can be cut in one cut.

The saw blade or dado head can also be used to make the spline groove. In fact, splines can be used to strengthen any miter joint. The spline itself is a thin strip of hardwood or plywood inserted in a groove cut in the two adjoining surfaces of the joint. The groove for the spline is commonly run in with the dado head, 1/4" being the usual for 3/4" stock (molding A), while a 1/8" spline, a single saw blade cut, is the best for molding B. The spline stock should be cut so that the grain runs at right angles to the grain of the joint. Since glue is used to hold the spline, no nails are required for this type of construction.

The sizes of the frames will depend on the size of the pictures, therefore, no materials list is given. Molding A (Photo 1) is used for larger pictures, while molding B (Photo 2) is used for smaller ones. The frames may be finished any way you desire.

Photo 2: Twin frames using molding B.

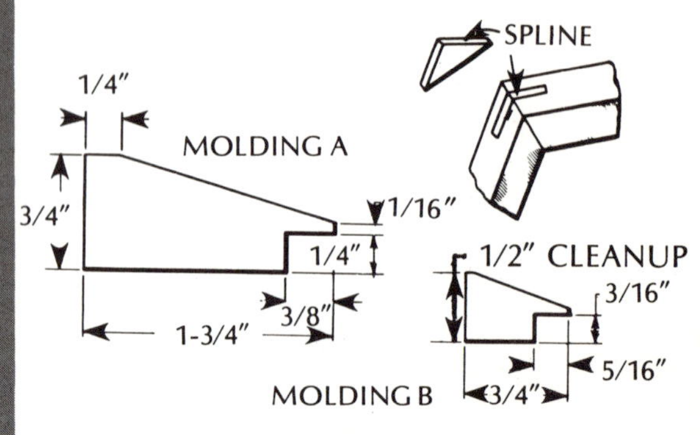

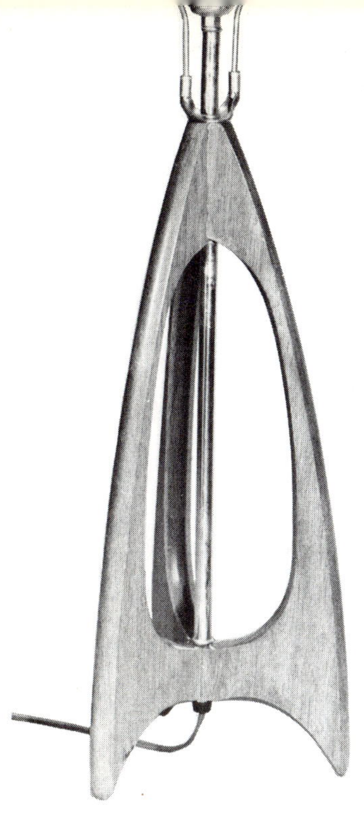

MODERN TABLE LAMP BASE

MATERIALS

Quantity	Description
3	13/16″ x 5″ x 18-1/2″ Lumber (legs)
1	1/8″ x 16-1/2″ Brass tube
2	Spacers
1	Lock nut
1	Lamp harp
1	Lamp socket
1	16″ dia. Shade
—	Fine abrasive
—	Glue
—	Polyurethane finish
3	Felt pads

This practical wood lamp with gleaming brass fittings will enrich any living room in any type of home. The graceful curved walnut legs are held together with a unique joint which should prove a challenge to any woodworker. A 16″ shade of white or tan textured grass cloth over parchment completes the project.

The base is made of three pieces of walnut stock 13/16″ thick, 5″ wide by 18-1/2″ long. Make a full size paper template of the leg. Before cutting the inside and outside curves of the leg pieces, make the joint cuts on the straight edge in two cuts, as shown in Figs. 2 and 3. The blade is tilted at 30° for both cuts, only the blade height is different (Photos 1 and 2). Dry fit the three pieces to make sure of a tight joint. Next, draw the curved portions with the paper template and proceed to cut out the pieces on either your band saw or scroll, (Photo 3). The stop rounded molded edges are made on the spindle shaper with a three winged cutter (Photo 4). Note the wood template and stop point marks as indicated in Fig. 1 of the drawing.

If strap clamps are not available for gluing the three legs together, use rubber bands (Photo 5). When the glue has set overnight, bore the holes for the brass tube from the top and the bottom of the assembly (Photo 6).

Sand all of the parts thoroughly, breaking any sharp corners with fine abrasive paper. For a natural finish, apply two coats of rubbed effect or satin effect polyurethane finish.

Felt pads can be added under each foot of the lamp for added stability. Bore a 3/8″ hole part way and insert the felt pads with glue.

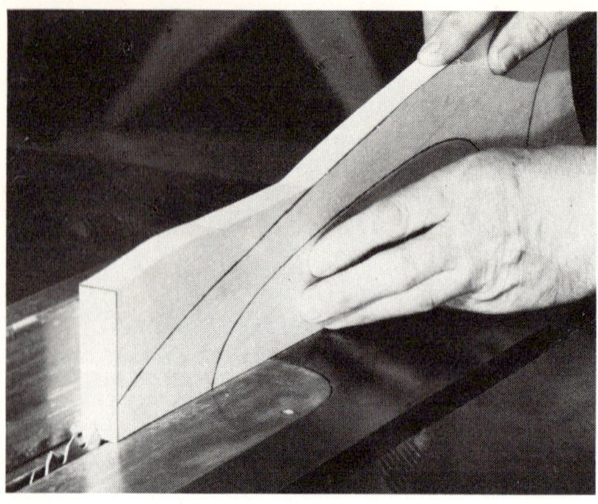

Photo 1: The first cut of the assembly joint is made on the table saw with the stock in an upright position and the blade set at a 30° angle. Note: The blade guard is removed for clarity.

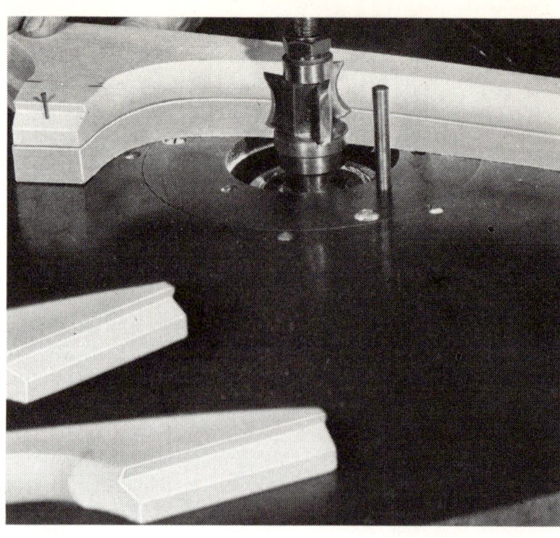

Photo 4: The edges of the legs are made on the spindle shaper using a three lip cutter. Note the wood template and molding stop points.

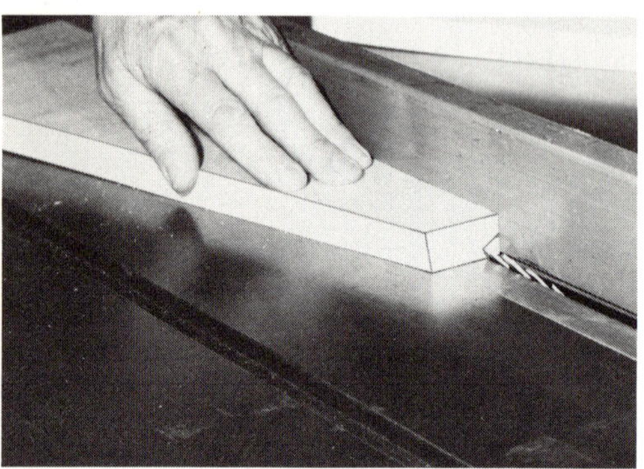

Photo 2: The second cut of the assembly joint is made on the table saw with the stock on its side and the blade again tilted to a 30° angle. Note: The blade guard is removed for clarity.

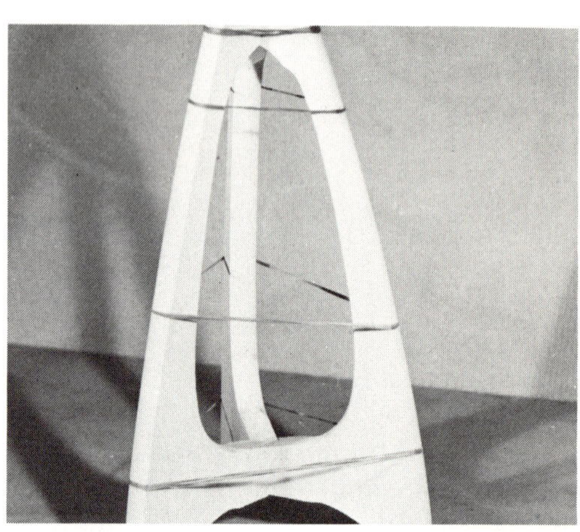

Photo 5: The three legs are assembled with glue and held together with rubber bands.

Photo 3: Inside and outside curves are cut on the band saw using a 1/4" skip tooth blade.

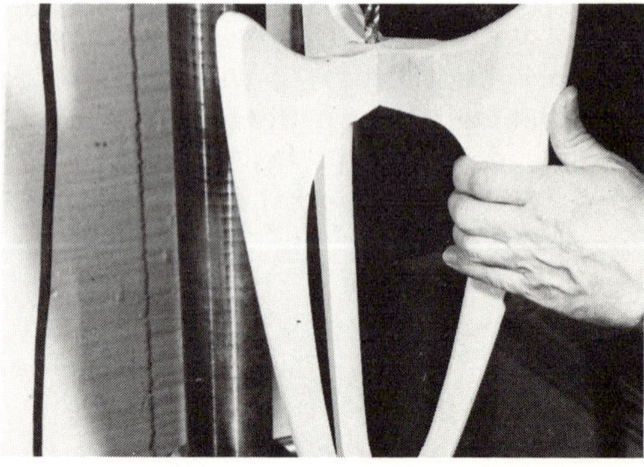

Photo 6: Holes for the brass tube are bored on the drill press with a 3/8" bit.

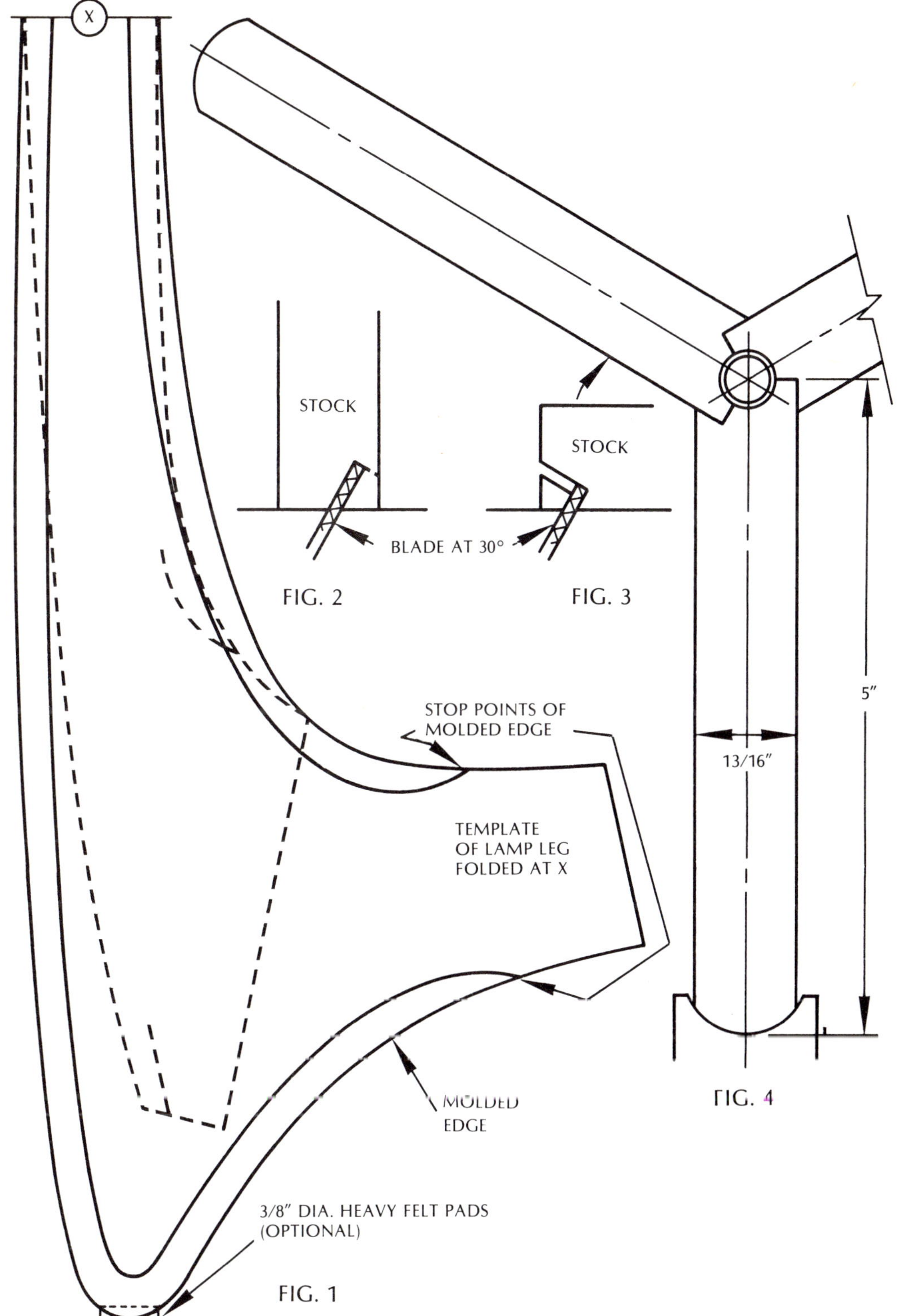
X
STOCK
STOCK
BLADE AT 30°
FIG. 2
FIG. 3
STOP POINTS OF
MOLDED EDGE
TEMPLATE
OF LAMP LEG
FOLDED AT X
5″
13/16″
MOLDED
EDGE
FIG. 4
3/8″ DIA. HEAVY FELT PADS
(OPTIONAL)
FIG. 1

SHAKER SMALL BENCH

The ingenious simplicity of Shaker joinery is well illustrated by the half-dovetail joints on this little bench. This construction results in a finished product that is surprisingly light and strong. It can easily be built by following these instructions:

1. Cut the boards to the sizes shown in Fig. 3, and cut half-circles in the legs.
2. Cut 1/4″ by 1/2″ dadoes in the top to fit the legs.
3. Miter the ends of the braces and cut notches as shown in Photos 1 and 2. (Glue the full-size template to one of the braces and use it to position a stopblock for each cut.)
4. Assemble one leg into the top without glue, lay a brace in position, and mark the cuts to be made in the top and leg (Photo 3). Repeat for the other braces. Make the initial cuts with a dovetail saw or backsaw.
5. Clean out the cuts using a dado blade with the miter gauge at 90°, and then at 45° (Photo 4).
6. Finish-sand all the pieces before assembly.
7. Assemble the bench with white glue and nails. The Shakers used square cut nails and left the heads exposed, which made an attractive detail. If ordinary brads are used, countersink them and fill the holes.
8. Trim the ends of the braces flush. A router with a self piloting bit will do this very quickly, but a block plane and/or rasp will also do a satisfactory job.
9. Break all sharp edges with a block sander and very fine abrasive paper. Finish as desired.

MATERIALS

Quantity	Description
1	1/2″ x 8″ x 17″ Pine
2	1/2″ x 8″ x 9-15/16″ Hard maple
4	3/16″ x 1-1/4″ x 7-1/4″ Hard maple
8	Cut nails or 1″ brads
-	White glue
-	Finishing materials

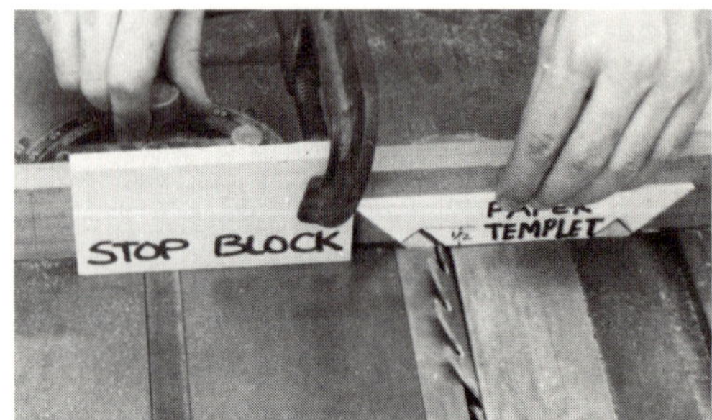

Photo 1: Starting the notches in the brace. Note: The blade guard is removed for clarity.

PAPER TEMPLET
STOP BLOCK

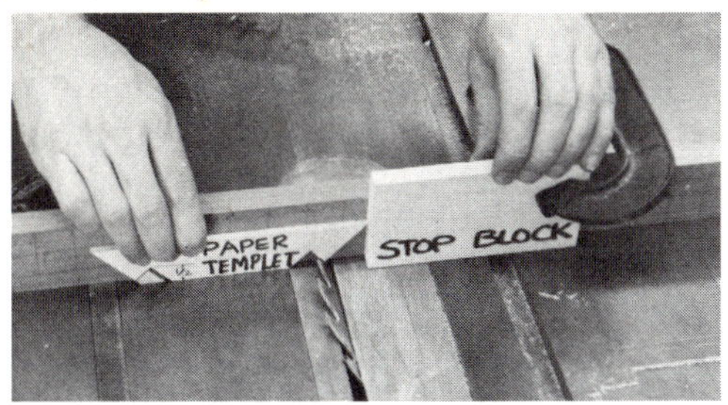

Photo 2: Completing the notches in the brace. Hold the work tightly; the blade may snag the scrap corner, producing a mild kick if it is held loosely. Note: The blade guard is removed for clarity.

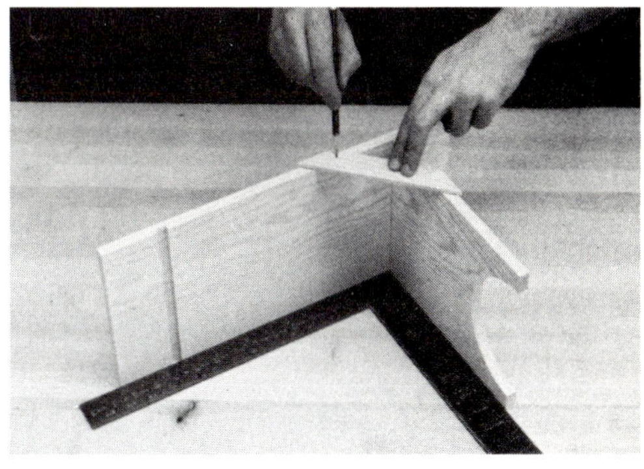

Photo 3: Marking the position of the dadoes in the top and leg.

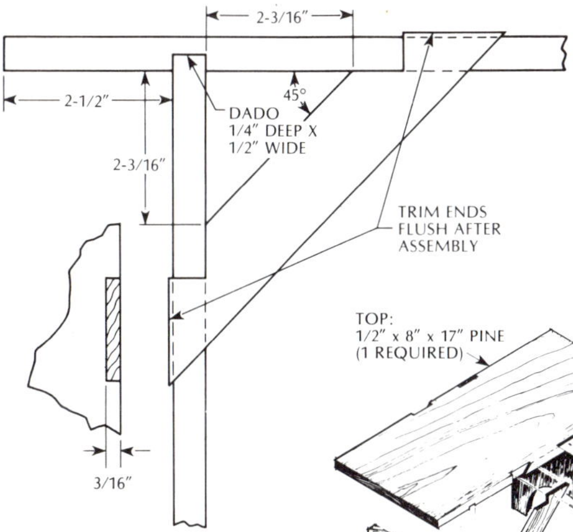
2-3/16"
2-1/2"
45°
DADO
1/4" DEEP X
1/2" WIDE
2-3/16"
TRIM ENDS
FLUSH AFTER
ASSEMBLY
3/16"

FIG. 1

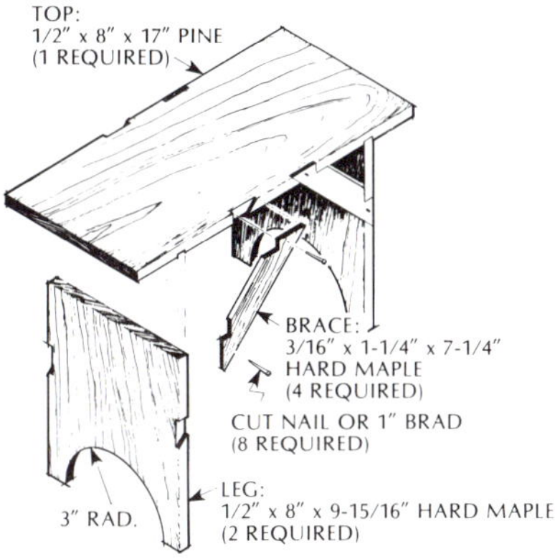
TOP:
1/2" x 8" x 17" PINE
(1 REQUIRED)
BRACE:
3/16" x 1-1/4" x 7-1/4"
HARD MAPLE
(4 REQUIRED)
CUT NAIL OR 1" BRAD
(8 REQUIRED)
3" RAD.
LEG:
1/2" x 8" x 9-15/16" HARD MAPLE
(2 REQUIRED)

FIG. 3

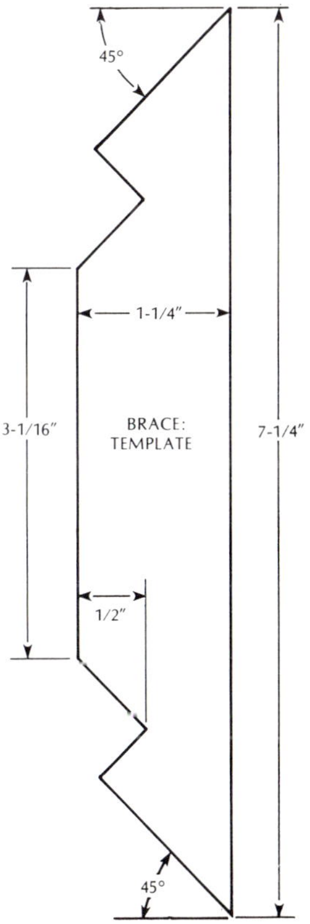
45°
1-1/4"
3-1/16"
BRACE:
TEMPLATE
7-1/4"
1/2"
45°

FIG. 2

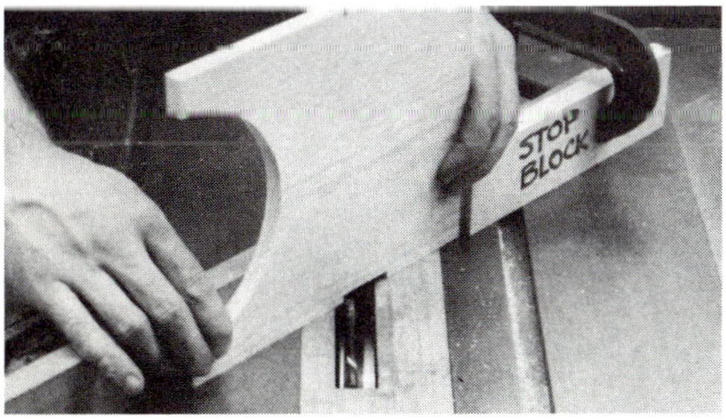
STOP BLOCK

Photo 4: Cleaning out the dadoes. The initial cuts were first made with a dovetail saw.

TROPHY MOUNTING BOARD

A very distinctive trophy mounting board can be made from pine or a hardwood, such as oak or walnut, finished in a dark stain. For larger trophies, the parts can be increased in size by using the squares method as shown in the drawing.

The backboard and front shelf are identical in shape, except for the thickness of the stock. Only the shelf board has the top edge molded with a flute cutter mounted on the spindle of a shaper, or in the chuck of a portable router. The shelf is nailed and glued to the 1/2" thick bracket as indicated in the drawing. The backboard has a groove routed on the top end over which a staple is mounted, used to hang the finished shelf on the wall. The backboard is screw fastened from the back with two 1-1/4" No. 6 flathead wood screws.

Sand the assembled shelf thoroughly with fine abrasive paper, breaking all sharp corners. Stain with a dark oak or walnut stain and apply a filler to close the pores of the wood. Two coats of polyurethane finish should complete the job. Of course, a penetrating resin finish may also be used.

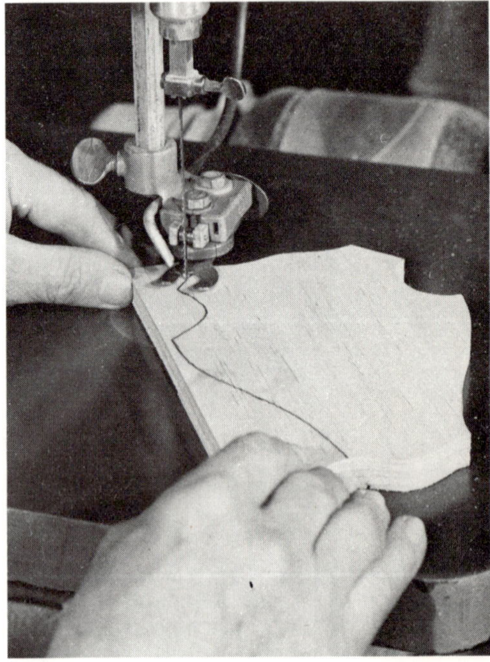

Photo 1: The three parts of the shelf including the base, shelf, and bracket can be cut on the band saw with a 1/8" blade, or on the scroll saw using a jeweler's blade. Lacking either of these tools, a portable jig saw may be used.

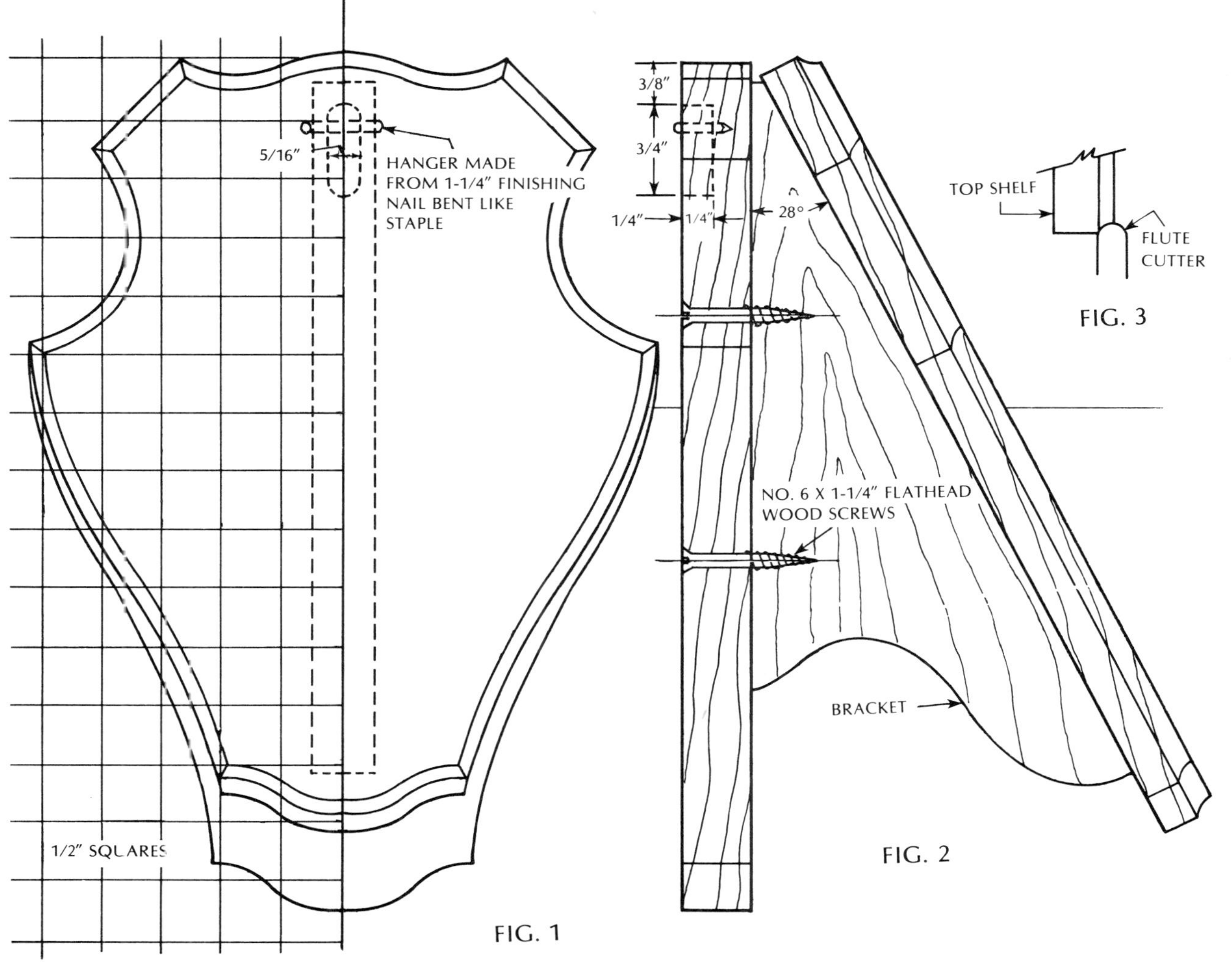

FIG. 1

FIG. 2

FIG. 3

TELEPHONE TABLE

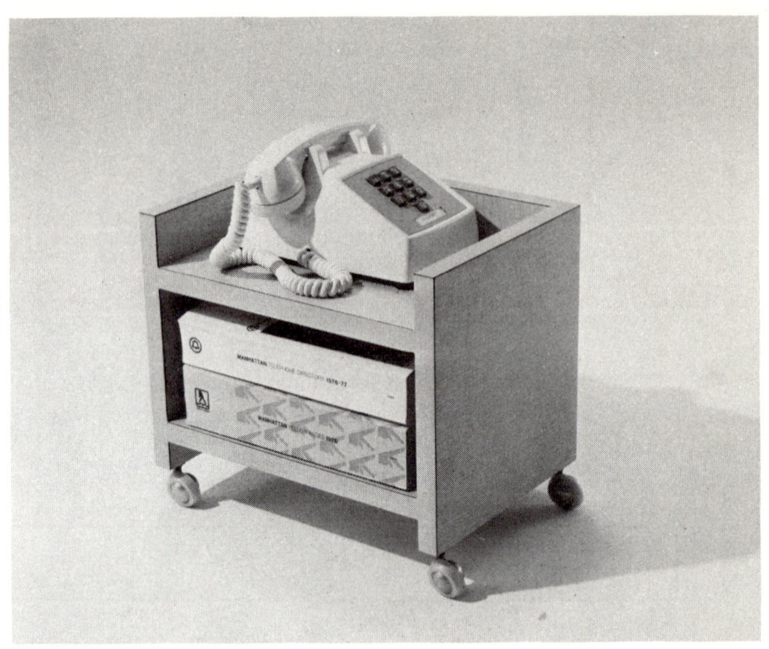

The simple telephone table illustrated here is constructed as follows:

1. Start by cutting all of the parts to size as shown in the drawing.

2. Next, using either a router, a table saw, or a radial saw, cut all the rabbets and grooves as indicated.

3. Using 4d finishing nails only, temporarily assemble the table to check for fit. Adjust the dimensions if necessary. Locate and mark the caster-stem locations; bore the holes for the stems per manufacturer's instructions. Disassemble the table.

4. Apply a laminate on this project *before* the final assembly. Start by bonding the material to the inside surfaces of the sides and back. Trim all the laminate overhangs with a router and a straight carbide cutter as outlined on page 10. At this time, also rout away all the laminate covering grooves and rabbets. Set these pieces aside.

5. Next, carefully and accurately, cut the plastic laminate for the shelves. Since the grooves and rabbets in the plywood are only 3/4″ wide, those portions of the shelves which will be fit into the grooves must *not* be covered with the laminate. To prevent laminating the side and rear edges, use a carpenter's square to draw the guidelines 3/8″ from the edges.

6. With all the large inside surfaces laminated, the table can now be assembled. Use white glue and screws, as shown, for the joinery. Bore the pilot holes with countersinks and make certain the screw heads are fully flush with the surface. To be safe, thoroughly sand the driven screw heads before covering the side and back exterior surfaces with the laminate.

7. The order in which the remaining laminate pieces are applied is important. Start by covering the outside back of the table. Trim all the laminate overhangs and then apply the laminate to both sides. Trim the laminate.

8. Next, using a single sheet — so there will be no joints — laminate the front edges of the sides and shelves simultaneously.

Rout away all the overhang. *Note:* In order to remove the laminate between the shelves, you must first bore an entry hole for the router cutter.

9. Finally, again using a single sheet, bond the laminate to the top edges of the back and sides. Trim the overhang.

10. Install casters in the predrilled holes. Clean up the project with an adhesive solvent recommended on the adhesive label instructions. Be sure to follow all the safety precautions and provide adequate ventilation.

MATERIALS

Quantity	Description
1/2	3/4" x 48" x 24" Plywood panel
2	9-5/8" x 13-1/4" Plastic laminate (shelf tops)
4	10" x 11" Plastic laminate (sides)
3	11" x 15" Plastic laminate
1	10-1/2" x 15" Plastic laminate
4	Casters
24	1-1/4" No. 8 Flathead wood screws
-	White glue
-	Fine abrasive paper
-	Contact adhesive
-	Adhesive solvent

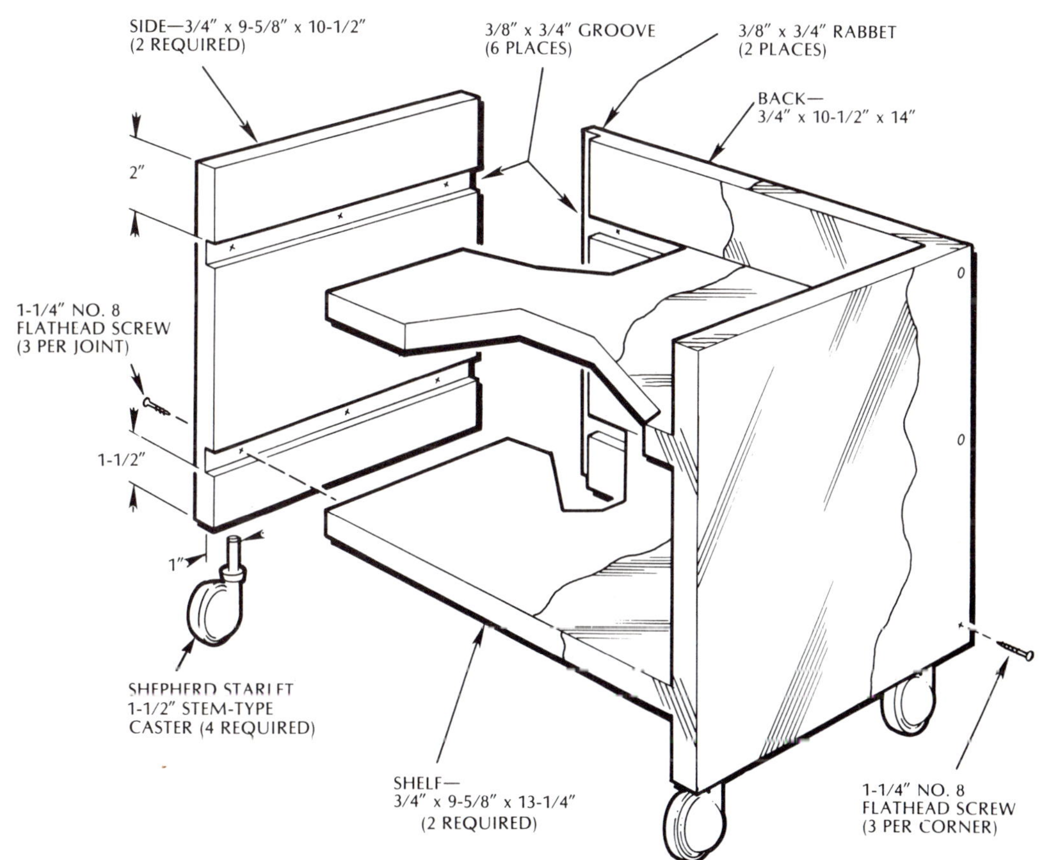

BIRD CENTERPIECE

MATERIALS

Quantity	**Description**
1	3/4" x 6" x 11" Lumber (base)
1	3/4" x 3" x 9" Lumber (bird)
1	3/4" x 7" x 2-1/2" Lumber (bird)
1	1/8" x 5" x 10" Plastic base insert (optional)
1	6" x 11" Felt material
1	1/8" dia. x 24" Copper or brass rod (legs)
—	Linseed oil

This piece will serve as a truly unusual centerpiece for a dining room table or a desk decoration. It is very inexpensive to make. Perhaps a good many of the materials can be salvaged from a scrap box.

Start the project by transferring the shapes of the birds and base to the material. Note that the grain direction of the wood on the upright bird runs the short way for added beak strength. Use the band saw equipped with a 1/8" blade to rough-cut to shape.

Finish shaping the birds on the drill press using both 3" and 11/16" diameter sanding drums and coarse grit abrasive sleeves. Change to a fine sleeve for the final machine sanding operation.

The router, equipped with a corner round bit, is used to round the edge of the free-form base. Use copper or brass rod for the legs.

If the project is made of a hardwood like mahogany or walnut, a hand-rubbed finish is recommended. Several coats of boiled linseed oil, or a penetrating resin, should do the trick.

Brown or green felt material, glued to the bottom of the base, completes the project.

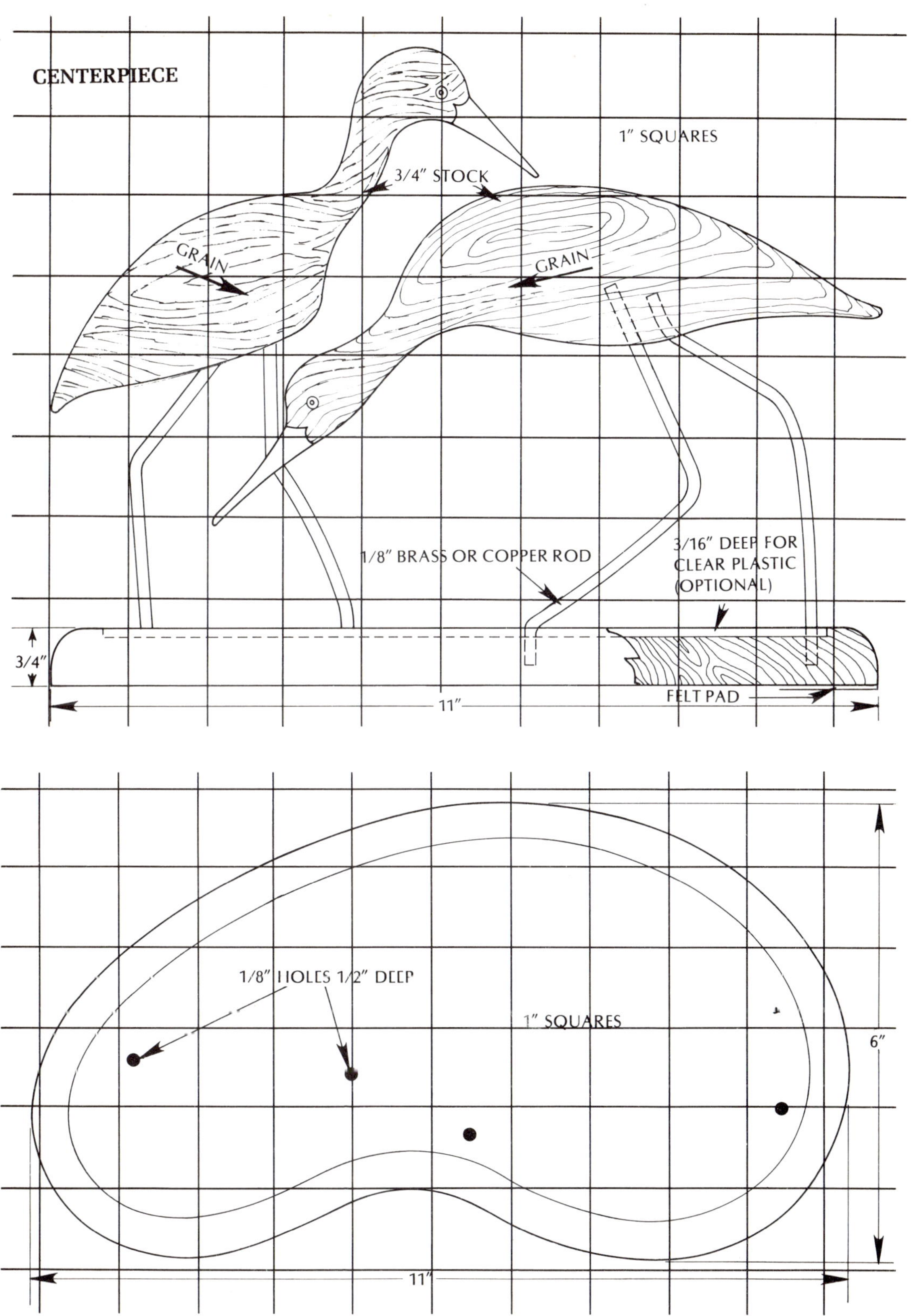
CENTERPIECE
1″ SQUARES
3/4″ STOCK
GRAIN
GRAIN
1/8″ BRASS OR COPPER ROD
3/16″ DEEP FOR
CLEAR PLASTIC
(OPTIONAL)
3/4″
FELT PAD
11″
1/8″ HOLES 1/2″ DEEP
1″ SQUARES
6″
11″

DOOR/WALL VALET

Photo 1: *This valet may be hung on the wall or the inside of a closet door. It folds up neatly, even with clothing on it. Note that the pants come off the hanger before the coat — a convenient detail.*

As was stated earlier, most of the projects given in this book are constructed by using several different construction techniques. The door/wall valet is a very good example of this. In fact, we have included two sets of plans, each using a different joint throughout. The joint in Plan 1 is easier to make, while the one in Plan 2 is stronger.

Whichever joint is used (Photo 3), make and assemble the frames (including the back) before making the hanger. If a table saw is used with the dado head, all the rabbet joints must be cut with the blade guard removed, so work extra-carefully.

To construct the frame, proceed as follows:

1. Saw the frame members to the overall sizes shown in Plan 1 or Plan 2. (Do not joint the edges yet.)

2. (*Plan 1 only.*) Using a dado head, cut the rabbets in all the horizontal members with the setup shown in Photo 4. (With a radial saw, the setup is similar; a stop-block is clamped to the fence and the rabbet is cross-cut.)

3. (*Plan 2 only.*) Use a dado head and the setup shown in Photo 5 to cut the 1/4″ grooves in all the horizontal members.

Photo 6 shows the setup for cutting the rabbets in the vertical members. Adjust the height of the blade till it leaves a tongue that fits the grooves in the horizontal members without being forced. (With a radial saw, similar setups are used for these two operations; in both cases, a stop-block is clamped to the fence and the groove or rabbet is cross-cut.)

4. Joint or hand-plane the edges of the frame members, cutting just deep enough to remove the saw marks.

5. Saw slots in the outer frame members to accept the back. They should be about 1/4″ deep and wide enough to fit the back with a little clearance (make trial cuts in scrap wood).

6. The back may be made from plastic laminate, hardboard (painted), or 1/8″ plywood that matches the frame material. Saw the back to 11-9/16″ by 21″ making sure the ends are square. Try assembling the outer frame around the back, and trim the back till it fits the frame with just a little clearance. This will keep the outer frame square during assembly.

7. Finish-sand the inner faces of all the frame members. Assemble both the frames

on a flat surface, using white glue. Clamp the frames lightly with bar clamps or heavy rubber bands. Check the inner frame with a square; if it is skewed, put one of the clamps on a little crooked to pull it square. It is *not* recommended to glue the back in place because it might cause the joints to crack if the frame tries to shrink a little.

8. When the glue is thoroughly dry, drill 1/4" holes in the locations shown in Plan 1 or 2 (Photo 7). Glue the dowels in, and cut them off about 1/32" above the surface. Do not force the dowels. If they will not go in with a gentle tap, sand or scrape them a little smaller.

9. Disc-sand, belt-sand, or file the dowels and protruding pieces of wood flush at the corners of both frames.

10. Finish-sand the frames. Stain and/or finish as desired.

11. Clamp the inner frame to the outer frame with the front edges flush and with a 1/4" gap between the frames at the top (Photo 8). Drill 1/4" frame pivot holes through the outer frame and into the inner frame. Remove the inner frame and redrill the holes in the outer frame to 5/16". Glue the two pivot dowels (Fig. 3) into the outer frame, pushing them in just far enough so the inner frame pivots freely without excessive play.

To make the hanger, proceed as follows:

12. Use the full-size template in Fig. 3 to trace the hanger onto a board at least 3/4" by 6" by 18-1/2". If a drill press is available, bore two 1" holes at the centers indicated to form the 1/2" radii. Cut out the hanger and round the edges. This job may be done by hand with a spokeshave and/or a rasp, but a router and 3/8" corner-round bit will do a quicker job. (Be careful not to "turn the corner" at the ends of the horizontal bar — they should not be rounded.)

13. Finish the hanger to match the frames.

14. Drill a 1/4" hole in each end of the hanger (Fig. 3). Drill a 5/16" hanger pivot hole in the frame (Plans 1 and 2). Glue the two tapered pivot dowels (Fig. 3) into the inner frame, pushing them in just far enough so the hanger pivots freely without excessive play.

To install the hardware and mount the door/wall valet units, proceed as follows:

15. Make and install a wood latch (Fig. 3) to hold the inner frame up.

16. For the stop chain, use an 11" length of any attractive chain, or a narrow strip of leather. Screw the chain or strap to the inner and outer frames as shown in Photo 1, positioning the screws so the inner frame will open 90°. When using fittings like those shown, leave the upper screw loose enough so that the fitting will swivel; otherwise the inner frame will not close.

17. Drill two 13/64" holes through the back and mount the valet on the wall or door with No. 10 round head screws. The hole location and screw length will be determined by the mounting requirements. If it is going on a wall, you might pick up two studs with holes 16" apart horizontally, or one stud with holes spaced vertically. If it is going on a door, check the door to find the best location for the holes.

MATERIALS

Quantity	Description
2	3/4" x 1-1/2" x 10" Inner frames*
2	3/4" x 1-1/2" x 21" Inner frames*
2	3/4" x 2-3/8" x 12" Outer frames*
2	3/4" x 2-3/8" x 22-1/2" Outer frames*
1	3/4" x 6" x 18-1/2" Hanger
1	3/8" x 3/4" x 1-1/2" Latch
1	11-9/16" x 21" Plastic laminate, 1/8" hardboard, or 1/8" plywood for back
3'	1/4" Dowel
6'	5/16" Dowel
1'	Chain or leather strap
2	No. 8 x 3/4" Round head screws
1	No. 8 x 1-1/4" Flathead screw
2	No. 10 Round head screws
—	Scrap wood for trial cuts, etc.

* Lengths approximate — see plans for exact lengths.

Photo 2: The valet in the up position.

Photo 3: The corner detail showing the two common rabbet joints.

Photo 6: (Plan 2 joint): Rabbeting the vertical members. The stop-block controls the width of the rabbet.

Photo 4: (Plan 1 joint): Rabbeting the horizontal members. The stop-block controls the width of the rabbet.

Photo 7: Drilling the 1/4" dowel holes in the corners. The masking tape on the drill bit indicates the proper hole depth.

Photo 5: (Plan 2 joint): Dadoing a 1/4" groove in the horizontal members. The stop-block controls the position of the groove.

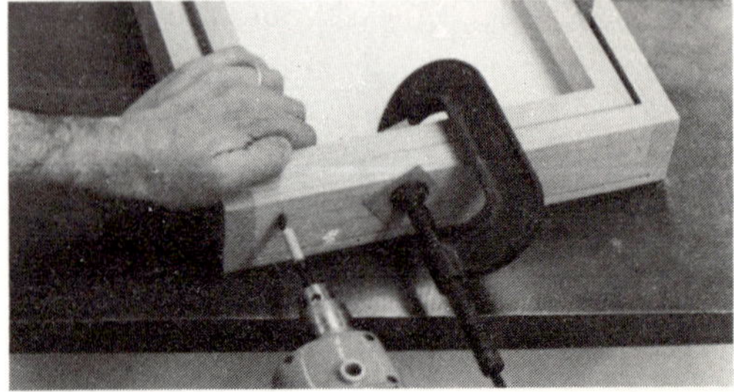

Photo 8: Drilling the 5/16" pivot holes in the frames. Note the use of cardboard pads to keep the clamps from marring the finish.

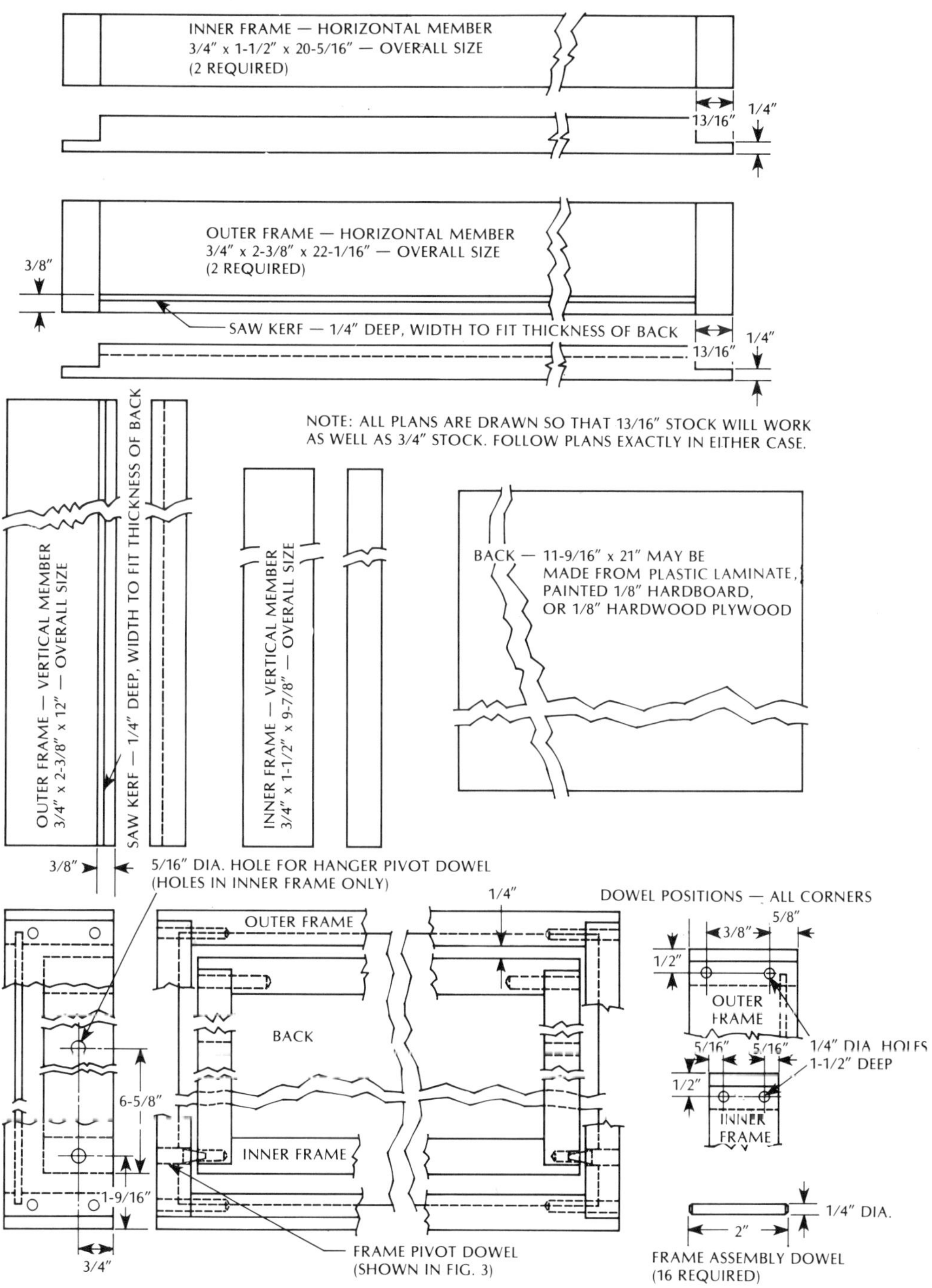

INNER FRAME — HORIZONTAL MEMBER
3/4" x 1-1/2" x 20-5/16" — OVERALL SIZE
(2 REQUIRED)
13/16"
1/4"
OUTER FRAME — HORIZONTAL MEMBER
3/4" x 2-3/8" x 22-1/16" — OVERALL SIZE
(2 REQUIRED)
3/8"
SAW KERF — 1/4" DEEP, WIDTH TO FIT THICKNESS OF BACK
13/16"
1/4"
NOTE: ALL PLANS ARE DRAWN SO THAT 13/16" STOCK WILL WORK AS WELL AS 3/4" STOCK. FOLLOW PLANS EXACTLY IN EITHER CASE.
OUTER FRAME — VERTICAL MEMBER
3/4" x 2-3/8" x 12" — OVERALL SIZE
SAW KERF — 1/4" DEEP, WIDTH TO FIT THICKNESS OF BACK
INNER FRAME — VERTICAL MEMBER
3/4" x 1-1/2" x 9-7/8" — OVERALL SIZE
BACK — 11-9/16" x 21" MAY BE MADE FROM PLASTIC LAMINATE, PAINTED 1/8" HARDBOARD, OR 1/8" HARDWOOD PLYWOOD
3/8"
5/16" DIA. HOLE FOR HANGER PIVOT DOWEL
(HOLES IN INNER FRAME ONLY)
1/4"
OUTER FRAME
BACK
INNER FRAME
6-5/8"
1-9/16"
3/4"
FRAME PIVOT DOWEL
(SHOWN IN FIG. 3)
DOWEL POSITIONS — ALL CORNERS
3/8"
5/8"
1/2"
OUTER FRAME
5/16"
5/16"
1/4" DIA. HOLES
1-1/2" DEEP
1/2"
INNER FRAME
1/4" DIA.
2"
FRAME ASSEMBLY DOWEL
(16 REQUIRED)

FIG. 1

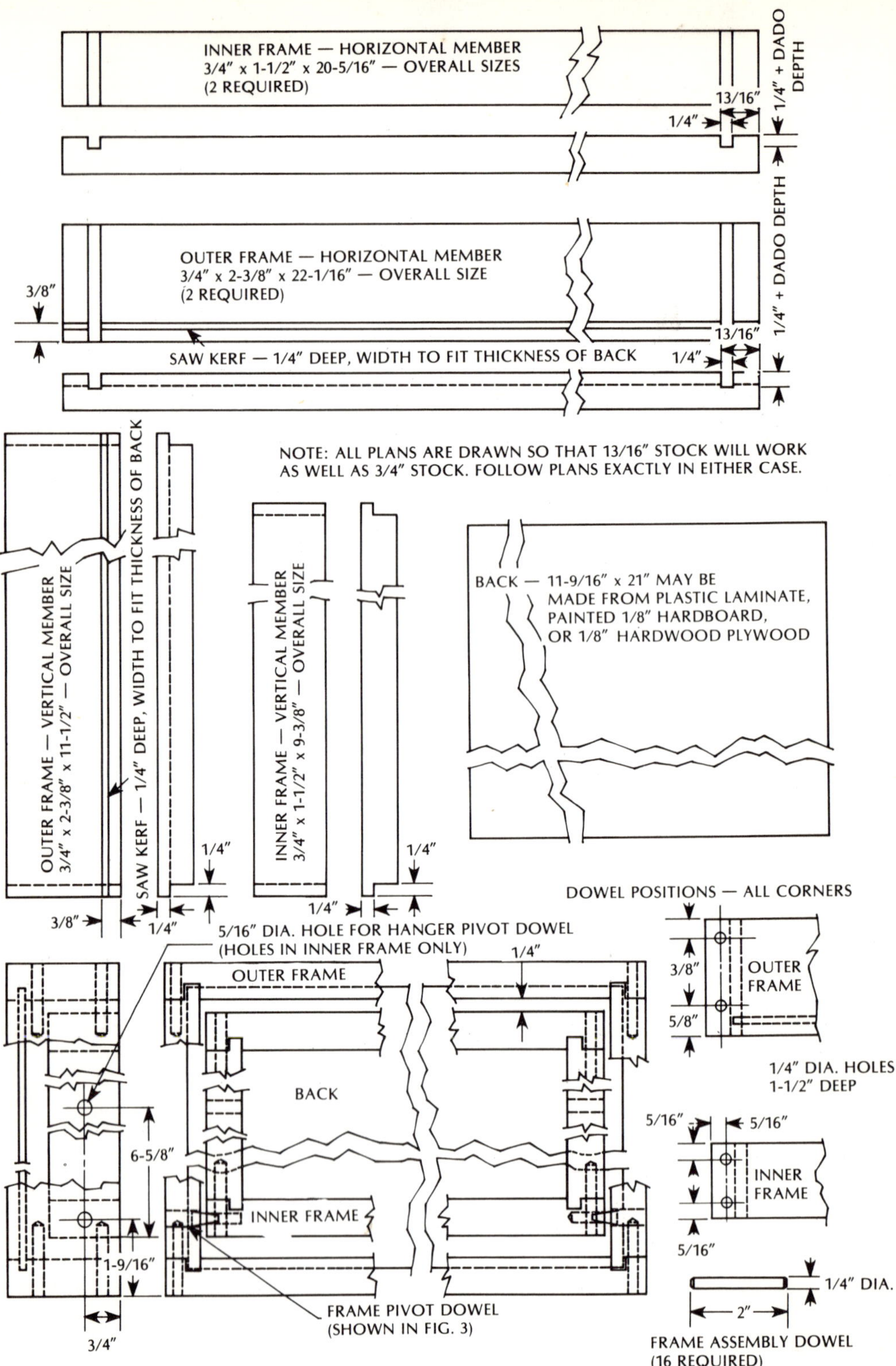
INNER FRAME — HORIZONTAL MEMBER
3/4" x 1-1/2" x 20-5/16" — OVERALL SIZES
(2 REQUIRED)
13/16"
1/4"
1/4" + DADO DEPTH
OUTER FRAME — HORIZONTAL MEMBER
3/4" x 2-3/8" x 22-1/16" — OVERALL SIZE
(2 REQUIRED)
3/8"
13/16"
SAW KERF — 1/4" DEEP, WIDTH TO FIT THICKNESS OF BACK
1/4"
1/4" + DADO DEPTH
NOTE: ALL PLANS ARE DRAWN SO THAT 13/16" STOCK WILL WORK AS WELL AS 3/4" STOCK. FOLLOW PLANS EXACTLY IN EITHER CASE.
OUTER FRAME — VERTICAL MEMBER
3/4" x 2-3/8" x 11-1/2" — OVERALL SIZE
SAW KERF — 1/4" DEEP, WIDTH TO FIT THICKNESS OF BACK
INNER FRAME — VERTICAL MEMBER
3/4" x 1-1/2" x 9-3/8" — OVERALL SIZE
BACK — 11-9/16" x 21" MAY BE
MADE FROM PLASTIC LAMINATE,
PAINTED 1/8" HARDBOARD,
OR 1/8" HARDWOOD PLYWOOD
1/4"
1/4"
3/8"
1/4"
1/4"
DOWEL POSITIONS — ALL CORNERS
5/16" DIA. HOLE FOR HANGER PIVOT DOWEL
(HOLES IN INNER FRAME ONLY)
OUTER FRAME
1/4"
BACK
6-5/8"
INNER FRAME
1-9/16"
3/4"
FRAME PIVOT DOWEL
(SHOWN IN FIG. 3)
3/8"
OUTER FRAME
5/8"
1/4" DIA. HOLES
1-1/2" DEEP
5/16"
5/16"
INNER FRAME
5/16"
1/4" DIA.
2"
FRAME ASSEMBLY DOWEL
(16 REQUIRED)

FIG. 2

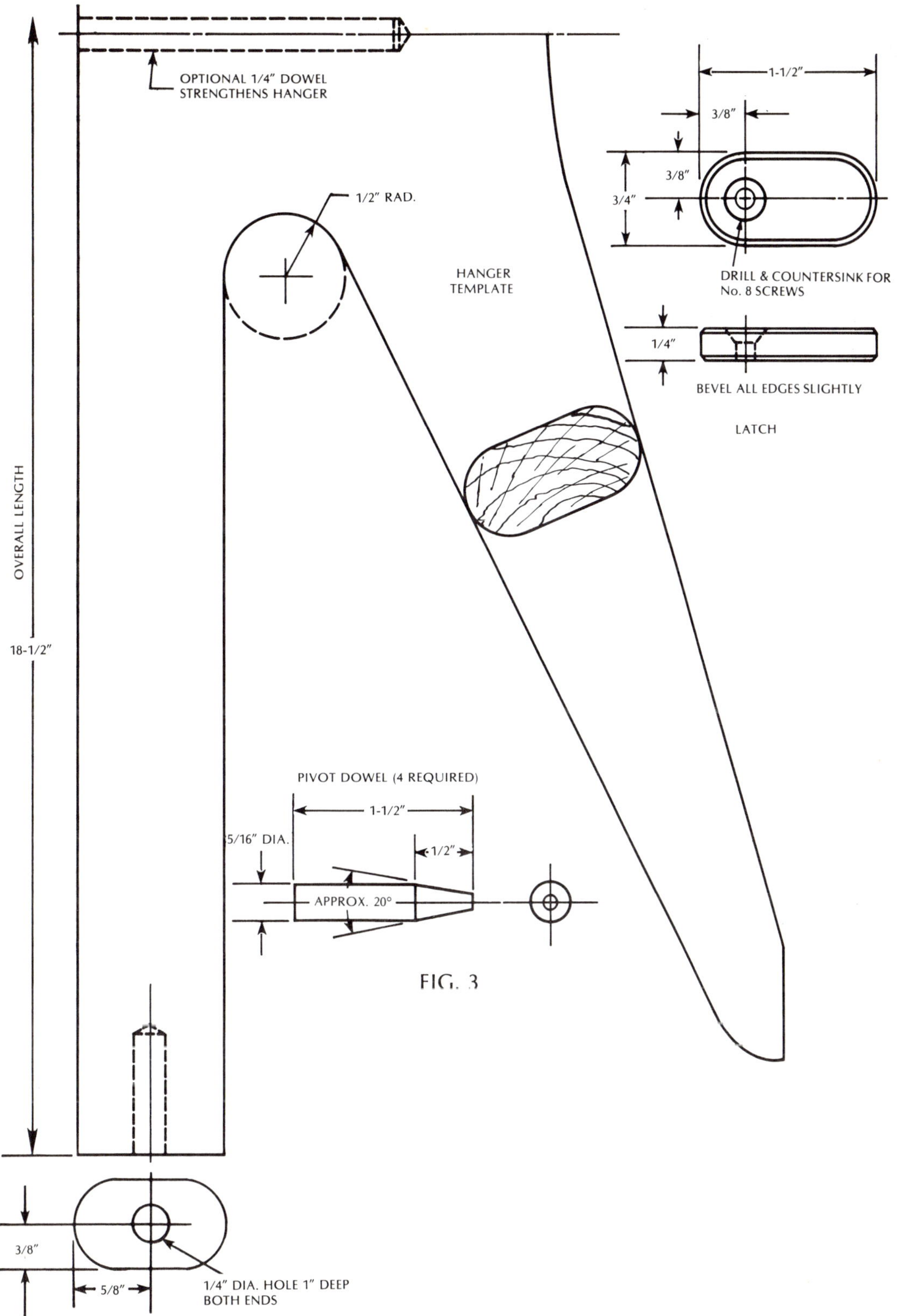
OPTIONAL 1/4" DOWEL
STRENGTHENS HANGER
1/2" RAD.
HANGER
TEMPLATE
OVERALL LENGTH
18-1/2"
1-1/2"
3/8"
3/8"
3/4"
DRILL & COUNTERSINK FOR
No. 8 SCREWS
1/4"
BEVEL ALL EDGES SLIGHTLY
LATCH
PIVOT DOWEL (4 REQUIRED)
1-1/2"
5/16" DIA.
1/2"
APPROX. 20°
3/8"
5/8"
1/4" DIA. HOLE 1" DEEP
BOTH ENDS

FIG. 3

DOOR STORAGE SHELVES

Put wasted space to use with this handy door shelf compartment! The unit can be made to fit the door of any bedroom, utility room, pantry, or kitchen. In addition, the shelf and dowel heights may also be varied to suit any storage requirements.

First, determine a convenient overall width and depth based on the dimensions of the closet and door on which the storage shelves will be mounted. Make sure it does not interfere with any closet shelves, etc.

For a 28″ wide door, the shelf should measure about 20″ wide. The length can vary according to individual needs. (For this reason, no materials list is included.)

The sides are made of 3/4″ hardwood or softwood plywood. If mounted on a closet door, the average shelf depth will be almost 3″ to 4-1/2″. The identical top and bottom scroll designs of the side pieces are either band or scroll sawed to shape as indicated in the drawing using the squares method as shown. Five dado grooves, 1/2″ wide by 1/4″ deep, are made in each side piece for the 1/2″ shelf stock. Five 1/2″ holes are bored 1/4″ deep in each side piece, 3/4″ from the front edge and 1-1/2″ above each shelf. The dowels fitted into these holes prevent items from falling off the shelf when opening or closing the door.

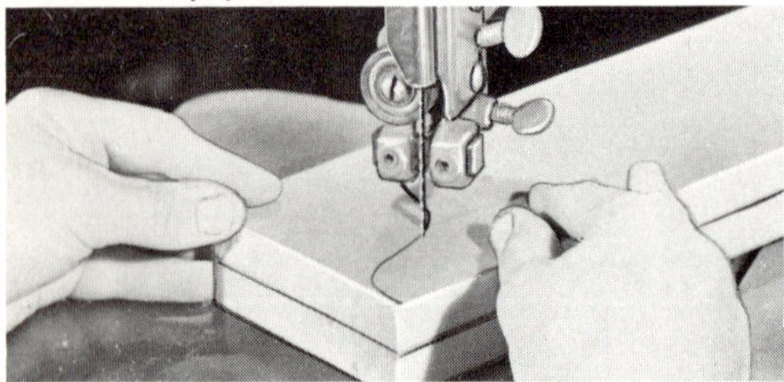

Photo 1: The two 3/4″ side pieces of the shelf can be tacked together when cutting the curved ends on the band saw using a 1/4″ skip tooth blade.

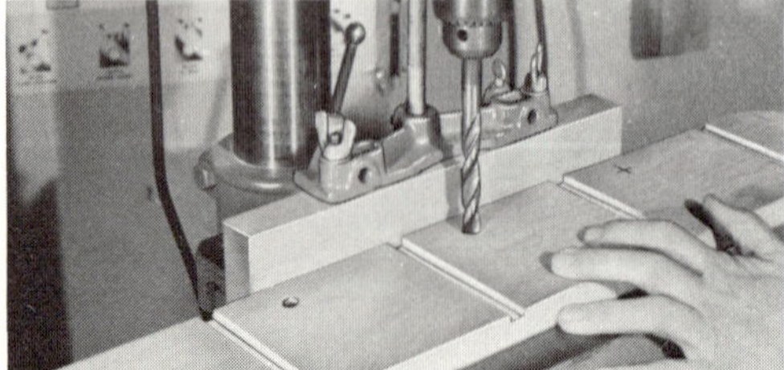

Photo 2: A fence is used on the drill press table for quickly drilling the dowel holes 3/4″ from the front edge of the side pieces. A 1/2″ bit is used for boring the holes.

Cut the 1/2″ shelf stock and the 1/2″ dowels to the desired lengths. Assemble the shelf with glue and 1-1/2″ finishing nails. If you use veneer core plywood, you can cover the edges with thin wood trim, or paint the edges to match the wood used.

Break all the sharp corners and sand them thoroughly. Finish natural with two coats of polyurethane varnish or enamel to match the door. For mounting, two metal hanger plates are screw fastened to the back edges of the side pieces as indicated in Figs. 2 and 3.

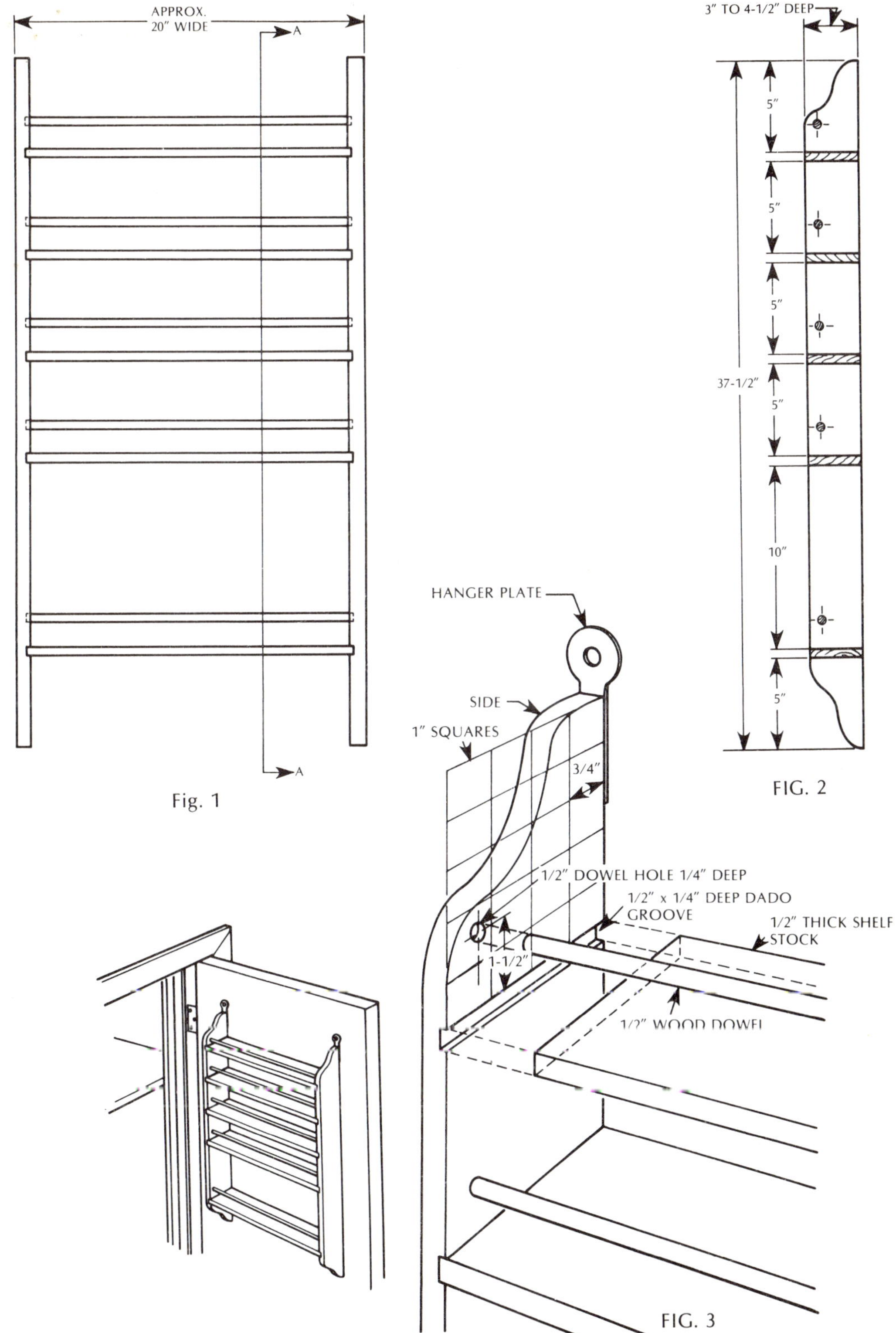
APPROX.
20" WIDE
A
A
Fig. 1
3" TO 4-1/2" DEEP
5"
5"
5"
37-1/2"
5"
10"
5"
FIG. 2
HANGER PLATE
SIDE
1" SQUARES
3/4"
1/2" DOWEL HOLE 1/4" DEEP
1/2" x 1/4" DEEP DADO
GROOVE
1/2" THICK SHELF
STOCK
1-1/2"
1/2" WOOD DOWEL
FIG. 3

CHEESE CUTTING BOARD

A very attractive cheese cutting board or a party server can be made of maple or cherry wood and finished with a dark cherry stain. The wire bladed knife is designed to fit right into the board. A bright colored ceramic round tile makes a perfect cutting surface.

The cutting board is made of two pieces of stock 5/16″ thick which are cut to size and shape as shown in the drawing.

Use a fine jeweler's blade on a scroll saw for cutting the finger opening in the knife. To start the cut, drill a hole on a drill press and then insert the jeweler's blade. The opening for the ceramic tile insert is cut the same way (Photo 1). Be sure to check the diameter of the tile when marking off the cutout opening, making sure the tile fits tightly. When all of the parts are cut and properly fitted, mark off the outline position of each piece with a pencil. Glue the pieces to the bottom board using wood hand screws, as shown in Photo 2. If a veneer press is available, use it instead. Glue all of the pieces to the board except the cutting knife.

Allow the glue to set overnight before doing any further work on the board. Holes for fastening the steel wire to the knife are bored at an angle with the aid of

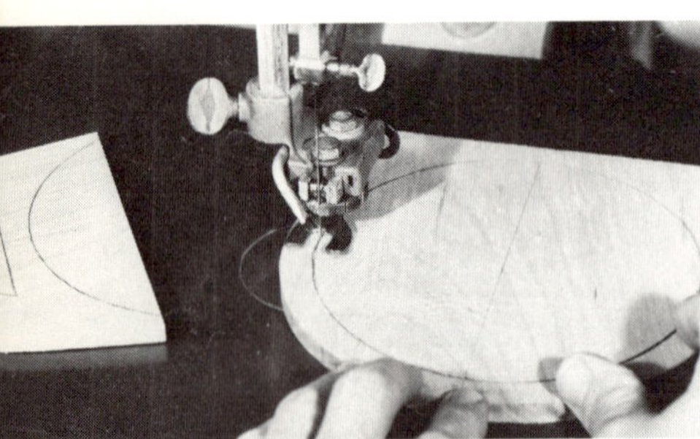

Photo 1: To make the knife finger opening and the opening for the tile insert, first drill starting holes and then use a fine jeweler's blade on a scroll saw to make the cutouts.

Photo 2: Wood hand screws are used for gluing the pieces to the bottom board. A veneer press would be better, if available.

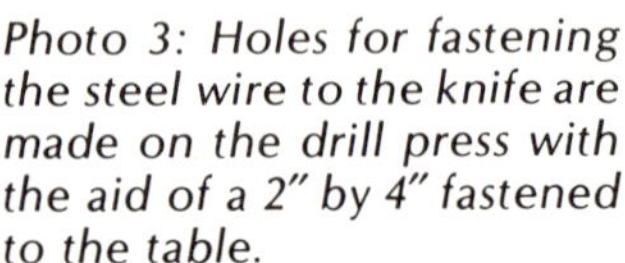

Photo 3: Holes for fastening the steel wire to the knife are made on the drill press with the aid of a 2″ by 4″ fastened to the table.

a 2″ by 4″ held on the drill press table with a hand screw (Photo 3).

Sand all the parts with a fine abrasive paper breaking all sharp corners. Finish with a desired wood colored stain. When dry, apply two coats of satin polyurethane finish or another synthetic varnish. Incidentally, a penetrating oil resin finish may be substituted as a top coat. Attach three small rubber headed nails to the bottom of the board to prevent it from sliding while in use.

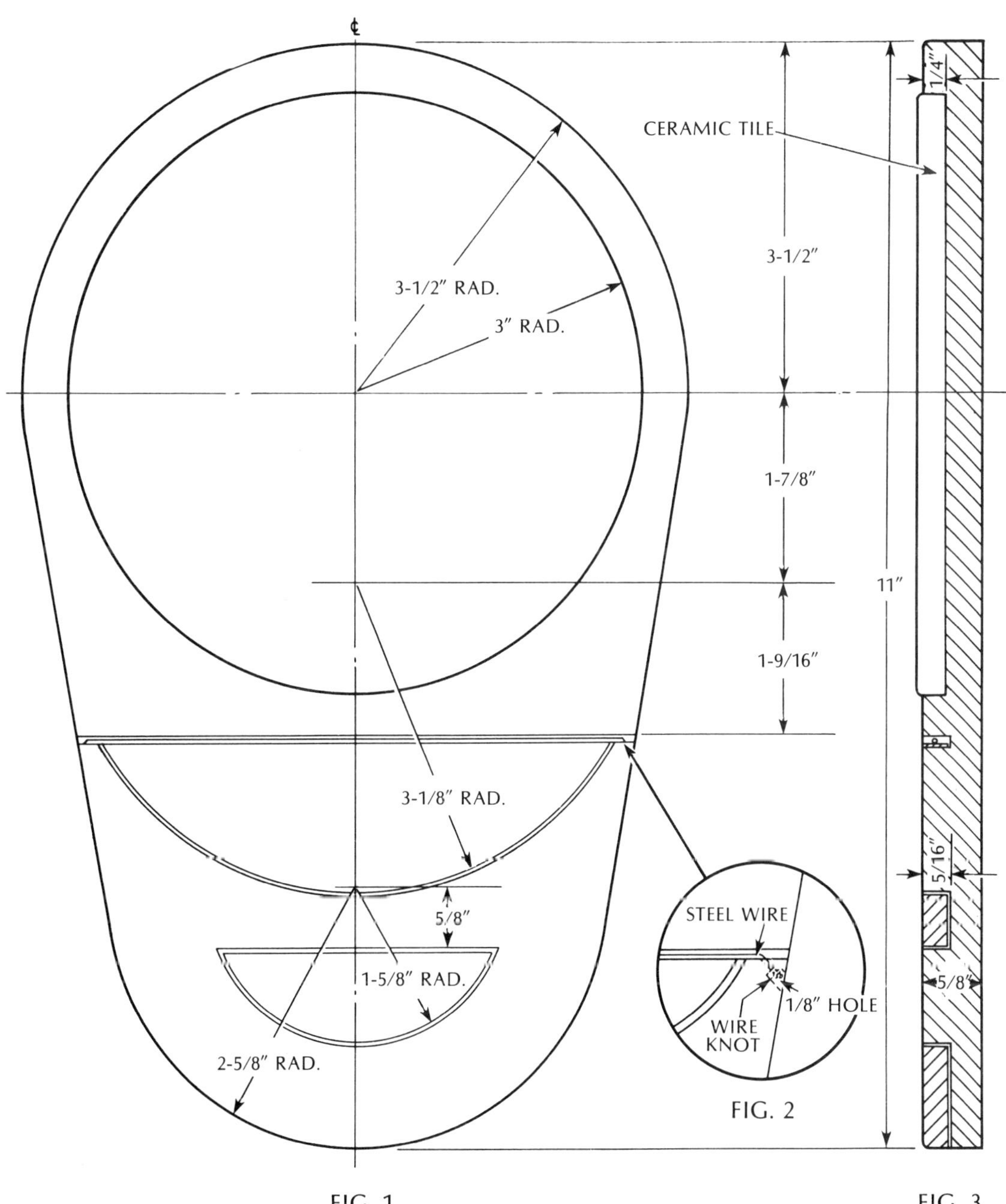

FIG. 1

FIG. 2

FIG. 3

FOLDING ANTIQUE HAT & COAT RACK

The hat and coat rack from which this project was copied was at least 150 years old. The white headed nails are beginning to turn a yellowish brown, as all antique porcelain ware does. No two pegs or hangers were the same size on the original rack.

It would be best to make all the wood parts from a hard wood like hickory or maple. The crosspieces could be made in long lengths and molded with two beads on the face side, with a beading cutter fitted into a high speed router, and later cut to the proper length as required. Half-inch peg holes are bored 1-5/16" from each end into the four short lengths with a center hole bored in each long length (Fig. 2).

The pegs are made from 13/16" square stock. By using the duplicator attachment on your lathe, you can turn three or more pegs at one time (Photo 2). Overall dimensions are given in Fig. 3. The dowel portion of each peg is nailed to the bottom stretcher piece with a 5/8" brad. The peg must work free on the top stretcher piece for opening and closing the unit. The white porcelain or rubber headed nails are not nailed into position until after the hanger is completely assembled and finished.

Break all sharp corners and sand all the parts thoroughly before applying a dark stain followed by a coat of satin finish polyurethane. The stretched out hanger can be hung on the wall using two shoulder hooks.

Photo l: The hat and coat rack folded for storage.

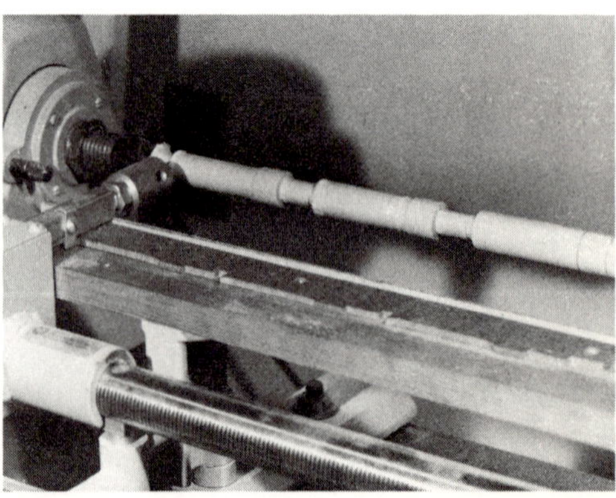

Photo 2: Several pegs can be turned at one time when using a duplicator attachment.

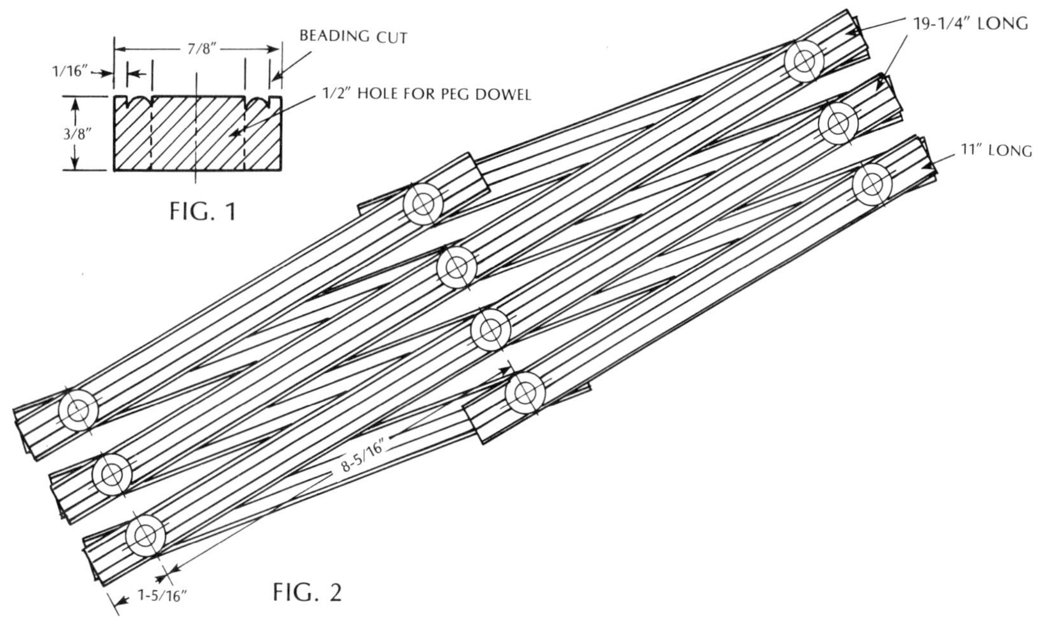

FIG. 1

FIG. 2

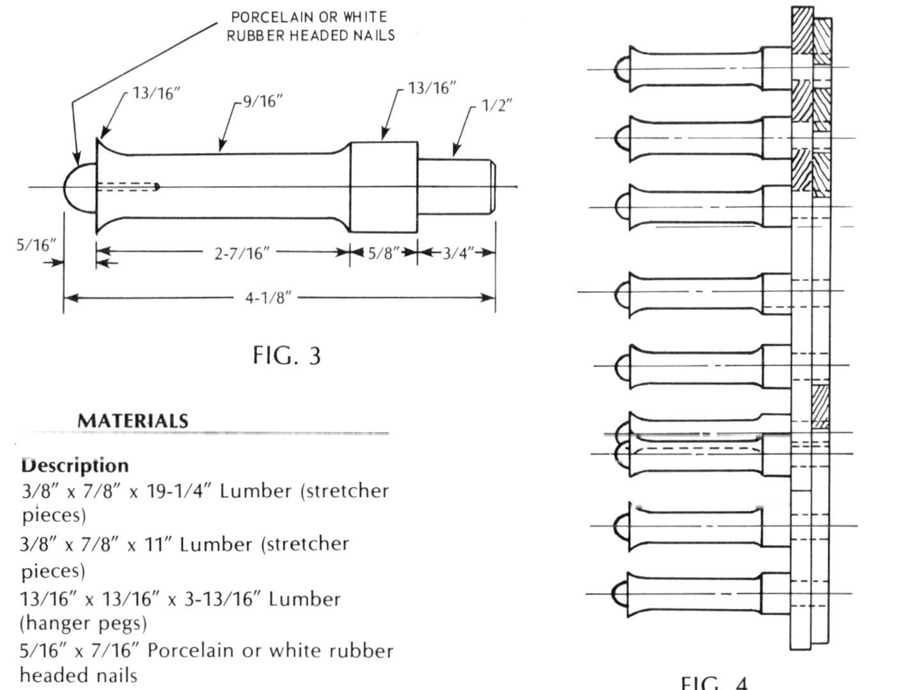

FIG. 3

FIG. 4

MATERIALS

Quantity	Description
4	3/8" x 7/8" x 19-1/4" Lumber (stretcher pieces)
4	3/8" x 7/8" x 11" Lumber (stretcher pieces)
10	13/16" x 13/16" x 3-13/16" Lumber (hanger pegs)
10	5/16" x 7/16" Porcelain or white rubber headed nails
10	No. 19 x 5/8" Brads
—	Fine abrasive paper
—	Woodstain
—	Polyurethane finish

DOLL HOUSE TOY CART

This sturdy toy cart, designed as a doll house, is perfect for the child in your family. To make this charming toy box, all you need is a 1/2" panel of A-B Interior or Medium Density Overlaid (MDO) plywood, some wood dowels and paint.

Here are building hints that should be followed when making the cart:

1. Cut out the rough square piece for each wheel; trace out each wheel; cut carefully. You may wish to cut out at least two wheels at a time, to assure uniformity when gluing each pair together. Use a powered jig saw to make all the cutouts and curved parts. Make sure the blade enters the good face of the panel.

2. Glue-nail the gussets to the bottom of sections (A) and (B) as shown in Fig. 1. Assemble the remaining pieces of the doll house.

3. Assemble the dowel-gusset-washer-wheel units. Sand as needed; paint. You may wish to paint the wheels and doors before you attach them to the doll house. Do not paint over dust, spots of oil, or glue. Any knots or pitch streaks should be touched up with sealer or shellac before painting. Use a water-base paint in a semi-gloss finish.

MATERIALS

Quantity	Description
1/2	1/2" x 4' x 4' Plywood panel
4 lin. feet	5/8" dia. Wood dowel (cut into two 24" pieces)
18 lin. inches	1-1/2" dia. Wood dowel
4	2" Washers for wheels
4	3/4" Door hinges
2	Door latches (if desired)
—	6d Finishing nails
—	Wood putty
—	Fine abrasive paper
—	White glue
—	Interior semi-gloss enamel paint

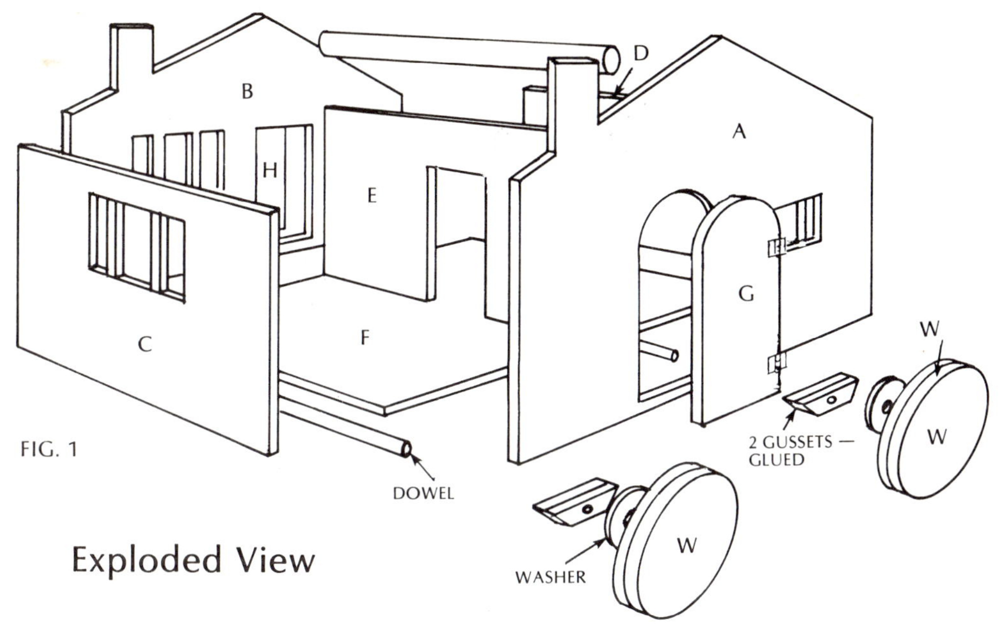

Exploded View

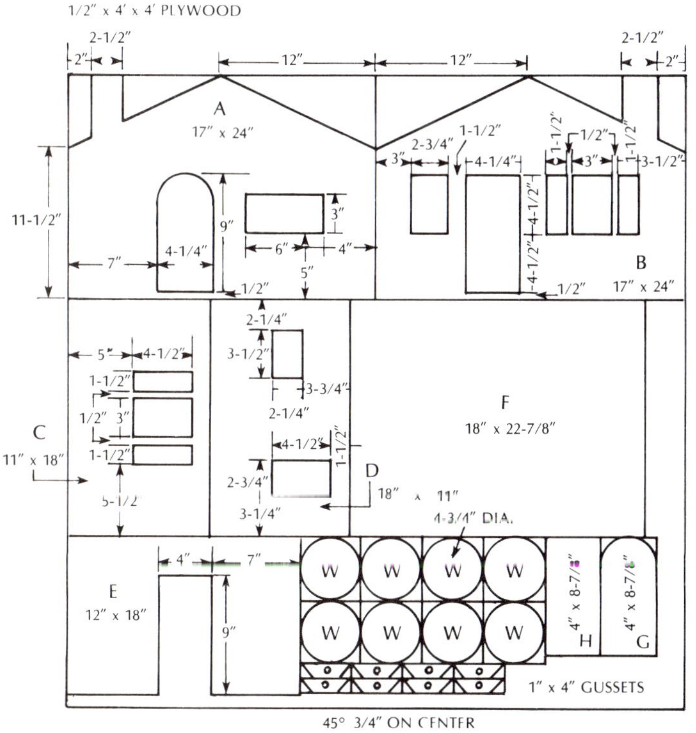

1/2" x 4' x 4' PLYWOOD

A
17" x 24"

B
17" x 24"

C
11" x 18"

D
18" x 11"

E
12" x 18"

F
18" x 22-7/8"

4-3/4" DIA.

4" x 8-7/8" H

4" x 8-7/8" G

1" x 4" GUSSETS

45° 3/4" ON CENTER

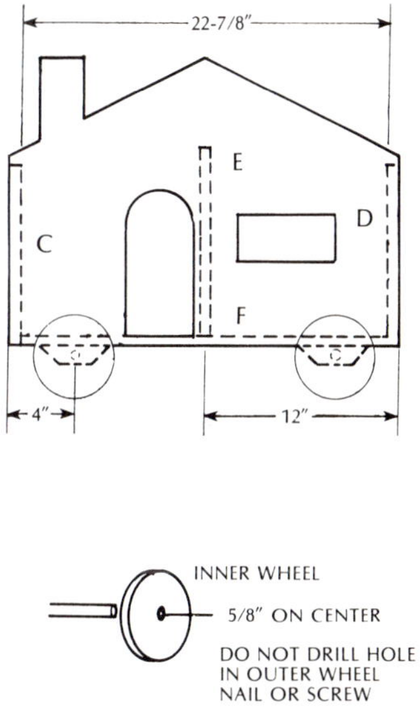

INNER WHEEL
5/8" ON CENTER
DO NOT DRILL HOLE
IN OUTER WHEEL
NAIL OR SCREW

A Side View

Panel Layout

DUCK DECOYS

Making and using duck decoys in this country dates back to the early American Indians. The main purpose for using decoys is to attract the ducks to the hunter's blind or ambush. Most good sportsmen would not attempt to hunt waterfowl without several decoys such as are featured here.

The two decoy designs shown were made of 1/2″ thick layers of white pine lumber, which is comparatively easy to carve. Some sportsmen prefer cedar lumber, but this is harder to work with because it splinters very easily.

The heads are band sawed according to the outline in the line drawing, from both the side and top views, after the 3/8″ hole has been bored for the dowel.

Rough cut the layer pieces on the band saw or scroll saw (Photo 1). It would be well to cut several pieces of the same shape to make up a number of the same kind of decoys. Note that the inside layers are hollowed out on a scroll saw or a portable jig saw to add buoyancy and also, make less weight for transporting. After cutting, the layers are assembled with nails and a resorcinol-type waterproof glue, and placed in clamps overnight (Photo 2).

Let the 3/8″ dowels extend about 2″ beyond the bottom of the decoy. The extended dowels are then inserted into a waste piece of 2″ by 4″ stock for holding the decoy for carving (See Photos 4 and 6).

No special skill is required to shape the decoys. All you need to do is trim the body down until the edges disappear (Photo 4). Another method for the quick removal of stock is on a sander/grinder (Photo 5). The rough effect on the decoys is accomplished with a bastard file or wood rasp (Photo 6).

To make sure the finished decoys float properly, add a lead keel as shown in Fig. 3. A screw eye is fastened on the forward end for attaching a mooring line. The eyes can be purchased from a local sporting goods dealer. See Fig. 2 for assembling the eyes to the head.

Most sportsmen have their own ideas about painting the decoys. For colors to use, check with sports magazines or the local museum. Apply two or three thin coats of sealer or shellac before putting on the colored paints. Be sure to use flat colors to avoid all shine on the finished decoys. Gloss enamels will give them an unrealistic effect which may frighten the wild game away from the decoys.

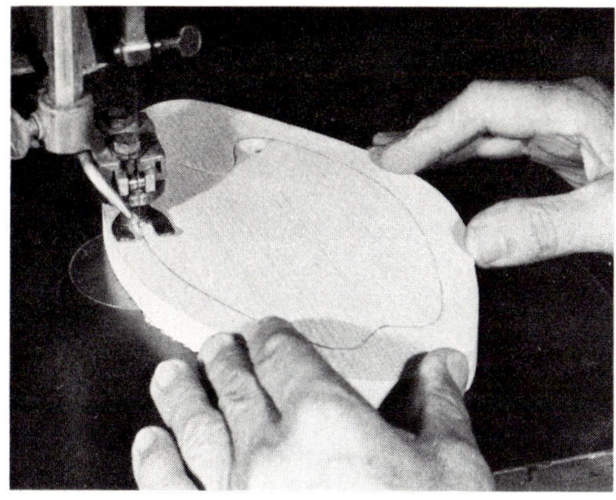

Photo 1: The layers of stock that make up the body of the decoys may be cut on a scroll saw, or with a portable power jig saw.

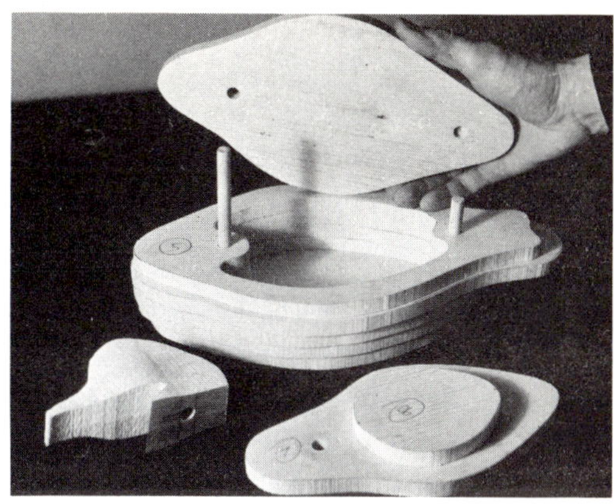

Photo 2. The layers are assembled over 3/8" dowels. Note the hollowed four layers.

Photo 3. The assembled body has been glued together and is ready for roughing out.

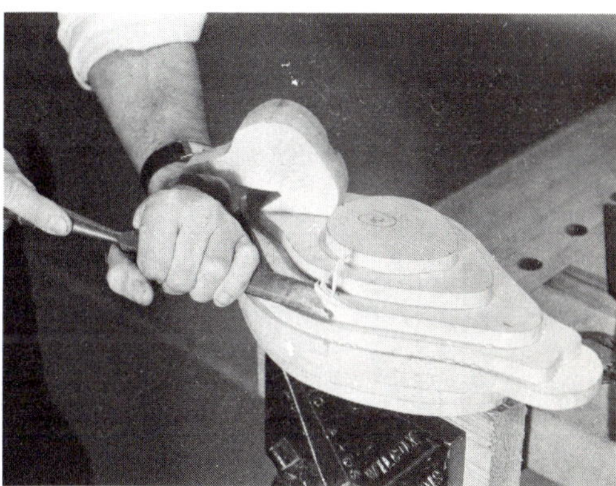

Photo 4. The assembled body can be roughed out or shaped with a 1" wood chisel.

Photo 5. A quicker method of roughing out or shaping the body can be done on a sander/ grinder using a rough belt.

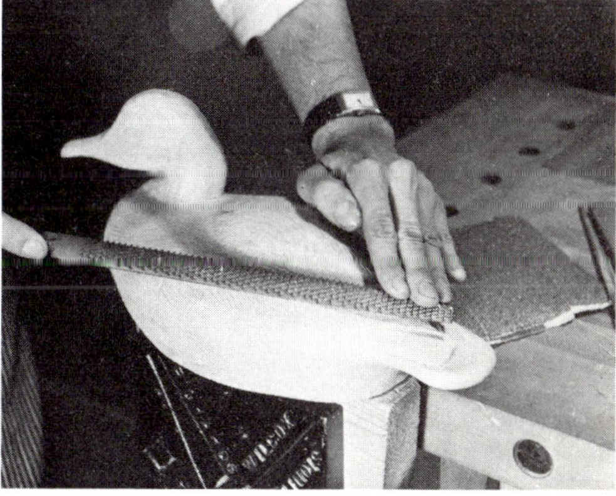

Photo 6. The final roughing effect which is essential to a good decoy is accomplished with a bastard file or wood rasp.

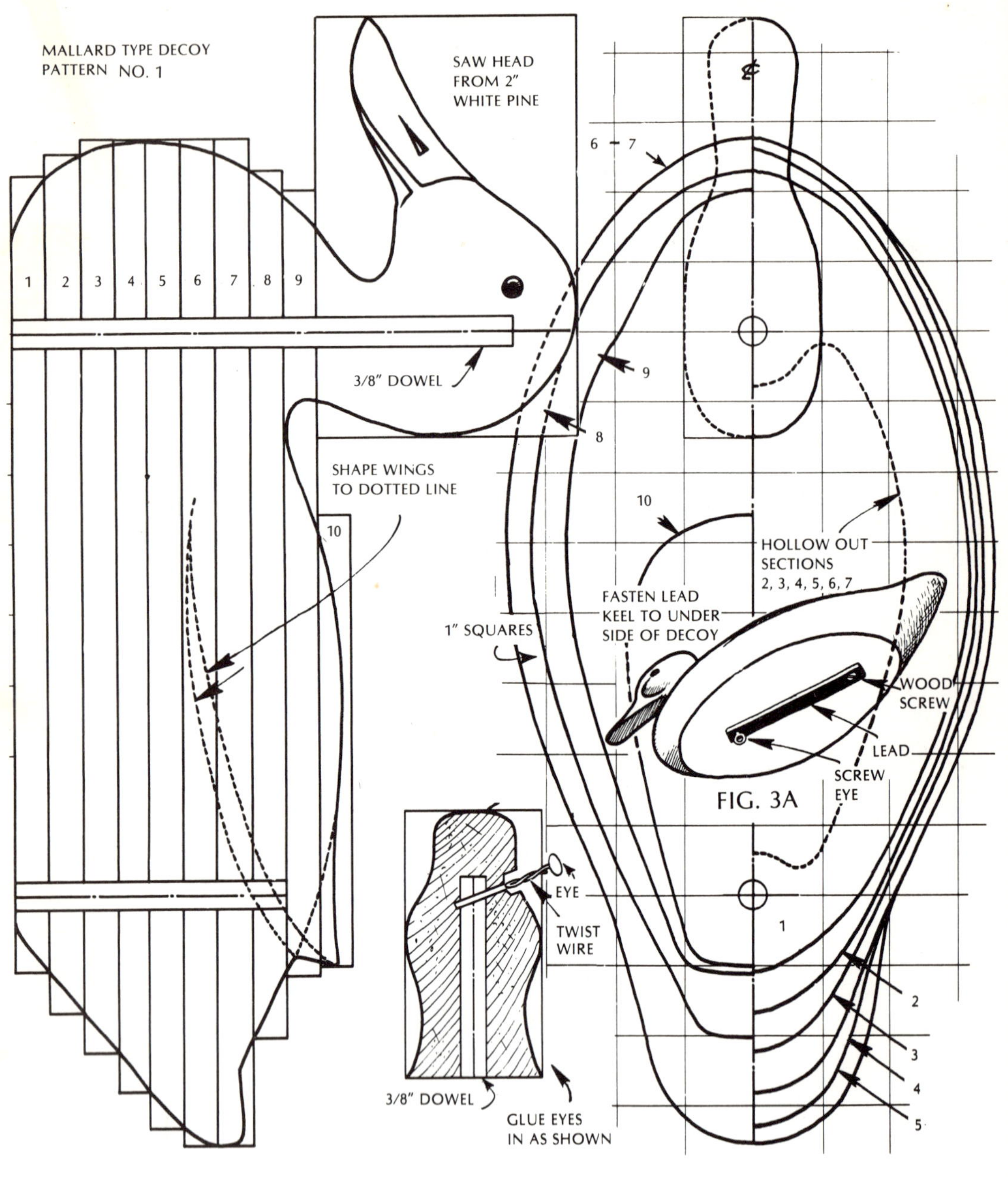

FIG. 1 FIG. 2 FIG. 3B

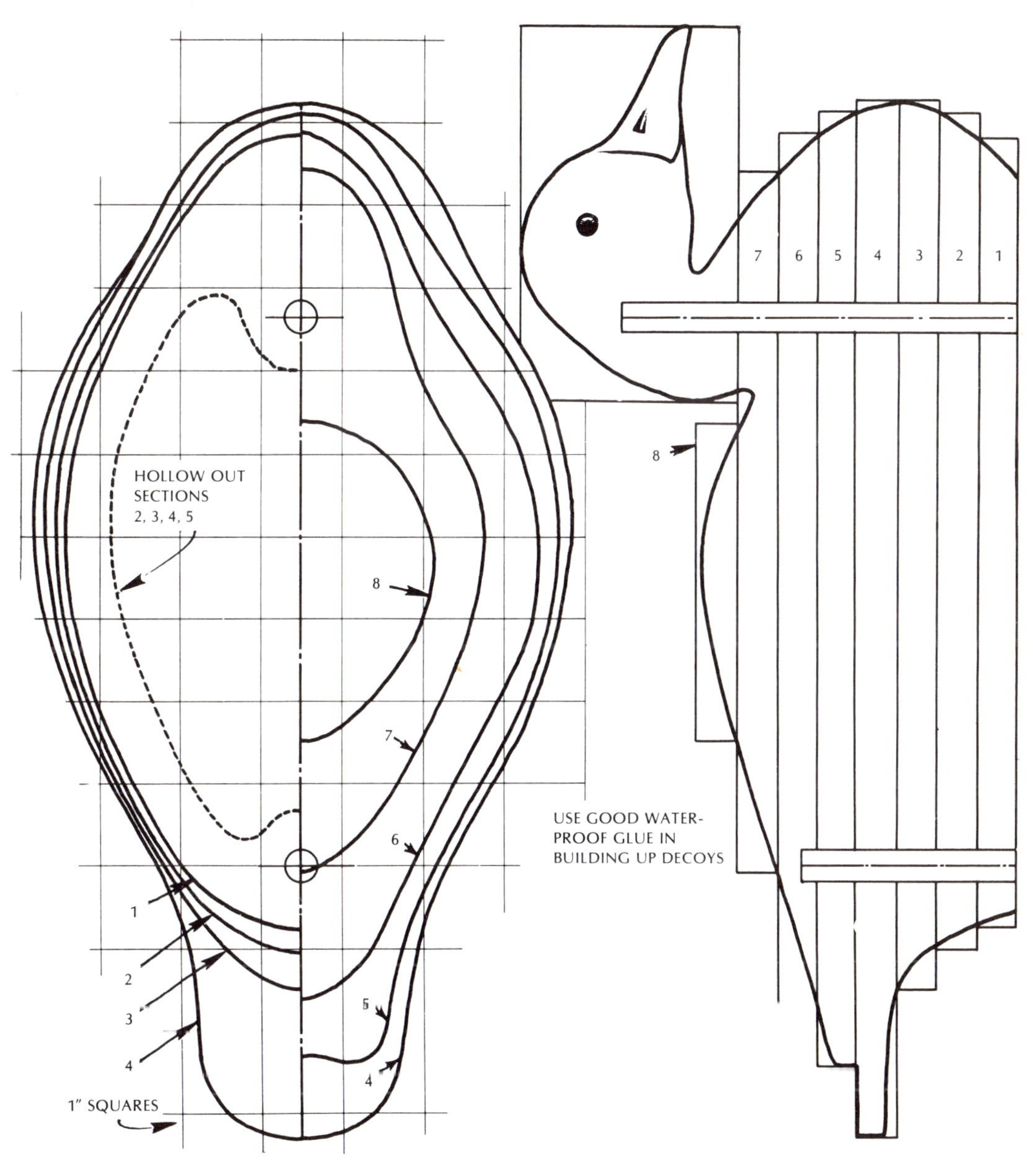
HOLLOW OUT
SECTIONS
2, 3, 4, 5
8
7
6
1
2
3
4
5
4
1" SQUARES
7
6
5
4
3
2
1
8
USE GOOD WATER-
PROOF GLUE IN
BUILDING UP DECOYS

FIG. 4

FIG. 5

FOLDING SAW HORSE

FIG. 1

Every home owner has many uses for a pair of saw horses. They are definitely a "must" in the workshop. The one featured here folds up and takes very little storage space.

All of the required details appear in the line drawing. The overall dimensions can be varied to suit the individual's need. The tapered cuts on the legs and the notches on the cross bar make the assembled horse very sturdy when the bolts are fastened. The holes for bolt tightening are bored at one time through both the legs and the cross arms with a 5/16" drill bit mounted in an electric drill.

Two coats of polyurethane finish will make it easy to keep them clean, as paint and grease can rapidly be wiped off without leaving a stain.

A window sash handle fastened to the underside of the top cross bar will make it easy to carry the horses.

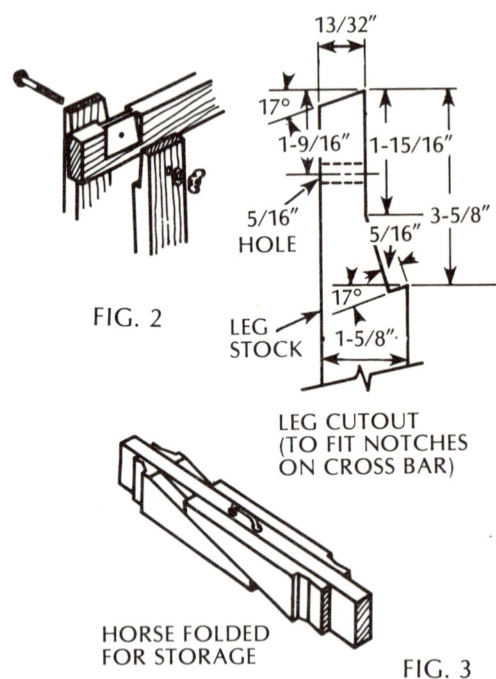

FIG. 2

FIG. 3

MATERIALS

Quantity	Description
4	1-5/8" x 3-5/8" x 27" Lumber (legs)
1	1-5/8" x 3-5/8" x Length of lumber as desired (crossarm)
2	5/16" x 3-1/2" Carriage bolts with washers and wing nuts
1	Sash handle
—	Polyurethane finish
—	Fine abrasive paper

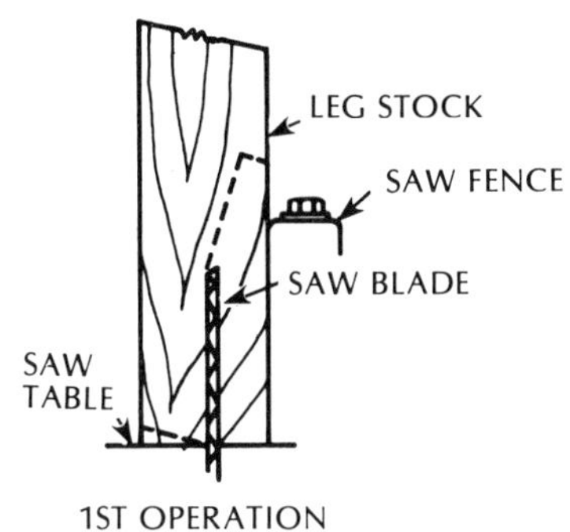

FIG. 4

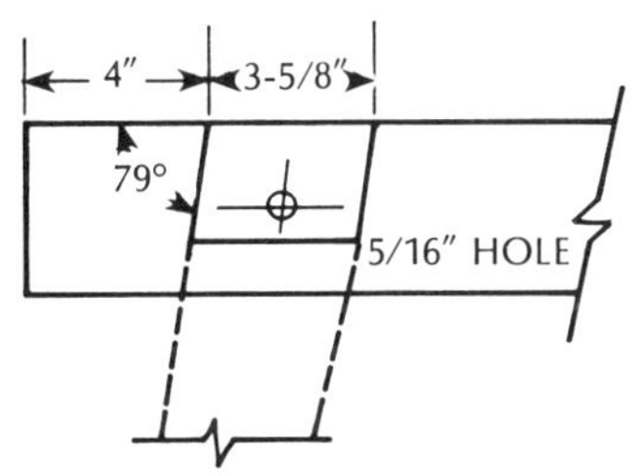

FIG. 6

FIG. 5

FIG. 7

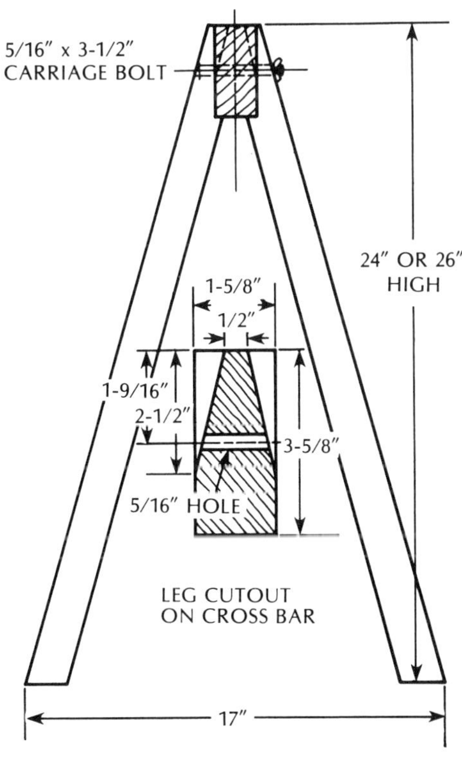

FIG. 8

CATWALK SHELF

Do you have a collection of plates, glasses, pitchers, or any curios you were given at some time or other which you would like to show off? Make this catwalk shelf with grooves in the lower and middle shelf for storing plates. Dowels can be set into the lower trim piece for hanging mugs or other utensils.

Since the shelf will display antique items it would be best to make it from pine or maple and finish it appropriately. The entire project can be made of 1/2″ or 3/4″ stock. If using the heavier stock, reduce the length of the shelf and trim the pieces by 1/2″. Tack both of the side pieces together and cut them out at the same time on the band saw (Photo 1). Stop dadoes, 1/4″ deep, for the shelves are made on the table saw (see Fig. 1A). The inside curves of the shelf sides as well as the top and bottom sander on the drill press (Photo 2). The outside curves of the shelf sides are finish sanded on the sander/grinder unit (Photo 3).

The dish slot grooves of both shelves are made with a 3/8″ core box cutter mounted in a high speed router. These grooves should be cut about 1-5/8″ from the back edge of the shelf stock (see Fig. 1A).

Assemble all of the pieces with glue and 6d finishing nails. Check for squareness with a try square or large steel framing square. Break all the sharp edges and finish sand all surfaces with a power block sander. Stain to suit and finish with two coats of satin or dull synthetic varnish. A penetrating resin finish may also be used.

MATERIALS

Quantity	Description
2	1/2″ x 7-1/2″ x 24″ Lumber (sides)
1	1/2″ x 7″ x 35-3/8″ Lumber (bottom shelf)
1	1/2″ x 3-5/8″ x 35-3/8″ Lumber (center shelf)
1	1/2″ x 1-1/2″ x 35-3/8″ Lumber (top shelf)
1	1/2″ x 3″ x 35-3/8″ Lumber (bottom trim)
1	1/2″ x 2-1/4″ x 35-3/8″ Lumber (top trim)
4	1/2″ dia. x 2-1/2″ Dowels (mug holders — optional)
—	6d Finishing nails
—	White glue
—	Wood putty
—	Fine abrasive paper
—	Wood stain
—	Polyurethane finish

Photo 1: By tacking both side pieces of stock together, they can be cut on the band saw fitted with a 1/4″ skip tooth blade.

Photo 2: While the pieces are still tacked together, finish sand all of the inside curves of the shelf sides on the drill press using a 3″ sanding drum.

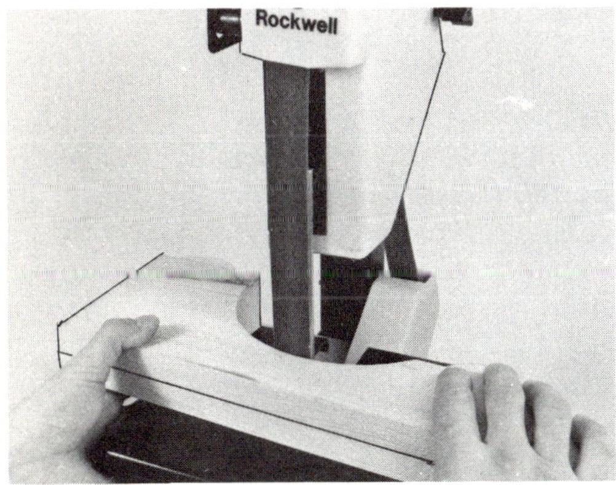

Photo 3: Outside curves of the shelf sides are sanded on the sander/grinder using a straight platen.

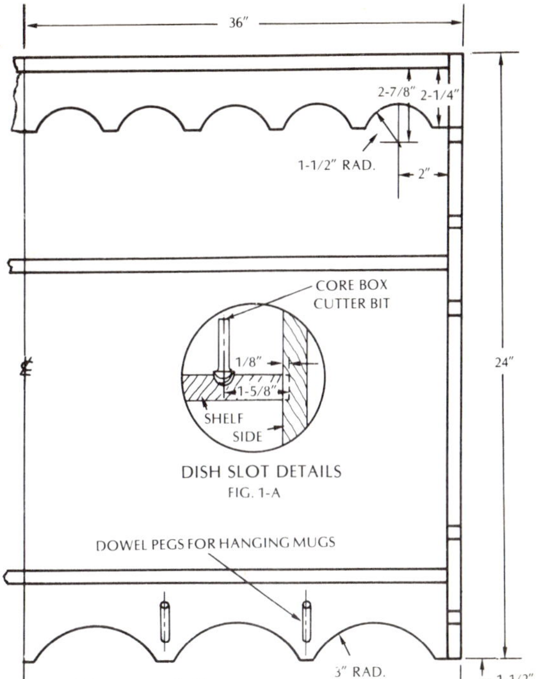

36″
2-7/8″
2-1/4″
1-1/2″ RAD.
2″
CORE BOX
CUTTER BIT
1/8″
1-5/8″
SHELF
SIDE
24″
DISH SLOT DETAILS
FIG. 1-A
DOWEL PEGS FOR HANGING MUGS
3″ RAD.
1-1/2″
3-3/4″

Front View
FIG. 1

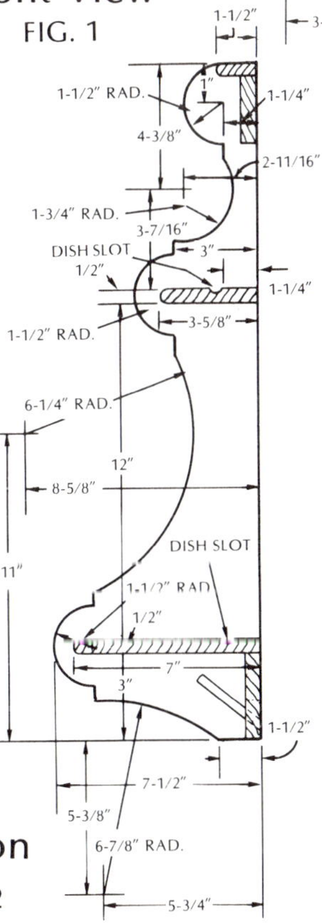

1-1/2″
1-1/2″ RAD.
1″
1-1/4″
4-3/8″
2-11/16″
1-3/4″ RAD.
3-7/16″
DISH SLOT
3″
1/2″
1-1/4″
3-5/8″
1-1/2″ RAD.
6-1/4″ RAD.
12″
8-5/8″
11″
DISH SLOT
1-1/2″ RAD.
1/2″
7″
3″
1-1/2″
7-1/2″
5-3/8″
6-7/8″ RAD.
5-3/4″

Cross Section
FIG. 2

COOKWARE RACK

MATERIALS

Quantity	Description
1/8	1/2″ x 1′ x 4′ Plywood panel
22″	5/8″ Wood dowels (cut into 6 pieces 3-1/2″ long)
22″	5/8″ Wood dowels (cut into 4 pieces 5-1/4″ long)
-	Fine abrasive paper
-	Interior semi-gloss enamel paint
-	Molly-bolts for fastening the rack to the wall, or screws for screwing it into wall studs.

Display and store your cookware with this smart pot and pan rack. Using only 1/8 of a panel of plywood and a few wood dowels, it is constructed as follows:

1. Lay out the pots, pans, and their lids on a rack piece before drilling the dowel holes. Dowel spacing may differ from the placement shown here, depending on the size of the pans and lids.

2. To assure alignment of the assembled rack pieces, drill the dowel holes for both pieces at once by laying one piece of plywood on top of the other.

3. Notch one end of the pot hanger dowels with a knife or saw to fit the rings on the pot handles so the pots cannot easily be knocked off the rack.

4. If necessary, adjust the diameter of the half-circles shown on the plan to the size of your lid knobs.

5. If you want the dowels painted, do it before assembling the rack. When all the painted pieces are thoroughly dry, gently pound the dowels in place.

The completed cookware rack may be either painted or stained. The latter may be used to obtain a natural looking finish of the plywood's grain. Two methods that give pleasing results are color toning, which uses companion stains and non-penetrating sealers; and light stain, which uses a pigmented sealer, tinting material (stain, thin enamel, or undercoat), and finish coat (varnish or lacquer).

Exploded View

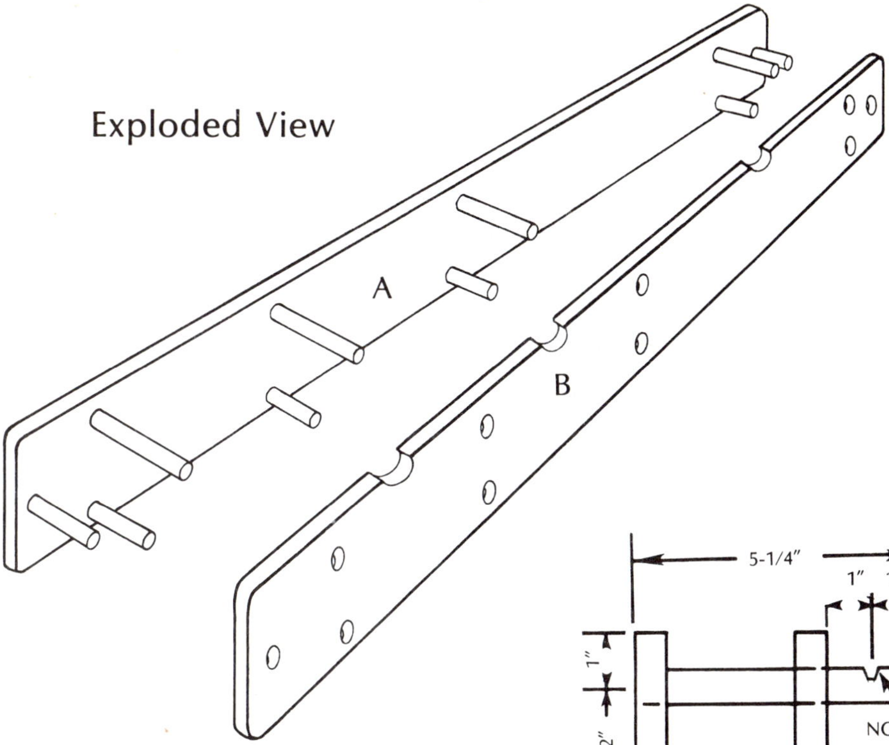

A

B

Side View

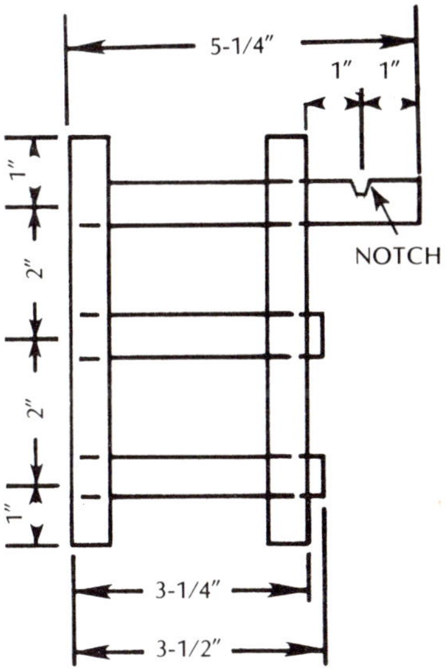

5-1/4"

1" 1"

1"

2"

2"

1"

NOTCH

3-1/4"

3-1/2"

Panel Layout

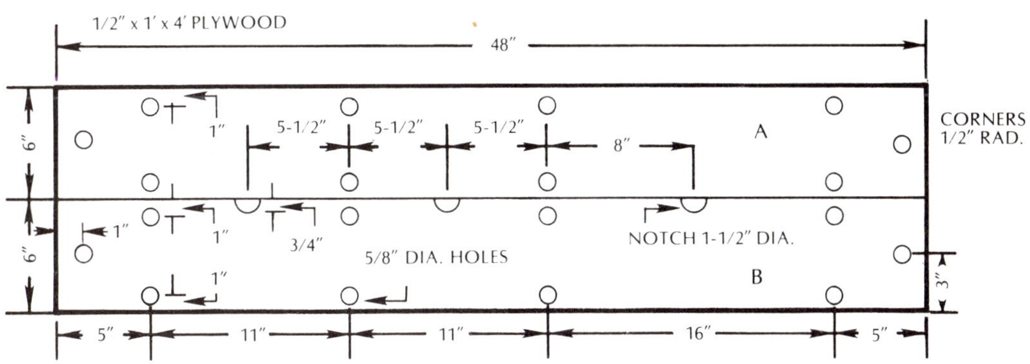

WORKSHOP STOOL

A stool with a double life! You can use this stool in the workshop or at the kitchen snack bar.

The stool top is made from a 2″ by 12″ by 12″ piece of stock. While it is still square, lay out the diagonal lines and space the four leg dowel holes on 6″ centers (Photo 1). Set the drill press table at a 7° angle. With an auxiliary board and two pieces of stock nailed at a 90° angle, drill all four 1″ holes while holding the piece to the table with a C-clamp (Photo 1). Cut the stool top round to size on the band saw. Finish the edge and dish out the center on the lathe, if desired, by fastening it to a 3″ or 6″ face plate (Photo 2).

The dowel ends of the stool legs are turned on the lathe (Photo 3) to fit the 1″ holes in the stool top. Make sure the dowel of the leg does not fit too tightly into the stool hole so as to allow for gluing. Break off the sharp corners on the portion of the leg just about 4″ below the dowel end. See the detail drawing (Fig. 2).

The 3/8″ by 1-1/4″ mortises to accommodate the stretchers are made on the drill press with the table tilted 7°. Make the mortises about 7/8″ deep. Make sure the dowel end of the leg stock is to the left with the drill press table tilted to the right.

Break all of the sharp corners with abrasive paper. Apply two coats of polyurethane finish. To complete the project, fasten 1″ furniture glides to the bottom of the legs.

MATERIALS

Quantity	Description
4	1-9/16″ x 1-9/16″ x 30-1/2″ Lumber (legs)
2	1-1/4″ x 1-1/4″ x 9-3/4″ Lumber (stretchers)
2	1-1/4″ x 1-1/4″ x 9-1/2″ Lumber (stretchers)
1	1-9/16″ x 11-1/2″ x 11-1/2″ Lumber (seat)
4	1″ dia. Furniture glides
—	White glue
—	Fine abrasive paper
—	Polyurethane finish

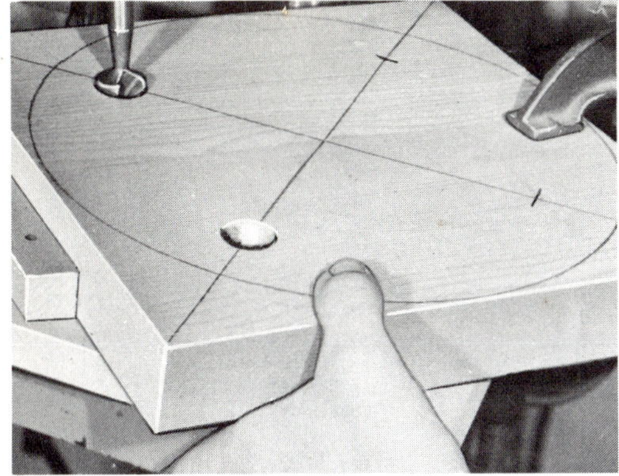

Photo 1: The dowel holes are bored on the drill press with a 1" multi-spur bit. Note that the auxiliary wood table is fastened to the drill press table with a C-clamp. The table is tilted 7°.

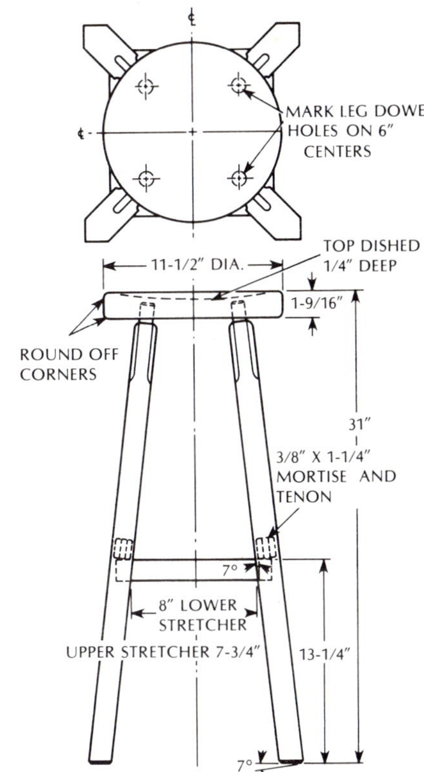

FIG. 1

Photo 2: The stool top is dished out on the lathe about 1/4" deep. The edges are rounded off with a 1/4" round nose chisel.

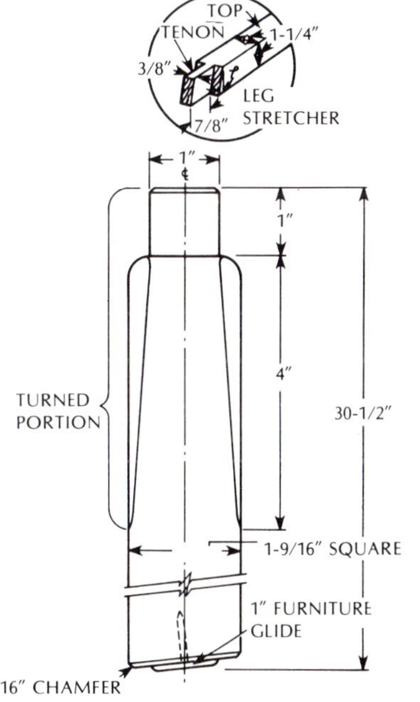

FIG. 2

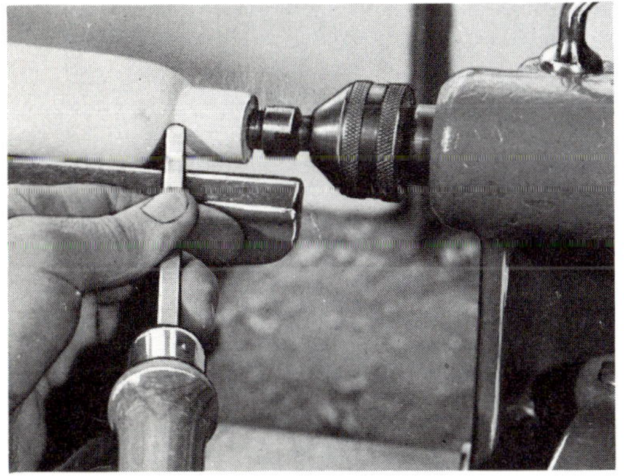

Photo 3: The end of the stool leg is turned down to fit the hole in the stool top. Part of the leg is turned down, about 4" below the dowel.

FIREPLACE BENCH

This smart fireplace bench provides all the extra seating you will need by the hearth next winter. Its simple contemporary styling complements any decor. Under the bench seat there is plenty of room for wood, kindling, and old newspapers.

To make the fireplace bench, first cut the parts from a 4′ by 8′ sheet of A—B Interior, A—C Exterior, or Medium Density Overlaid (MDO) American Plywood Association grade-marked plywood as indicated in Fig. 1. Then proceed as follows:

1. Glue-nail the two (F) parts to each side (A) to form the side pieces.
2. Glue-nail sections (E) to sections (B).
3. Glue-nail the 1-1/2″ half-round to the front edge of sections (A) as shown in Fig. 2.
4. Glue-nail the 3/4″ half-round to section (B) base, as shown in Fig. 2.
5. Assemble the rest of the bench pieces, glue-nailing the 3/4″ quarter-round between the sections (A) and (D) and (A) and (C), as shown in Fig. 2.
6. Cut each end of the top edge 1-1/2″ half-rounds at a 45° angle to form the corners, as shown in Fig. 3.
7. Glue-nail these top edge half-rounds as shown in Fig. 4. Fill the joints with wood putty as needed; sand as needed; paint.

3/4" x 4' x 8' PLYWOOD

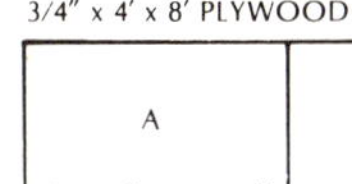

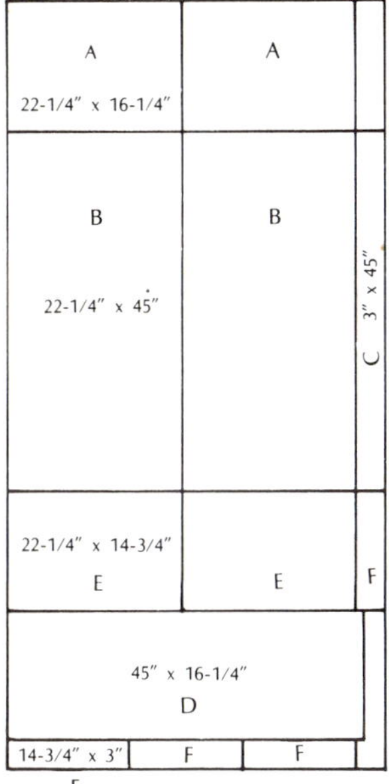

Panel Layout

FIG. 1

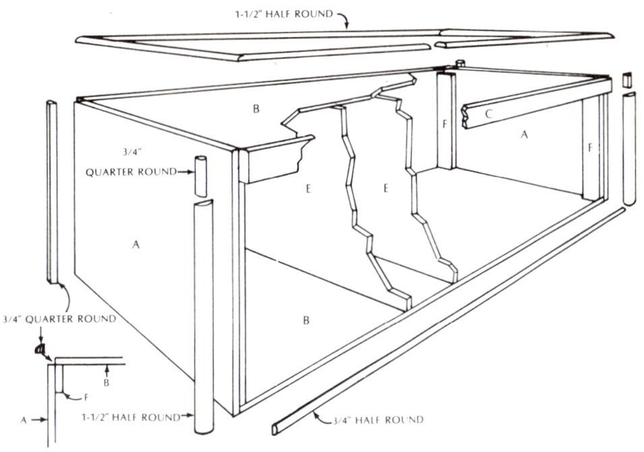

Exploded View

FIG. 2

MATERIALS

Quantity	**Description**
1	3/4" x 4' x 8' Plywood
15'	3/4" Wood half-round
4'	3/4" Wood quarter-round
1	22" x 46" Cushion top
—	8d Finishing nails
—	Fine abrasive paper
—	Wood putty
—	White glue
—	Interior semi-gloss enamel paint

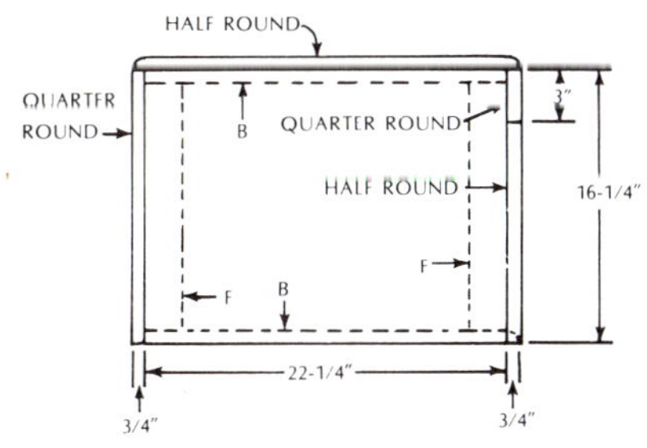

Side View

FIG. 3

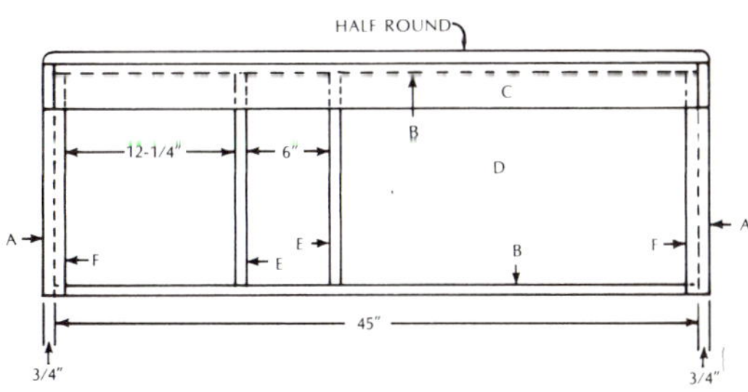

Front View

FIG. 4

KITCHEN REMINDER BOARD

This project with its peg board is a reminder of the kitchen of our youth. A very practical paper pad was added so that you wouldn't forget what you wanted when you got to the store. A piece of 1/4" thick plywood cut to the shape indicated in the drawing will fill the bill. Finish it natural with a coat of satin finish varnish. Lettering and feature lines of the chef can be painted with a fine brush and black paint.

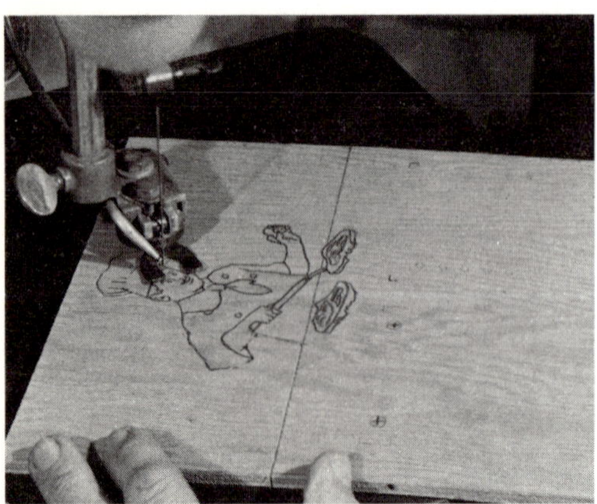

Photo 1: The chef design of the reminder board is cut with a portable jig saw or a scroll saw.

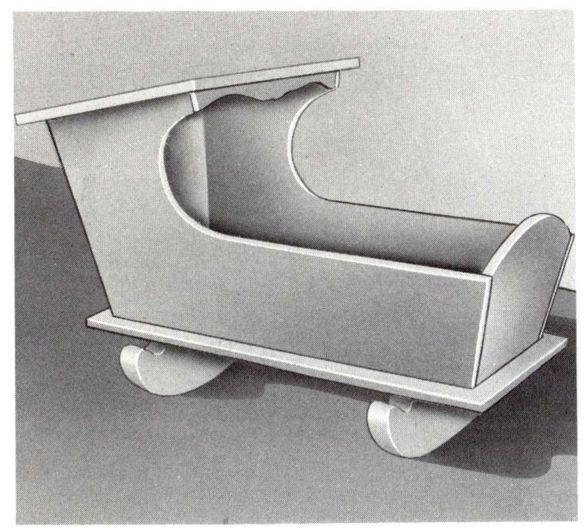

DOLL CRADLE

Any little girl will be delighted to have this toy cradle for her favorite doll. The 3/8″ plywood parts are assembled with glue and nails. The 3/4″ rockers are held together with glue and screws.

Fill all of the holes with wood putty. Then, break all of the sharp corners and sand the entire project with fine abrasive paper. Finish it with a light oak oil stain followed by a coat of plywood sealer. The top coat may be either shellac or synthetic varnish.

MATERIALS

Quantity	Description
2	3/8″ x 9-1/4″ x 17-1/4″ Plywood (sides)
1	3/8″ x 8-9/16″ x 8″ Plywood (headboard)
1	3/8″ x 7″ x 5-1/4″ Plywood (footboard)
1	3/8″ x 7-5/8″ x 16-1/2″ Plywood (bottom)
1	3/8″ x 8-5/8″ x 10-7/8″ Plywood (top)
1	3/8″ x 7/8″ x 9-1/8″ Plywood (top trim)
2	3/4″ x 2-5/8″ x 12-3/8″ Plywood (rockers)
-	Fine abrasive paper
-	White glue
-	Nails
-	Screws
-	Wood putty
-	Finishing materials

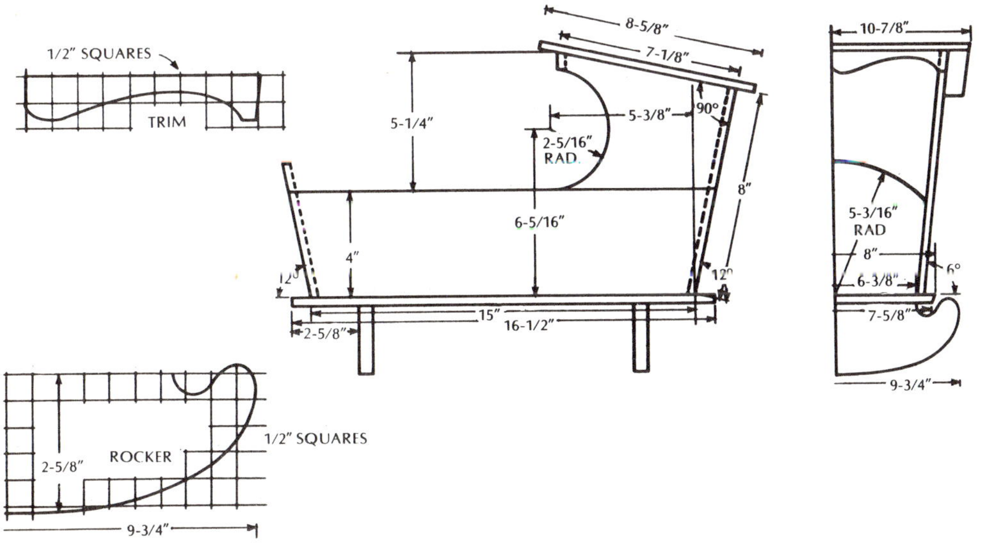

PEN AND PENCIL HOLDER

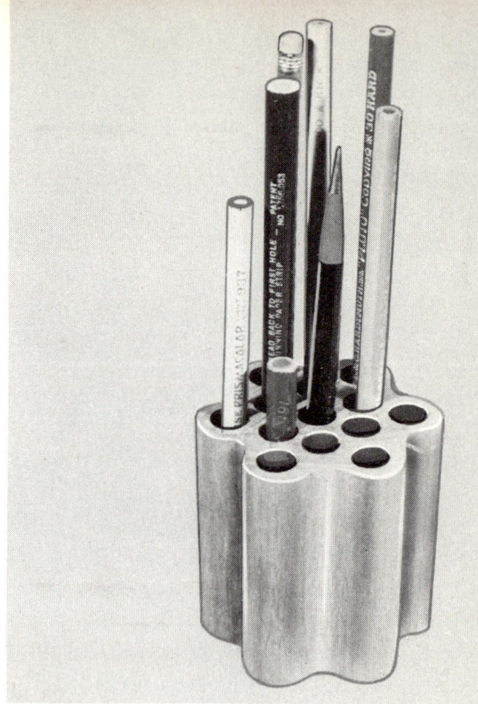

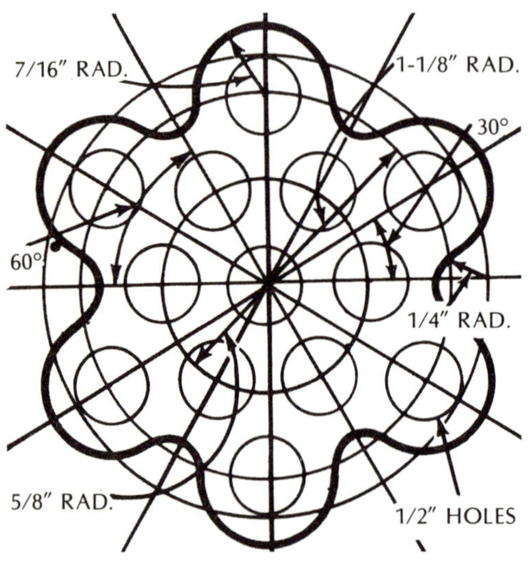

A solid block of walnut or mahogany, 3-1/8" square by 2-7/8" high, is used to make this practical pen and pencil holder. Trace the drill hole positions and the outer edge cutout design using the full size line drawing. The 1/2" holes are bored 2-5/8" deep and the cutout design is cut on the band saw using a 1/8" blade, then sanded as in Photo 2.

Fine sand the block with a very fine abrasive paper. Apply rubbing oil or boiled linseed oil for a natural finish. Follow with two coats of white shellac.

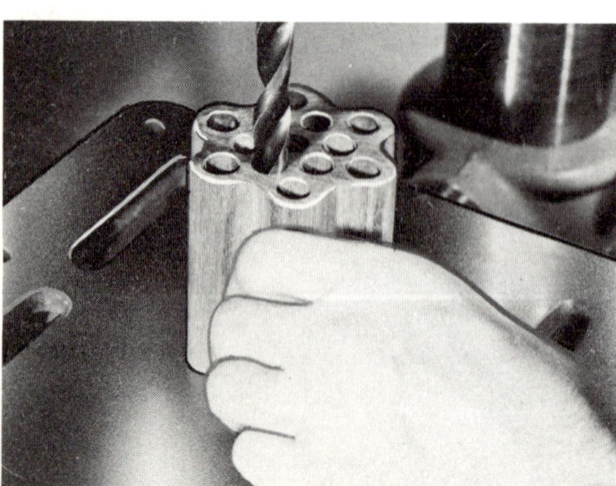

Photo 1: After cutting the outside section on a band saw, the 13 holes are bored 2-5/8" deep on the drill press.

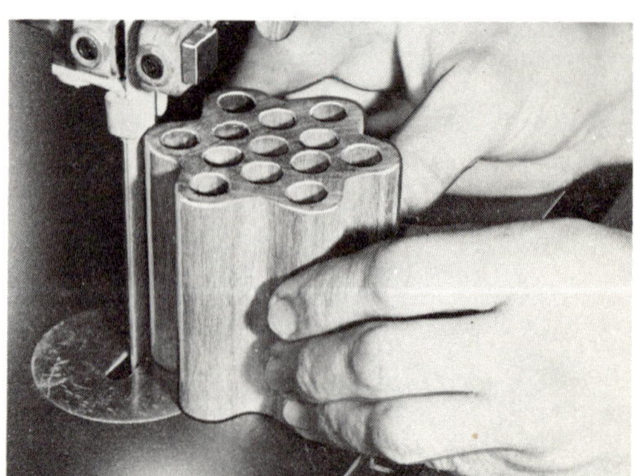

Photo 2: To sand the outside curves use the belt sanding attachment with a fine belt on the band saw.

COOKIE JAR

A cookie jar is a cheerful touch in the pantry or kitchen for keeping the goodies fresh. If you are not up to trying your hand at painting a decoration on your cookie jar, you can do it the easy way, with decals.

Hardwood, either maple or birch, can be used; 3/8" for all but the lid which is 3/4". Box joints for the entire project can be cut at one time by tacking the side pieces together in a staggered manner (Photo 1) with the alternate ends indented 3/8", the width of the dado groove. Cut the dado grooves on the table saw using two outside dado cutters and one 1/8" inside cutter, with paper shim washers between them. Equal spacing of the grooves is accomplished by attaching an auxiliary wood fence fitted with an indexing pin to the standard miter gauge. After sawing this piece, remove the saw from the arbor and mount a dado cutter to cut the thickness of the stock. Hold the auxiliary facing firmly against the miter gauge and run it across the dado head somewhere near the center. Remove the facing and mark the position of a second cut (D), in Fig. 3, spacing this from the first cut, (C), the same width as the groove. At the same time mark lines (A) and

MATERIALS

Quantity	Description
4	3/8" x 6-1/2" x 7-3/8" Lumber (sides)
1	3/8" x 6" x 6" Lumber (bottom)
1	3/4" x 6-1/2" x 6-1/2" Lumber (cover)
2	7/8" x 7/8" x 1-1/8" Lumber (knobs)
-	White glue
-	Fine abrasive paper
-	Satin polyurethane finish

(B), centering them as shown. Nail a close-fitting guide pin into this first dado cut. It should be long enough to project two stock thicknesses out from the face of the auxiliary facing. Then, make the second dado cut, (D). Line up the second cut, (D), with the dado cutter and screw fasten the auxiliary facing to the miter gauge. Accuracy is important in spacing the second cut, (D). You are now ready to make the box joint.

To make the box joint, set two pieces of stock that are to be joined against the auxiliary facing. Place the edge of one piece even with line (A), and the edge of the other piece even with line (B). Push the work across the cutter and then shift it so that the groove just cut sits over the guide pin. Make the second cut. Set the second groove over the guide pin and make a third cut. Continue in this manner until the whole width of the work is cut. It is important that the two pieces of stock maintain the same position throughout the operation. This is easily effected if the guide pin is made long enough to catch both pieces. If desired, the two pieces can be nailed together lightly or clamped together. Adjustments can be made by moving the auxiliary facing slightly to the right or left.

The baseboard is assembled to the sides with a 1/8" by 1/8" tongue and groove joint (Fig. 1). Glue the box sides and the baseboard in one assembly. When the glue is set, round off the edges of the box sides.

The top lid has a finger knob which is turned on the lathe. The rabbet of the lid can be made on the table saw in one operation with the dado head, or in two operations using a hollow ground blade.

Finish only the *outside* of the jar with two coats of satin polyurethane finish.

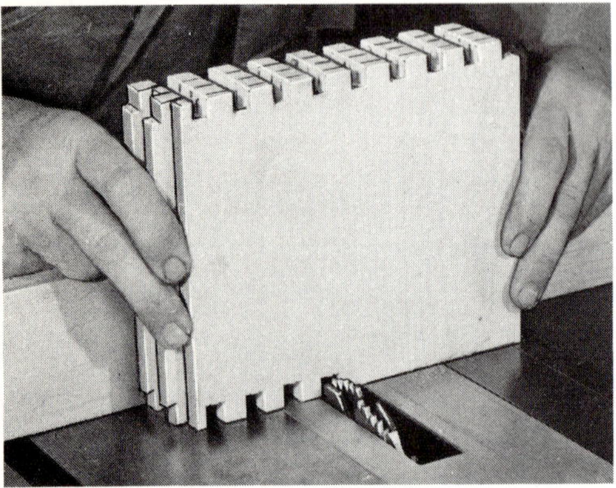

Photo 1: Box joint grooves are cut on all four side pieces simultaneously. Pieces are staggered and tacked together. The auxiliary fence with indexing device is attached to the miter gauge.

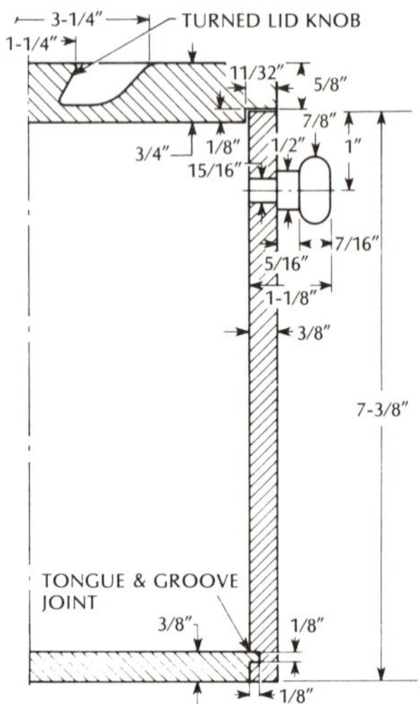

FIG. 1

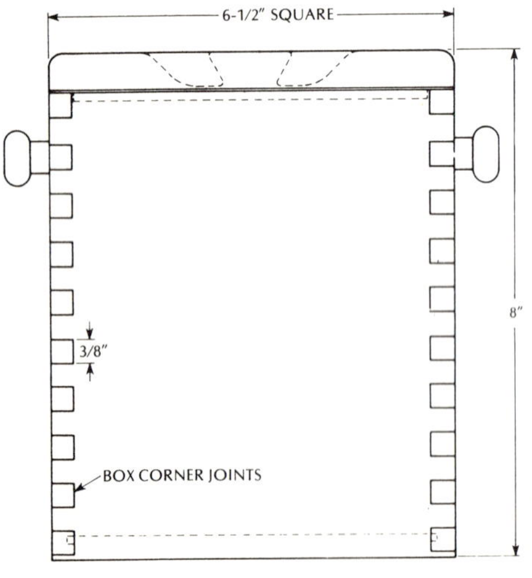

FIG. 2

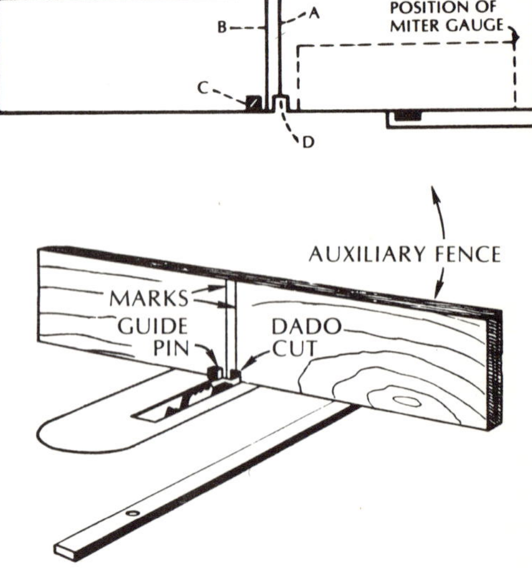

FIG. 3

This imaginative and distinctive statue of a circus performer was sculptored completely with power tools. Lauan (Philippine mahogany) is best suited for any carving or pattern work. If it is not available, sugar pine will work satisfactorily. The size of stock required for the carving should measure approximately 1-1/8″ thick by 6″ wide by 16″ long.

SCULPTURING WITH POWER TOOLS

Lay out the pattern on brown wrapping paper using the squares method (see line drawing), and draw the outline on the wood stock (Photo 1). Rough cut the outline of the figure on the band saw using a 1/8″ blade. Be sure to cut away from the finished line to allow enough stock for final detailing (Photo 2). The cut outs under the arms are made on the scroll saw with a 1/8″ blade (Photo 3). A portable jig saw may be used in place of the scroll saw.

The major portion of the carving can be done on the drill press with rotary rasps. Photo 4 shows a cone shape rasp being used to start the rough cutting of the figure. Be sure to hold the work firmly while applying pressure against the rotating rasp. The drill press should run at the second highest speed, or 2400 rpm. A variety of shaped rotary rasps are available from your local hardware or tool supplier.

After the figure has been carved to the finished shape desired, it can be sanded with small sanding drums made for this purpose (Photo 6). These drums are also available in several sizes to enable you to sand in the hard to get places. Leaving a few rough carving marks will make the figure look more like an authentic hand carving.

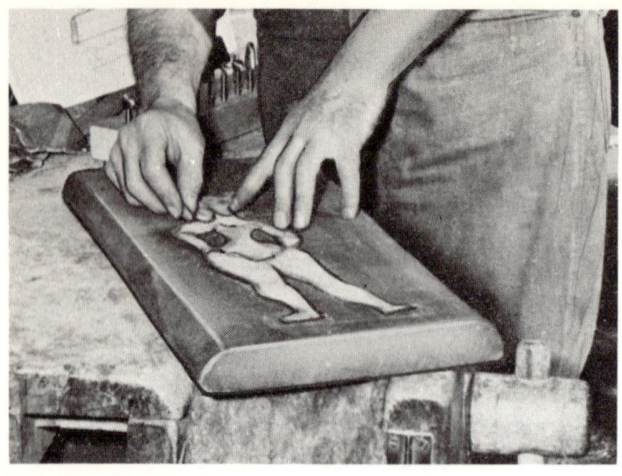

Photo 1: After drawing the figure on paper, it is used as a template to trace the outline on the wood stock.

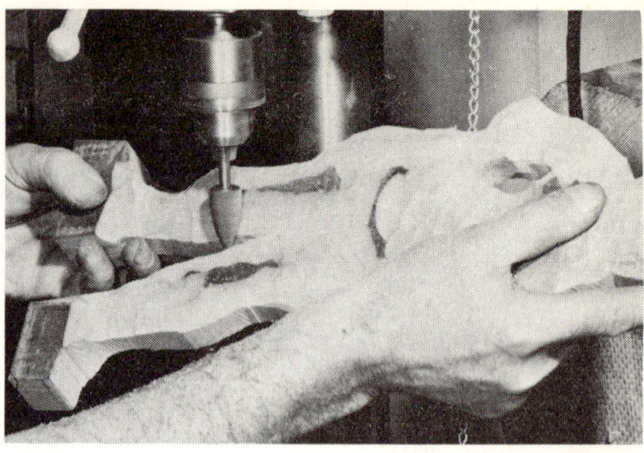

Photo 4: A rotary rasp, mounted in the drill press running at the second highest speed, will remove the stock on the carving in a relatively short time.

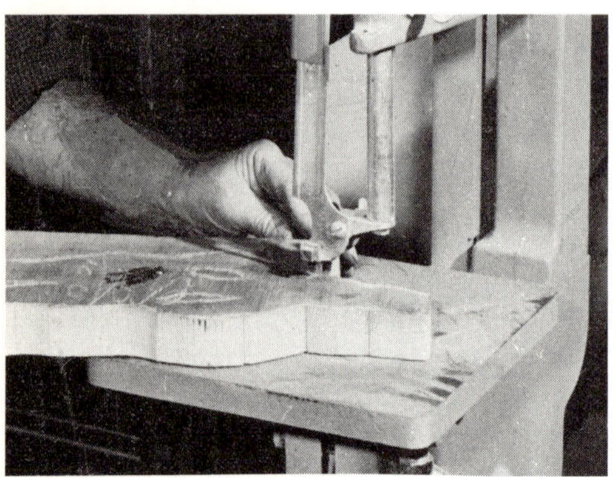

Photo 2: Rough cutting the outline of the carving is done on either the scroll or band saw with a 1/8" wide blade. Cut away from the line to allow for the finish carving.

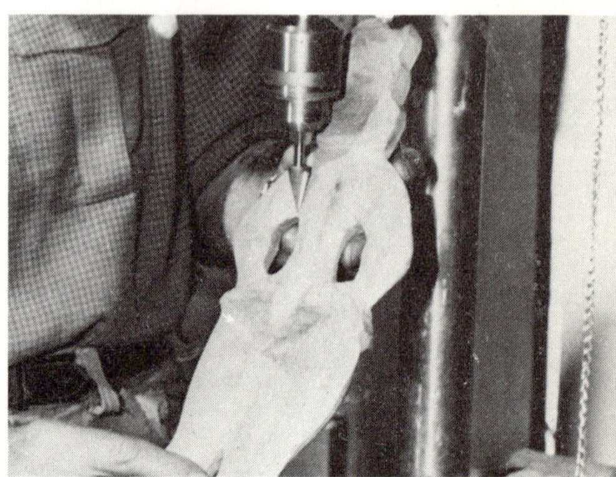

Photo 5: Finish carving in hard to get places is done with a sharp pointed cone shaped rasp on the drill press. Guide the work carefully toward the cutter to prevent overlap cuts.

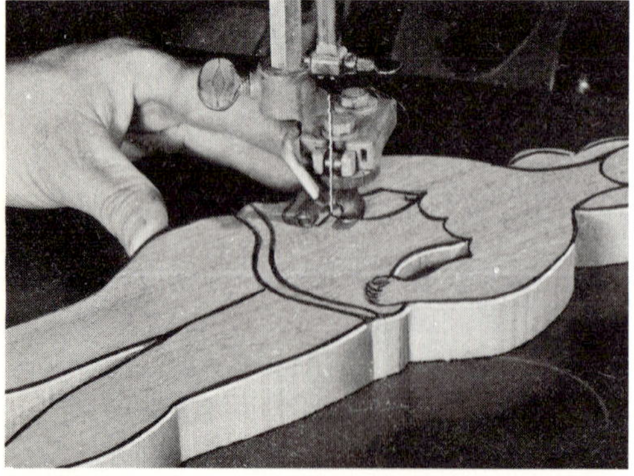

Photo 3: Under arm cutouts are made on a portable jig saw or a scroll saw. When using the latter, cut with a jeweler's blade at 1725 rpm.

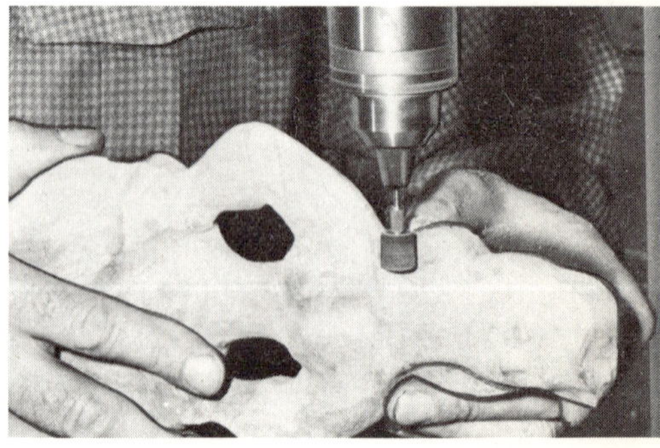

Photo 6: A lot of hard sanding can be eliminated with the use of small sanding drums mounted in the spindle of the drill press. In this case, run the press at about 1250 rpm.

Photo. 7 (left): The figure leg block is carefully fitted into the base block by trimming it to size on the band saw.

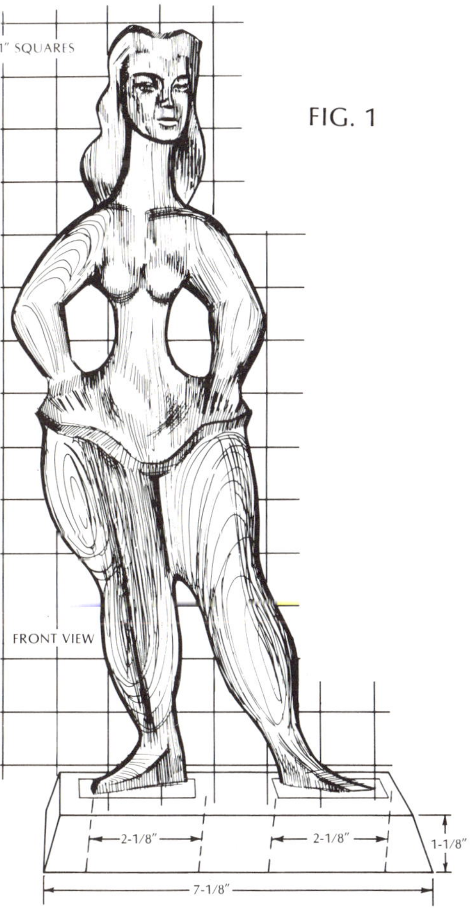

FIG. 1

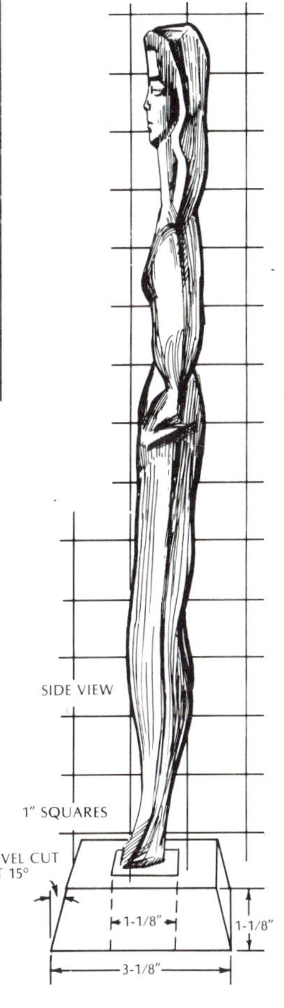

FIG. 2

Trim the foot blocks on the band saw (Photo 7) to fit into the mortises of the base block. Glue the foot blocks into the base, making sure to wipe off all the excess glue before it sets.

Give the carving a natural finish with white shellac, sanding between coats. The final coat should be rubbed with fine steel wool (Photo 8), and then rubbed with paste wax. If you wish to give color to the sculptored piece, use a penetrating resin finish, followed by a coat of wax.

INCH/MILLIMETER CONVERSIONS

INCHES TO MILLIMETERS
Multiply inches by 25.4

MILLIMETERS TO INCHES
Multiply millimeters by 0.03937

INCHES	MILLIMETERS	INCHES	MILLIMETERS	MILLIMETERS	INCHES
.001	.025	17/32	13.4938	.001	.00004
.01	.254	35/64	13.8906	.01	.00039
1/64	.3969	9/16	14.2875	.02	.00079
.02	.508	37/64	14.6844	.03	.00118
.03	.762	19/32	15.0812	.04	.00157
1/32	.7938	.6	15.24	.05	.00196
.04	1.016	39/64	15.4781	.06	.00236
3/64	1.191	5/8	15.875	.07	.00276
.05	1.27	41/64	16.2719	.08	.00315
.06	1.524	21/32	16.6688	.09	.00354
1/16	1.5875	43/64	17.0656	.1	.00394
.07	1.778	11/16	17.4625	.2	.00787
5/64	1.9844	.7	17.78	.3	.01181
.08	2.032	45/64	17.8594	.4	.01575
.09	2.286	23/32	18.2562	.5	.01969
3/32	2.3812	47/64	18.6531	.6	.02362
.1	2.54	3/4	19.050	.7	.02756
7/64	2.7781	49/64	19.4469	.8	.0315
1/8	3.175	25/32	19.8438	.9	.03543
9/64	3.5719	51/64	20.2406	1.0	.03937
5/32	3.9688	.8	20.32	2.0	.07874
11/64	4.3656	13/16	20.6375	3.0	.11811
3/16	4.7625	53/64	21.0344	4.0	.15748
.2	5.08	27/32	21.4312	5.0	.19685
13/64	5.1594	55/64	21.8281	6.0	.23622
7/32	5.5562	7/8	22.225	7.0	.27559
15/64	5.9531	57/64	22.6219	8.0	.31496
1/4	6.35	.9	22.86	9.0	.35433
17/64	6.7469	29/32	23.0188	1 CM	.3937
9/32	7.1438	59/64	23.4156	2 CM	.7874
19/64	7.5406	15/16	23.8125	3 CM	1.1811
.3	7.62	61/64	24.2094	4 CM	1.5748
5/16	7.9375	31/32	24.6062	5 CM	1.9685
21/64	8.3344	63/64	25.0031	6 CM	2.3622
11/32	8.7312	1.0	25.4	7 CM	2.7559
23/64	9.1281	2.0	50.8	8 CM	3.1496
3/8	9.525	3.0	76.2	9 CM	3.5433
25/64	9.9219	4.0	101.6	1 DM	3.937
.4	10.16	5.0	127.0	2 DM	7.874
13/32	10.3188	6.0	152.4	3 DM	11.811
27/64	10.7156	7.0	177.8	4 DM	1 Ft., 3.748
7/16	11.1125	8.0	203.2		
29/64	11.5094	9.0	228.6		
15/32	11.9062	10.0	254.0		
31/64	12.3031	11.0	279.4		
1/2	12.7	1 Ft.	304.8		
33/64	13.0969				

ABBREVIATIONS
MM-Millimeter(1/1000)
CM-Centimeter(1/100)
DM-Decimeter(1/10)